A Dirty, Wicked Town
Tales of 19th Century Omaha

A DIRTY, WICKED TOWN
Tales of 19th Century Omaha

David Bristow

CAXTON PRESS
Caldwell, Idaho
2009

First printing May, 2000
Second printing July, 2002
Third printing April, 2006
Fourth printing February, 2009

Library of Congress Cataloging-in-Publication Data

Bristow, David (David L.) —
    A dirty, wicked town: tales of 19th century Omaha / David Bristow.--1st ed.
        p. cm.
    Includes bibliographical references and index.
    ISBN 978-0-87004-398-7 (trade pbk.: alk. paper)
    1. Omaha (Neb.)--History--19th century--Anecdotes. 2. Frontier and pioneer life--Nebraska--Omaha--Anecdotes. 3. Vice--History--19th century--Anecdotes. I. Title.
    F674.O557 B75 2000
    978.2'254--dc21   00-029494

Photos in this book credited to the Durham Western Heritage Museum are from the Bostwick-Frehardt Collection, owned by KMTV and on permanent loan to the Durham Western Heritage Museum, Omaha, Nebraska.

Lithographed and bound in the United States of America
CAXTON PRESS
Caldwell, Idaho
177802

CONTENTS

ILLUSTRATIONS

Prologue

No Sound Save One's Own Breathing

Standing at the corner of 102nd and Center, in Omaha, Nebraska, I am guessing that the world began about 1965. If anything existed before then, I see no trace of it here.

I am standing beside a stoplight, where residential 102nd crosses West Center Road's four lanes of sport utility vehicles and cellular phone conversations. Center runs east-west across the southern half of the city and intersects 102nd at a hilltop. Now and then the stoplight brings Center's traffic to a halt, but mostly the cars roar by with a constant rushing noise and blur of colors. On either side of the road, the houses look new whatever their age, while the chemically-treated lawns are uniformly green and homogeneous, well-trimmed, and shaded by large trees.

This place—busy, familiar, prosperous, and above all, unremarkable—is where I choose to begin my book about nineteenth century Omaha.

Take a look around. To the west, Center descends into dust and orange construction signs around the I-680 viaduct. To the south, 102nd leads into a quiet residential neighborhood. To the east, Center disappears over another rise, after which it drops off toward the valley of the Big Papio Creek—really just a big drainage ditch lined with steel towers and powerlines buzzing with high-voltage electricity. To the north lies another residential neighborhood, which grows more and more posh as it approaches the Happy Hollow Country Club.

A man who has long since died once stood on this hill and looked out at a world which has long since changed beyond recognition. Here is what he saw:

The prospect was grand and sublime unlike anything I ever saw or my fancy ever imagined. In a north-west direction the eye could follow for twenty miles the course of the Pappio ma[r]ked by the few trees that skirted its banks[.] in every other direction as far as the eye could see was a wide expanse of rolling prairie, unmolested by the hand of Man[.] it lay in silent slumber just as it was left at the creation[.][1]

He called it Rock Brook Farm. Located six miles west of Omaha, the 240-acre claim was a farm only in imagination. Partly wooded, mostly prairie, it lay near the junction of the Big Papillion and Ninnabah (Rockbrook) creeks. There the otters played in the water; there that morning six swallow-tailed eagles had perched in a walnut tree; there, worn into the ground by the Omahas, was a trail along the Papio, leading northwest "into the heart of the Buffalo country." There at the base of the bluffs, carved into the soft sandstone, were "many devices by the Indians," who had long used the area as a campground.

It was evening on the first day of August, 1857. There was no breeze. Even at the hilltop, the air hung hot and sticky and still—and utterly silent:

no signs of human life was visible. no looing herd was seen on the hills. no tinkling bell of the flock was herd as it wended its way to the foald. no tired husbandman sought his cottage on the prairie. no domestic fowl was heard to crook or cackle not even the robin or sparrow is known here, no sound save ones own breathing is heard. The same stillness characterizes morning, noon, and night, you rise with the first approach of light and listen until the sun has commenced his march in the heavens. No crowing cock salutes the morn, no rumbling wheels or baying watch dog is heard. the same continued death like stillness prevails as at the beginning of time. Who shall mark the change ten years hence in this garden of the world?

This is the world in which our story begins. Our unlikely starting point has turned out to be unfamiliar and exotic after all.

This is not a work of historical fiction. All of the stories in this book are true and are based on careful research. I do not pretend to have written a comprehensive history of Omaha, but what is here is as accurate as I could make it. I consider this type of book a supplement to, and not a substitute for, conventional history.

This may be to your benefit. To enjoy this book, you don't even have to *like* history. You don't need to live in Omaha, either. If you like a good story, that's enough. In fact, for the time being, put aside everything you know about today's Omaha. The Omaha that emerges from these pages is a different animal.

Remember, it isn't so much a matter of *where* as a matter of *when*. Consider: On the west bank of the Missouri River, at forty-one degrees, fifteen minutes north latitude, is a city called Omaha. This has been so since 1854. But the Omaha of 1854, the Omaha of 1900, and the Omaha of today differ so radically from each other that they can hardly be thought of as one city.

It is as though present-day Omaha is the great-great granddaughter of a long-forgotten town of the same name and location; a town which once upon a time sprang up out of the virgin prairie, worked, played, swindled, dreamed, and brawled along the banks of the untamed Missouri; a town full of stories so strange and outlandish that they may as well have come from a distant land; a town neither pretty, nor clean, nor safe, nor well-governed, nor chaste, nor sober, nor particularly honest, nor "good" in any moral sense, but which—perhaps in spite of its innumerable faults, but more likely *because* of them—makes for good reading for those of us at the safe distance of more than a hundred years.

No project of this kind comes together without the assistance and encouragement of others. I would like to thank Thomas

Heenan and the staff of the History and Social Sciences Department of the Omaha Public Library, The Historical Society of Douglas County, and my friends Kira Gale and Margie Lukas. But mostly, I want to thank my wife, Danette, on whose support and valuable comments I have come to rely. This book is lovingly dedicated to her.

DLB
Omaha, Nebraska

Prologue notes

[1] Erastus Beadle, *To Nebraska in '57: A Diary of Erastus Beadle,* New York: The New York Public Library, 1923, 72.

Chapter One

THE FIRST DAY

July 4, 1854

It began with a party. Bearing picnic baskets and distilled refreshments, about three dozen Council Bluffians crossed the Missouri River in a ferryboat. As they looked backward in time to celebrate their country's seventy-eighth birthday, they wished also to look forward in time by holding the celebration in a new city in a new territory.[1]

As an "organized" territory, Nebraska was less than two months old. The Kansas-Nebraska Act, which opened Nebraska to settlement, also provided a territorial governor (to be appointed by the president), and a territorial legislature (to be elected by the people).

All but the act itself was still in the future. On July 4, Nebraska had no governor, no legislature, no capitol, no laws, and nothing that much resembled government. What it had was a few would-be towns springing up along the Missouri River. One of these was called Omaha City.

Omaha was, from the very start, a scheme. For about a year, some Council Bluffs men had been dreaming about the proposed transcontinental railroad and plotting to get it built through their town.

The railroad would cross the northern states; that had been part of the deal behind the Kansas-Nebraska Act. This meant not only that the rails would have to cross the Missouri somewhere, but also that land near the crossing would greatly increase in value. The Council Bluffs men figured that having a booming town right across the river from them—preferably a territorial capitol—would increase their odds of becoming a railroad city. So they began planning a new town.

Already, Omaha City was well under way. It had street names, town lots, and stock certificates. It had—-or would soon have—its own city map, beautifully lithographed by a St. Louis printer. It had a postmaster (A. D. Jones) and a post office (A. D. Jones' stovepipe hat). Within a few weeks, it would have its own newspaper, the *Omaha Arrow*. It had, in short, everything a frontier town needed, except buildings and residents.

Carried across the river by a leaky flat-boat ferry, the picnickers landed at the foot of Davenport Street. Though it had been surveyed and staked out, Davenport was still, like Omaha itself, a pleasant act of fantasy. The name of the ferry's landing point, Lone Tree Landing, required much less imagination.[2] Aside from the tree, an ocean of tall prairie grass lay before the picnickers, covering a mile-wide plateau of high bottomland that lay between two creeks. Looking west, the plateau rose into a line of hills about half a mile away. Such was the townsite.[3]

There must have been at least a few other trees nearby, for the group built a cabin—for fun, apparently. Working under the July sun, they put up sturdy log walls, but ran low on ambition before a roof was added.

It didn't matter. No one could move in yet, anyway. A marshal had come along to make sure no one did, not until Congress ratified the recent Indian treaty for this part of the territory. Enough of a sense of fair play existed for the government to insist on "proper" treaties before taking Indian land. This sense wasn't strong enough to prevent the constant violation of old treaties and the signing of new, more restrictive ones, but such as it was, it created some sense of restraint.

In other words, cabin or no cabin, everyone knew they'd be returning to Council Bluffs that evening. The first real settlers wouldn't set up housekeeping for another week. Still, this was a beginning of sorts, a date as good as any to reckon as Omaha's

A. D. Jones was Omaha's first postmaster. In the early days he carried the mail in his stovepipe hat. The "Big Six" was an early Omaha general store.

birthday. With their little cabin, the group seemed to realize this.

They moved on to the hills. With a wagon and a team of horses, they fought their way through grass as tall as a horse's bridle, heading west on "Davenport Street."

Postmaster A. D. Jones (the fellow who carried the mail in his hat) pointed to the highest hill and advised a youthful companion, "Young man, take a claim up on that hill and it will make you rich some day."

Not seeing the desirability of land on a steep hill outside of town, the young man ignored the advice. He would regret it later.

The group halted atop Jones' impressive hill. From there, they could see for miles in every direction. In the valley below them, the little unfinished cabin looked lonely and insignificant. Atop the hill, where Central High School now stands, they held their celebration.

It wasn't enough just to have a picnic. It was the Fourth of July. It had to be done with style. Grand toasts were drunk, such as, "Nebraska—May her gentle zephyrs and rolling prairies invite pioneers from beyond the muddy Missouri river to happy homes within her borders, and may her lands ever be dedicated to free soil, free labor and free men."

True to the democratic spirit of frontier America, the group also adopted resolutions, fired a salute, and called for speeches. Like the picnic itself, a nineteenth century speech had to be performed with a certain attention to style. The group was small enough that they could have been addressed in a normal, conversational manner. This wouldn't do. Instead, the speaker chose to stand in the wagon bed so he could tower above his audience. If he was any kind of orator at all, he assumed the proper stance, stiff, chest out, almost sway-backed, keeping one hand behind him at the small of his back, and gesturing broadly with the other hand. The reader who has ever seen a bad performance of Shakespeare will have some idea of how it was done.

Bringing out his best adjectives, the speaker "commenced a spread-eagle speech." We don't know what he said, but it was probably some elaboration on some such phrase as "Westward the star of empire takes its way." It doesn't matter much. He never finished the speech.

It seems that the gunpowder salute a few minutes earlier had produced some unintended consequences. The party on the hilltop got the feeling they were being watched. In the distance, Indians appeared.

One participant recalled that "the women became frightened," which of course implies that the men did not. It was, therefore, purely for the ladies that the speech was suddenly cut short, that the food and belongings were hastily piled into the wagon, that the horses were hitched up, and that the whole group suddenly couldn't wait to get back across the river. The Indians watched as team and wagon went rattling and bouncing down the hill, followed closely by about three dozen white (probably very white) people.

Soon the ferryboat departed, and Omaha—a city of staked ground and one roofless cabin—was once again deserted.

And there was evening, and there was morning—the first day.

Chapter 1 notes

[1]Except where noted, this chapter is based on Alfred R. Sorenson, *History of Omaha from the Pioneer Days to the Present Time*, Omaha: Gibson, Miller & Richardson, Printers, 1889, 51-53. All quotations are from p. 52.

[2]Federal Writers' Project, *Omaha, A Guide to the City and Its Environs*, Washington, D.C., Works Progress Administration, 1939, 108.

[3]The original townsite lay between Nicholas and Jones streets on the north and south, and between the river and 12th Street on the east and west. The two creeks mentioned have long since been filled in, the steep hills long since cut down to a gentler grade. See Federal Writer's Project, 106.

Chapter Two

A JOURNEY TO OMAHA

March 1857

Words from a diary:

> *March 9th, 1857 — Left home with the inten-*
> *tion of being absent longer than any previous trip*
> *I had ever taken from my own fireside. Still I had*
> *none of those feelings which usually possess me at*
> *parting with my nearest and dearest of friends*
> *and relatives. I had no realizing sence of any pro-*
> *tracted absence more than I would feel on going to*
> *my daily business. Days previous to my departure*
> *however were days of deep thought and reflection.*
> *The simplest acts of my children were unusually*
> *interesting to me and remarks that at any other*
> *time I would barely notice would make my heart*
> *swell and tears start unbidden in my eyes.*[1]

His name was Erastus Beadle—the same pioneer quoted in the prologue. He was thirty-five years old, married, and had two children. He lived in Buffalo, New York, but hoped to start a new life in the West. He hoped, too, that early success—or at least the promise of such—would allow him to send for his family before too many months passed.

So he departed. But his was no rugged expedition on the order of Lewis and Clark: he had nearly $100 in his pocket and the convenience of modern travel at his disposal. Still, he was bound for Omaha City, Nebraska Territory, a destination which lay hundreds of miles to the west—on the very frontier of civilization—and which, for all the time and expense involved in getting there, might as well have been located on another continent.

The first part of the journey was easy. Beadle traveled by rail, then ferry, then rail again, wending his way to Cincinnati, Ohio, by a roundabout route through Ontario, Michigan, and Indiana. While traveling through the latter state, Beadle gazed out the car windows with morbid fascination as mile after mile of miserable cornfields, family graveyards, and "the poorest kind of logg huts" rolled by. Indiana was "a 'Hoosier' state in earnest," he concluded.

At Cincinnati, Beadle found the river city booming. Down at the river, the levee was crowded with export goods for the West—whiskey, pork, and ready-made buildings chief among them. It was "the busyest place I ever saw." And there he boarded a steamboat, planning to follow the Ohio River down to its junction with the Mississippi, then up the Mississippi to St. Louis.

The passengers were mostly Southerners, and Beadle—a life-long resident of upstate New York—was fascinated with them. Though he found them "extremely warm hearted," he noted that "they consider the use of the revolver as honorable a way of settling a dispute or punishing an insult as any plan that can be adopted." But he got used to it: A fight in which some well-lubricated Mississippians "used their revolvers and bowie knives" to settle their card game receives only a short paragraph in Beadle's diary.

Beadle liked his new Southern friends, but left the steamer at Louisville after becoming frustrated with day after day of travel delays. Now, it was back to the railroad and on west to Jefferson City, Missouri, where he boarded a Missouri River steamboat.

He was not alone. In Missouri, Beadle found himself part of a vast movement to the new territories of Kansas and

Durham Western Heritage Museum
Steamboats at Omaha Landing in 1865.

Nebraska. The steamboats were packed with emigrants eagerly making their way to the territories, while at the levee people stood shoulder-to-shoulder as they sought to find a place on the crowded boats. When Beadle's train arrived in Jefferson City, "every person had their carpet sack in hand to make a spring for the boat when the cars should stop. And when they did stop down they went in a mass like a flock of sheep tumbling over each other in the dark . . ."

Once aboard, the struggle didn't cease. A "stateroom," meaning a tiny room with a few bunks, was to be had only by a limited number of first-class passengers. Everyone else slept on the cabin floor. Or tried to:

> *About this time the porters comenced turning down the chairs along the state room doors completely blocking up the entrance or exits through the door. This being done they brough in a lot of Mattresses arranging them along one end on the chair backs to serve as a pillow. I took the hint and made fast to one then came a general strife to see who should have a bed About one half were accommodated. Some had a mattress some a*

pillow others a blanket. Covering about two thirds
of the cabin floor, one would laugh another sing
and a third curse, those that could get no chance
to sleep done all they could to prevent others from
sleeping and kickt up a general uproar until they
got exhausted and we at last got to sleep. I was
soare from laughing at the vanity of disposition,
one was for fun another kept up a constant growl.
those however who said least fared best. I have
often heard people tell of a crowd, but this beat
all.

In short, they were "jamed into our cabin like stage coach passengers." During the five days' upstream journey to Leavenworth, Kansas, the passengers tried to make the best of life on the overcrowded steamboat. The food was bad, the mattresses were few and fought over, and the progress against the swollen current was painfully slow—especially when the boat got stuck for a day on a sandbar, or when a collision with another steamer resulted in a smashed-in wheelhouse. All this while on board a "blackleg" gambler prowled the decks, swindling those passengers who were foolish enough to play cards with him. At least one man lost all his money, and another nearly fought a duel with the "blackleg."

But such was the optimism of the frontier that no hardship could suppress it. Beadle was in high spirits as he watched the rising river, observed the deer and wild turkeys along the banks, and made the acquaintance of Daniel Boone's great-granddaughter, an intelligent Missouri woman who could "talk of wild scenery different from any one I ever conversed with."

All about the steamer, hundreds of business contacts were being made, plans conceived, friendships begun. At every town, the levees were crowded with people, all coming or going or engaging in one bold enterprise or another. The boat's clerk said that since the river had opened—just weeks earlier—some 12,000 emigrants had come by boat, and "as many more by land."

Of these overland travelers, Beadle writes:

every ferry we came to was crowded from Morning to Night. Such a tide of emigration was never before known. They are pouring in one continual stream to every town and ferry on the east bank of the river and stand in large groops of men, women, children, waggons, horses and oxen awaiting their turn to cross into the promise land. They tell us they are only pioneers and have but to write home favorable to bring parties of from ten to twenty for every individual now entering the Territories. They are covering the territories like a swarm of locusts.

Arriving in St. Joseph, Beadle found "the Hotels filled and accommodations poor." He needed to switch boats in order to get to Omaha, but the next boat was full. Rather than wait, Beadle and a few others decided to finish the journey by stagecoach. Council Bluffs, they were told, lay at the end of a thirty-six-hour ride.

Next morning at 8 a.m., they set off from St. Joe, eleven men crowded inside the coach, the driver atop it, traveling "at a snail pace up one bluff and down another tiping and pitching in all directions." At two that afternoon, they bogged down in a mud hole. It took all twelve of them—driver and passengers alike— an hour's work to get unstuck.

That evening, they continued on after stopping for dinner and fresh horses. The passengers got out and walked, enjoying the evening, hiking up and down the steep hills. Sunset found them beside a large cornfield, which:

was alive with Wild Geese and ducks that were coming in to feed on young wheat which was just starting up and to roost The ground was covered with them and the air filled with others hovering over. The noise made by their wings and their con-stant squaking was almost deafening and shook the ground like distant thunder. Their number could not be estimated.

After dark, a broken tongue (the part of the coach to which the horses were harnessed) forced a twelve-hour delay. Fortunately, the owner of a nearby farmhouse agreed to take them in for the night while the driver journeyed back to the last town to have a new tongue made.

The second day of the stage journey brought a new, more formidable challenge: the Tarkio River, now swollen out of its banks with snowmelt from the north. Leaving the stage behind, the driver swam the river on horseback. On the other side, he learned from an agent where the best crossing lay. Then he had to swim the river again, backtrack with the stagecoach to a different bridge several miles away, and then—after crossing the bridge—drive horses and coach through *"four Miles* of river bottoms where the water was from three feet to six inches in depth all the way. Some of the time the horses could with difficulty draw the coach."

It was long after dark when the travelers reached the end of their detour. But the day's travel wasn't over yet:

> *It was now four miles to our station being 36* [miles] *our team had to go, one of the horses will probably never go it again as we believe he is used up. The last four miles was hilly and we walked much of the way, which was delightfull The prairie was on fire in all dirictions, and presented a most Magnificent sight. The grass was dry and tall and a gentle wind blowing which kept the fire steadily marching on like an army of Soldiers.*

Beadle was enchanted. The fire burned gently in the night, advancing slowly "in wavey motions like the undulations of the sea." Scattered fires were visible in all directions, and in some places the coach passed so near the flames that the passengers could read by firelight.

Excited as a schoolboy, Beadle ran to a high bluff nearly half a mile ahead of the coach, and stood gazing out at the reddened clouds above and at the eerily lit landscape below. He counted twenty different fires—including one he'd set himself with a match—and he watched the slow approach of the stagecoach and its entourage of passengers walking alongside. "The glare from the burning prairie," he wrote, "gave them an unearthly look which was wild and romantic in the extreme."

And they traveled on through the night.

Morning came cold and raw, threatening snow. It was March 30. After breakfast, they crossed the Nishnabotna in a scow—and none too soon, for the river had risen a foot overnight, and was ready to spill out of its banks like the Tarkio. A cold drizzle began falling.

As slow rains often do, this one lasted all day and into the night. The road—or trail, if one is honest—grew muddy, and travel slowed as they made their way north through southwest Iowa. Still, by six o'clock that evening, Council Bluffs lay just twelve miles away. The stagecoach was lighter now, and less crowded, six of the eleven passengers having departed at Sidney. The driver thought he could make the final leg of the journey in two and one-half hours.

But from here, the road took to the river bottom and "was in a bad state." Night fell before they had gone six miles:

> *At this point was a sluce some twenty feet wide and about as deep. the watter was out of the banks and overflowed a large space of the bottoms both sides of the bridge. In the midst of the water before reaching the bridge the horses got set and could not move the coach. We were all obliged to get out and into the water three feet deep and wade to dry land. The water was cold as ice. our boots were full and more was pattering down on our heads while a cold north wind sent its chilling blasts almost through us.*
>
> *We stood a few minutes in this condition while the driver tryed to make his horses draw out the empty coach, but without success. What was to be done! No house was near, and to stand still was not deemed safe, in our wet and chilling condition. The driver wished us to wade in and unfasten his horses, while he remained on the Coach,*

thus enabling him to get on one of the horses and
get away without his getting in the watter We
declined however . . .

They were stuck. Now the only way forward was on foot.

Wading back to the stagecoach, the passengers grabbed their carpetbags and waded back to the bridge. They rested a minute, then "plunged in on the other side," wading for "near one hundred rods" (about a third of a mile) in icy water "knee deep and some of the way up to the seat of our pants."

Not daring to stop for long, they kept on through the rain and darkness, traveling "as best we could with our heavy Carpet Sacks boots filled with water, clothes wet and stif, and at every step our feet sticking like tar to the muddy prarie soil."

They hadn't gone far when they saw a light in the distance, "glimmering faintly through the darkness of the night and the falling rain." One man thought it was Council Bluffs, but the others dismissed the suggestion. Council Bluffs was still four miles away. Could the glow of a lantern or candle or fireplace really penetrate that far to beckon them on? Four miles—it was too discouraging a prospect, and they decided that the light must be coming from no farther than one and a half miles away. It had to be a farmhouse, a nearby farmhouse, standing alone on that endless prairie and waiting to shelter them for the night:

We draged ourselves along for one whole hour
until it seemed we could go no farther. Still that
deceptive light receded from us as fast as we
traveled, and we could not discover that it was
any nearer than when we started I could easily
imagine how one benight[ed] on the prarie in a
snow storm would become disheartened and lay
down and take his last sleep while the winter
wind covered him with pure white sheet of snow.

Another half hour and instead of one light we
could discover some dozen or more. this animated
us afresh at the same time we had another hun-
dred yards to wade in mud and water above our

knees. Our last half mile we paid no attention to the best part of the road so we made headway. At ten o'clock we reach the Paciffic House Council Bluffs. My head was dizzy and I could barely see while my arms seemed pulled down to the ground by my heavy satchel. We had walked six miles.

The source of the light had been Council Bluffs after all. Such was the darkness of the prairie—the moon and stars walled off by clouds, the grass fires snuffed out by rain—that the empty hills and valleys were enveloped in a vast and lonely blackness so intense that even the poor, flickering firelight in the windows of Council Bluffs homes shone like a beacon across four miles of rainy gloom.

And so the journey was all but over. Beadle arrived in Omaha City the next morning—a cold and foggy day—after traveling from Council Bluffs by omnibus and ferry. The journey from Buffalo had taken twenty-two days and all but nine of the nearly one hundred dollars with which he'd started out. He had come more than 1,200 miles by rail, river, and prairie—a hard journey, but he had arrived at last.

What did he find once he got there? What was it like to be so far away from home—out on the edge of the civilized world—in 1850s Omaha?

Chapter 2 notes

[1]This chapter is drawn entirely from Erastus Beadle, *To Nebraska in '57*, 3-23. Though I have not altered Beadle's spelling or grammar, I have added paragraph breaks to some of the lengthy quotations.

Chapter Three

A Long Way From Home

1850s

W hen Erastus Beadle at last saw Omaha City on the morning of March 31, 1857, it lay shrouded in fog. Still exhausted from his grueling journey, he gives us no further description of his entry into the city. But another early emigrant can tell us what it was like. And so, we will leave Mr. Beadle for a while and catch up with him later.

Emily Doane was seeing Omaha City for the first time. It was a bright, blustery, late autumn day in 1859, and Emily was aboard a steam ferry, crossing the wide, choppy Missouri River.

She was young, educated, well-born, and lately married to the new district attorney. They traveled together, William and Emily, a brilliant young couple ready to take their place in Omaha society. To them, the world was fresh and the future vast and uncharted, and it all lay spread out before them like a vast expanse of prairie.

Which is mostly what they could see from a distance. "The little settlement of houses, clustered about the new Herndon House at Ninth and Farnam streets" Emily wrote years later, "looked as though fallen down from the skies on to the bare plains."[1]

But soon the ferry landed, and Emily took her first step on

Nebraska soil. At just that moment, a gust of wind blew the cape of her poplin dress up over her head. As she pulled it down, the effect was something like an unveiling, or a curtain-raising at a theater. For the first time, she saw Omaha clearly, and the impression would linger for a lifetime:

> *And when I pulled it down and looked about me, I saw streets that were mostly a sea of mud, for there were no pavements and only one side-walk in town, a makeshift affair that surrounded the Herndon House. Here and there, a thoughtful citizen had laid a plank or two for the comfort of pedestrians, but these were few and far between.*

In short, Omaha looked "rough and unfinished." Still, Emily found (though she may have been working hard to perceive it) "a certain cosmopolitanism about the place." Looking past the crude conditions, she remembers the early settlers as "mostly college bred men of fine family" whose "adventurous spirit had guided them to the west."

There was something to this, at least among the Doanes' circle of friends. Upon their arrival, William Doane and Emily moved into the aforementioned Herndon House, Omaha's only real hotel at the time. At the Herndon, the residents did their best to transplant the lifestyle of Eastern society out onto the plains:

> *At the dances and evening parties, it was most unusual to see a man not in full dress suit, while women wore spreading skirts containing yards and yards of material, and the low-cut bodices of Victorian times. The skirts were long and had trains, for no lady would have allowed an ankle to be seen in those days . . .*

No one seemed to question whether or not the dress suits or the skirts with their flowing trains made much sense in such a place. Civilization was at a premium in early Omaha, and the "well bred" grabbed for it wherever they could.

Frank Leslie's Illustrated Newspaper, November 6, 1858
Omaha in 1858.

Emily was no exception. One night a dance was to be held. Emily loved dancing, loved parties, and was determined to go. Trouble was, the party was being held in another part of town, and the couple's horse and buggy were on loan to a friend. Undaunted, Emily set out on foot. That night, she was a picture of frontier civilization: a young woman in full dress, carrying her heavy skirts while gingerly picking her way through ten sparsely-inhabited blocks of unpaved streets, across bare ground rutted by wagon wheels and littered with manure, her path lit only by a single lantern carried by her husband, who walked ahead of her to guide her delicate, cultured, and indominatable footsteps.

And they arrived safely at the dance, and apparently had themselves a good time.

No Herndon House existed for Erastus Beadle when he arrived in Omaha. The lodging he found was of the log cabin variety, and even that was at a premium, costing a man eight dollars a day for room and board, an outrageous sum. At first, he took lodging at the house where his business associate, Mr. Cook, was staying. Beadle describes the conditions:

> *The Family where Mr Cook boards consists of
> the man and wife with nine children the oldest is
> a Son Married whose wife also lives in the same
> family, they also have five day boarders and they
> only occupy one room, without a closet pantry or
> any out house² and live up stairs. A curtain
> divides the room in the center one side is the din-
> ing room the other has a bed cook stove and all
> kitchen furniture. At night the beds are spread
> over the floor for the family and in the morning
> piled up in a corner. Such is Cook's boarding
> house without the least exageration.³*

Beadle soon learned, however, that living conditions in
Omaha weren't as bad as he thought. Which is to say that he
soon learned that the earliest settlers had had it even worse.
Consider, for example, the first Omaha home of Experience
Estabrook, Attorney General of Nebraska. Beadle relays the
description given him by Mrs. Estabrook:

> *They lived in what they now use as a barn, (it
> is not fit for horses) it is very low, and at the time
> the family occupied it, its only roof was made by
> putting a few small polls lengthwise and covering
> them with prairie grass, had no boards on the
> floor but covered the ground with hay and spread
> down a rag carpet and put in such furniture as
> they could procure, the house being on descending
> ground when it rained the water would run
> through the hay under the carpet and pass out on
> the other side. One night during a thunder storm
> a hole broke through the hay rooffing, the rain
> poard in faster than it would run out and they
> were forsed to use a wash tub most of the night,
> carrying it out as often as it filled which was every
> few minutes.⁴*

"How would Mrs. Beadle like this mode of living[?]" he asked
in his diary.

You have to wonder. Throughout his stay in Omaha, Beadle kept a diary and mailed completed sections off to his family at regular intervals. Scattered throughout the chronicle of his day-to-day affairs is a rich catalog of frontier experiences: breathing the dusty air when it was dry and windy; waking up to find the cabin floor covered with an inch of water when it rained; hearing news of a large wolf that had had the "impudence" to wander into town; killing rattlesnakes; meeting a Pawnee chief who was said to have killed many whites; hearing men call for the "extermination" of the Pawnees after an Indian scare; buying a claim and imagining what a fine farm it would be; casting a vote under the watchful eye of an illiterate election judge; 'booming' a new town.

It was this last activity that occupied most of his time. Though his professional background was in publishing, Beadle came to Omaha to work for the Saratoga Town Company. Saratoga was a would-be Omaha rival, located just a few miles to the north.[5] Beadle found the Saratoga townsite far superior to that of Omaha, and he worked hard to attract settlers and businessmen to the new city. Part of his job was to give away town lots to anyone who would build on them. He gave away plenty, and that summer the town grew rapidly. Though he continued to live in Omaha because of boarding arrangements, he was firmly convinced that the future would favor Saratoga. His was the boundless optimism and grandiose vision shared by all pioneers.

But truth be told, Erastus Beadle was not happy. It wasn't the frontier or the hardships. Those things intrigued him—amused him, usually—and Saratoga truly did excite him. But the distance from home and from loved ones, the weeks of travel which separated them, the slowness of the mail, the knowledge that accident or disease could strike in his absence—these are the things which made him miserable.

Five weeks and a day after leaving Buffalo, Beadle received his first letter from home:

A mingled sensation of joy and fear possessed me, were they all well if not well were they all liv-

ing, had disease or death been there? There had
been time for many sad changes.
    I took the letter unopened and went down to my
boarding house. Mrs. Estabrook knew I had a let-
ter as soon as she saw me. threw down the letter
on the table went down in the basement washed
my face and hands and brushed my clothes, then
went up into the sitting room and carefully
opened the letter. there was a letter enclosed from
each one . . . I read each one a number of times
which answered for my supper that night . . . I
slept but little althoug all were well at home.[6]

    This would be a recurring theme throughout Beadle's travel
diary—the nagging thought that he might have seen one or all
of his loved ones for the last time. Usually he expresses this fear
by complaining that he wasn't receiving enough letters; sometimes, he expresses it more openly, as on April 25:

    Another Sad Chapter in My diary. Among the
passengers that came up the river when I did was
a Mr Baker his wife son and daughter from
Western New York . . . His son was eleven years of
age and his daughter seven. The little girl on the
boat was taken down with the Whooping Cough .
. . one Eye was red as blood from Coughing which
had strained her Eyes very much. The boy had
been taken with the hay fever and was confined to
his bed.
    Yesterday [I learned that] *both children were*
dead and it was then time for the funeral. The girl
had died at noon and the boy at evening of the day
previous. I attended the funeral, and you may
readily imagine it was a heartrending scene. The
only children of the family a boy and girl lay side
by side in their . . . seperate coffins. The little girl
had on, in her coffin, a string of coral beads to
which was attached a little lockett. You cannot
conceive the feelings the sight gave me. The bal-

ance of the afternoon was a gloomy one to me. Oh how homesick I was[7]

Five days later, Beadle complained of nightmares. In a series of dreams, various friends and relatives came to him, one after another, to tell him of the death and burial of his daughter Sophia. In fact, Sophia was alive and healthy, but her father had no way of knowing that. All he knew was that he had just seen a couple—who like him were from western New York, and like him had two children, a boy and girl—lose them both within twenty-four hours.

And they weren't the only ones. During his journey to Omaha, Beadle attended the funeral of a little girl who had died in Weston, Kansas. Her parents—steamboat passengers bound for the territories—had no choice but to bury her and leave her behind. More recently, Scarlet fever was spreading through the Omaha area, and a number of local children had died with it.

"My mind is this morning in Buffalo," he wrote.

He first saw the woman from a distance, across a crowded room. The month of May was getting old, and Beadle had gone to a party held aboard the steamboat *Washington City*. A "fluttering a dresses" had caused him to turn around, and then he saw her—"a woman a perfect Degareotype of my wife in features."[8]

He did not dance with anyone that night, nor did he meet the woman—but he learned her name, Miss Clark, and he thereafter looked for her at every social occasion. A few weeks later, when another dance was being held, "I decided I would saunter down to the boat after the dance should commence and see what I could see." On the way he met his friend and roommate Cook, and "I told him I was going to the boat to see a lady. Cook laughed and said something about how good calico looked in Nebraska."

A few days later, when Cook had moved into a new house, Beadle no longer had to share a bed at night—for the first time since he had entered the territory. "I am glad to without a bedfellow," he wrote, "unless it be of a different sex from what I have had since I left Buffalo."

He continued to go to social gatherings in hopes of "feasting from a distance on the attraction of Miss Clark." What was going on here? Beadle wrote about Miss Clark repeatedly during that spring—yet did so in diary entries which he mailed off faithfully to his wife.

For all his watching, Beadle did not bother to actually *meet* Miss Clark, for that wasn't the point. Besides, "on a *close* view [she] did not bear the happy resemblance to my wife she did when distant the length of the Hall." So he continued to enjoy her from a distance, but—for Mrs. Beadle's sake—noted repeatedly how friends who had seen her photograph also noticed the resemblance, "so it cannot be attributed to her personal charms, sufficient to make my wife jealous if she *does* resemble her."

And so, of course, Erastus Beadle went home. At times, he had thought his family might be on their way, but learning that they were not, he decided in late August to go back. It wasn't that things had turned out badly. The future was bright and the tide of emigration strong. It was just that the money wasn't yet coming in fast enough. And with September coming on, the thought of spending the winter in Omaha—with no family and little income—was too much to bear. So he sold his Saratoga interest (but held on to Rockbrook Farm), and bought steamboat passage for St. Louis.

And on his way home, the upstate New Yorker discovered—somewhat to his surprise—that he had become a frontiersman. Arriving in St. Louis, he gagged at the stench of the big city's filthy air—an aroma he had not noticed on the westward journey. Nearing home and meeting old friends, comments such as "you look like a returned Californian" or "you are a regular border ruffian in earnest" made plain to him how much his appearance had changed. He was thinner now, his clothes badly worn, his hair unkempt, his complexion weathered.[9]

Beadle says almost nothing about his reunion with his wife and children in Cooperstown, where the family was now living. Though it was doubtless a heartfelt moment, it was not the triumphal meeting he had envisioned. The Saratoga scheme had not paid off. Worse, in a national economy that was starting to crumble, a local bank failure had destroyed the family's savings. Calculating his expenses for the year and his meager resources, Beadle concluded that for the time being, he had no choice but to stay in Cooperstown, "as all is now gone and I have no hopes."[10]

Still, he dreamed of returning to the West. Just past his thirty-sixth birthday, he was without direction, lost in the midst of the economic crisis soon to be known as the Panic of 1857. In the final day's entry of his travel diary, he says bitterly that "my friends and relatives have become scattered and I myself am out of business and unsettled and may take up my residence in the far west."[11]

In time, the West made Erastus Beadle a wealthy man. But it was not in Omaha City, but rather in New York City, where this happened. And it was not the West of reality—the West of Beadle's diary—but rather the West of myth that made his fortune. In 1860, Beadle and a partner began publishing a series of inexpensive books known as "Beadle's Dime Novels." They, and their imitators, were to become an American institution. These melodramatic tales of high adventure helped romanticize the West and laid the groundwork for the Wild West shows, the rodeos, and the Western movies of the future.

There's another Omaha connection here that's worth noting: Some of the dime novel heroes were people from real life, and so it happened that one-time Omaha resident Erastus Beadle helped to make a legend of a brave and talented Army scout named William Frederick Cody, a man who was to have an important Omaha connection of his own.[12]

Chapter 3 notes

[1] Ralph M. Wardle, "Territorial Bride," *Nebraska History*, Vol. 50, No. 2 (Summer, 1969), 210-215.

[2] "Out house" here refers to an outbuilding, not to a privy.

[3] Erastus Beadle, *To Nebraska in '57*, 22.

[4] Beadle, 26.

[5] The Saratoga townsite lay between modern-day Locust and Fort streets on the north and south, and between Carter Lake and 36th street on the east and west.

[6] Beadle, 30.

[7] Beadle, 35.

[8] Beadle and Miss Clark: 48, 52-53, 59-60. A daguerreotype was an early type of photograph.

[9] Beadle, 85.

[10] Beadle, 87.

[11] Beadle, 89.

[12] Beadle's dime novel career: Beadle, 3 (Introductory Note); Albert Johannsen, *The House of Beadle and Adams and Its Dime and Nickel Novels: The Story of a Vanished Literature*, Vol. I. Norman: University of Oklahoma Press, 1950.

Chapter Four

A Bushel of Donuts

1850s

Mathilda Peterson was alone and defenseless when the Indians entered her cabin. They came—we don't know how many there were—unannounced, and entered without knocking. That was the Indian way. Mathilda was terrified, of course, but refused to panic.

She was a young bride, lately come to Nebraska Territory with her husband, John. They had settled in Omaha City, building their cabin on the bank of the Otoe Creek, near what was to be the corner of Ninth and Jones.[1] John Peterson was an ambitious man. He was going to build a hotel, and not just a log cabin, but a real frame building. Just now he was away, cutting timber.

The Indians, saying nothing, sat on the cabin floor. Mathilda was frying a batch of donuts. Not knowing what else to do, she continued working as though nothing was out of the ordinary. But she was nervous, and soon accidentally dropped a donut. It rolled around on the floor, stopping in front of the leader of the Indians.

We don't know if Mathilda recognized the leader, but he lived nearby and was known in the community. He went by the name "No Flesh," and was said to be "no good." He also was hungry. Though the boiling-hot donut still sizzled, No Flesh snatched it up off the floor—and just as quickly dropped it with a howl of pain. Sticking his burnt fingers in his mouth, he realized that . . . his fingers tasted unnaturally good. The donut lay on the floor, cooling, and No Flesh picked it up again and tasted it.

It was delicious. He ate the donut, then called for more.

For more than an hour, the donuts disappeared as fast as Mathilda could make them. Working quick as she could, she kept a nervous eye on her shrinking store of provisions. What would the Indians do to her when the donuts ran out?

At last, and just as the supply was being exhausted, John Peterson arrived home. He entered the cabin to find his wife frantically slaving over the fire while No Flesh and his companions happily stuffed themselves with donuts.

Quickly, Peterson drove the Indians out of the cabin. Mathilda, safe at last, collapsed.[2]

In the 1850s, Omaha City was a new town in a new territory, but the settlers were by no means the first or the only residents of the area. In the early years, settlers were reminded of this daily. One early resident said that upon his father's arrival in 1855, "there seemed to be more Indians than white men in Omaha."[3]

In fact, five tribes lived in the vicinity: Pawnee, Omaha, Ponca, Otoe, and Missouria. Of these, the Omaha and Ponca were closely related, while the Otoe and Missouria had virtually merged into a single tribe. Though the tribes had their differences, they all shared an appalling poverty. Our friend Erastus Beadle described the following scene in his diary:

> *The Pawnee Indians are camped near here. The old men women and children. The strong and healthy are out on a Buffalo hunt. Those remaining here hang about the houses begging their living, stealing cats, dogs, and the refuse of the slaughter houses. Some one trying what he could do with his revolver shot a fine dog about a week ago. today the indians found it, and although it had commenced putrifying, they squat down skined it and carried it off to cook. Such is about*

Durham Western Heritage Museum
Indian Wigwam Store, 1870s, Farnam Street between 11th and 12th.

the best food the filthy Pawnees get while the hunters are away.[4]

On another occasion, Beadle found a place where "a mud hut of the Pawnees had been during the winter. The ground in the vicinity was strewed with bones of animals of various size including skulls of cats, dogs, deers, horses and cattle. The vicinity resembled the entrance to a wolfs den more than that of a human habitation."[5]

What neither Beadle nor most of the other settlers realized was that the Indians' extreme poverty was a relatively new condition. Life for the eastern Nebraska Indians had changed dramatically over the past generation, and generally not for the better. Though the changes were mainly the result of the United States' westward expansion, most settlers were unaware of the connection. They were unaware because most of the effects of westward emigration were felt in the region long before the first Nebraska settlers arrived.

Here's how it happened: As the frontier of white settlement advanced from the Eastern seaboard to the Appalachians in the seventeenth and eighteenth centuries, and then across the mountains and on into the Mississippi Valley in the late eighteenth and early nineteenth centuries, more and more native peoples were pushed west ahead of settlement and compressed into a smaller space. For instance, of the five eastern Nebraska tribes, only the Pawnees lived in the region prior to the eighteenth century. The other peoples migrated westward from the Great Lakes region. The Otoe, for example, had come west across southern Minnesota and northern Iowa, pressured by the Dakotas (Sioux) from the north and by the Sauk and Fox from the east. The migration took place gradually, over the course of many years. Finally, in the early 1700s, the Otoes crossed the Missouri and moved into what is now eastern Nebraska. The Omahas, Poncas, and Missourias, facing similar pressures, arrived later that century.

These groups did not find peace in their new homeland. More people were competing for fewer resources. Wild game became more scarce. Inter-tribal warfare became more common.

And then there was disease. Smallpox, diphtheria, cholera, and other maladies had existed among European peoples for centuries. Many had died, but over the generations the Europeans had built up some tolerance to these diseases. The Native Americans, isolated as they had been from the rest of the world, had no such tolerance. When the outside world began at last to trickle in, the effect was devastating.

By the time Lewis and Clark traveled up the Missouri River in 1804, all five tribes had been ravaged by recurring epidemics. The Omahas, for example, had numbered more than 2,000 in 1795. By the time of Lewis and Clark's visit, a smallpox epidemic had reduced their numbers by more than one half.

With such terrible mortality rates from disease, the Indians found themselves even less able to provide for themselves—with the result that malnutrition followed the epidemics. Thus weakened, the Indians of eastern Nebraska were more vulnerable to attack from their more numerous and better armed enemies to the north, the Lakotas.

All this would have been traumatic enough, but there was

more. Years ahead of the white settlers, and just behind the explorers, came the traders. To be sure, the traders brought with them guns and iron tools from which the Indians benefited, but they also brought whiskey.

The effect of alcohol on the already struggling native peoples can hardly be overstated. Alcoholism was rampant on the frontier, among whites and Indians alike, but while alcohol and its effects had long been known in the outside world, it was new to the Indians. Had smallpox been sold by the jug in liquid form, it could hardly have been more deadly. Smallpox could kill only the body; whiskey destroyed souls and cultures.

Wherever whiskey was introduced, violence and social disruption followed quickly behind. Moderate drinking was unknown. Once a village procured a barrel or two of spirits, they would drink as much as they could, and as quickly as they could. Under the influence of alcohol, acts of shocking cruelty were committed, even as more whiskey was purchased from traders instead of desperately needed provisions.

"They are complaining of starvation," wrote missionary Moses Merrill in Bellevue, "and at the same time leave their families to give away their little means of subsistence for whiskey at an extravagant price."[6]

By the time Omaha's first settlers began arriving, the local Indian tribes were but a shadow of what they had once been. Politically, they were losing their independence; economically, they had long since become dependent on trade goods and provisions from the whites; culturally, they were disintegrating; demographically, they were dying off. It's probably no accident that Omaha City's first grave, dug by William Snowden, Omaha's first settler, was for "the remains of an old Otoe squaw, who had been abandoned to die by the roadside."[7]

In short, the degradation—poverty, drunkenness, beggary, thievery—was appalling, but to the new residents of Omaha City, it appeared to be nothing other than the Indians' natural state. And what was natural was not to be mourned—especially if it was funny. Frank Burkley, an early-day resident, recalled one form of joking to which the illiterate Indians were subject:

Some of the Indians who were around Omaha
carried with them certificates of good character
given them by some waggish white acquaintances.
These were not always what the Indians thought
they were. I remember seeing one which certified
that the bearer was an adept at lying and stealing
and would carry off anything but a red hot stove.
He handed this around with much pride.[8]

At times, it grew more serious. "Indian atrocities" were frequently reported, and such news always caused great excitement among the settlers, who—for all their disdain for the
Indians—still feared them. In April 1857, Erastus Beadle
recorded the following in his diary:

Great Excitement on the frontier! Attack upon
the settlers by the Pawnees!! A Pawnee shot!!!—
Mr. John Davis, Justice of the peace at Salt creek
Lancaster Co. N. T. arrived here this Morning
about 10 o'clock calling upon The Governor for
Melitia to assist in exterminating the Pawnees.
Mr. Davis reports that depridations have been fre-
quent during this fall, winter and present Spring,
untill they have lost their oxen horses cattle and
in fact every thing the Indians could drive or run
off.
On Tuesday a number of Pawnees came to Salt
creek, painted and in war costume, demanding
the lands and pay for the deer and woolves the
whites had killed or they would kill and scalp
them, that they had taken the fort and scalped the
people, that there was a party of one hundred and
fifty Pawnees in the rear which would soon be up.
The present party continued in the vicinity all
night hooting and yelping.
About daylight they approached the house of
Mr. Davis with threatening signs, one of the
Pawnees raised his gun apparently in the act of
shooting—but was not quick enough as a ball

from Mr. Davis gun killed him on the spot. The
balance fled.[9]

Fortunately for the Pawnees, the governor wanted to learn
more of the affair before he sent in the militia. Beadle noted
that "this was not wholly satisfactory to Mr Davis who wanted
to raise a company of volunteers and exterminate the whole
race of Pawnees."

In those days, Mr. Davis was far from being alone in his sen-
timents. That such wholesale slaughters were generally avoided in the West may be due to the realization—among those settlers who looked closely enough—that there was another side to
the stories told about the Indians.

Erastus Beadle was one of those who grew in his understanding. About a month after Mr. Davis's Pawnee scare,
Beadle had the opportunity to meet a Pawnee war chief at the
home of a prominent Omaha citizen. The chief's name was
Corax, a friend of Beadle's host, Experience Estabrook. "What
he could not speak in english he made known by signs which
were made the most gracefull and almost seemed to speak, they
were so plain any one could understand them."[10]

Beadle was impressed by Corax's noble bearing and graceful
manner. Beadle noted that "It is said of him that he has probably scalped more white people crossing the plains than any
Pawnee of the tribe." Beadle seems to have been impressed,
rather than appalled, by this. Immediately, he adds, "He is however a most noble specimen of the Indian, and is at peace and
friendly with the whites." And then, just a few sentences later,
he admits:

> *The Indians have been greatly wronged, and as*
> *a general thing when there is Indian depredations*
> *the Whites are the first aggressors.*
>
> *The Pawnees were once numerous and very*
> *powerfull, and most to be dreaded of all the west-*
> *ern indians. In their wars with the Sioux and*
> *their intercourse with the Whites they have*
> *become as week as they were once powerfull, and*

are the most low filthy and degraded race in the west.[11]

We don't know if Mathilda Peterson knew any of this at the time she was frantically playing hostess to No Flesh and company. It's a safe bet that if she did know, she didn't much care.

No Flesh, meanwhile, couldn't have been more pleased with Mathilda. Later, he spoke with Mr. Peterson and proposed that they trade wives. No one-to-one trade, this: No Flesh offered three Indian women in exchange for the donut-frying wonder. Mr. Peterson, understanding the offer to be a friendly (and complimentary) joke, showed what a good sport he was by agreeing to the bargain.

Trouble was, No Flesh was serious. Soon, when Peterson was again away and Mathilda home alone, along came No Flesh with three squaws in tow. Mathilda, knowing nothing of any bargain—joking or otherwise—fled the cabin in terror. No Flesh then saw his future happiness, the true desire of both his heart and stomach, tearing off across the prairie under a full head of steam. He gave chase.

Mathilda ran a quarter mile to a neighbor's home, reaching the cabin ahead of her would-be husband.

"Save me!" she cried. And they did.

Historian Everett Dick wraps up the story in this way: "No-Flesh was stopped at the muzzle of a rifle and explanations were demanded. It took a council of war and a bushel of doughnuts to heal the breach."

Of course Mathilda would soon have learned the truth: that her husband, her bridegroom, her beloved, had agreed to trade her in, to swap, to horse-trade, to barter, to engage in a little commerce. And John Peterson could make no answer to this charge but to retreat to the feeble and spindly-legged argument that he had merely been *joking* when he agreed to sell her off like an extra mule. Whether any council of war or bushel of donuts, or flowers, or even gold coins could have saved Peterson from the awful wrath that awaited him, Professor Dick does not say.

Chapter 4 notes

[1]Location of the Peterson cabin: Federal Writers' Project, *Omaha: A Guide to the City and Its Environs*, Washington D.C.: Works Progress Administration, 1939, 116.

[2]Everett Dick, *The Sod-House Frontier 1854-1890*, Lincoln, NE: Johnsen Publishing Co., 1937, 167-168. The original source of this story (and thus its accuracy) is unclear. I found it only in Dick and in the Federal Writers' Project city guide. Neither book cites a primary source.

[3]Frank J. Burkley, *The Faded Frontier*, Omaha: Burkley Envelope & Printing Co., 1935, 70.

[4]Erastus Beadle, *To Nebraska in '57*, 27.

[5]Beadle, 33.

[6]Background on Nebraska Indians: David J. Wishart, *An Unspeakable Sadness: The Dispossession of the Nebraska Indians*, Lincoln: University of Nebraska Press, 1994, 1-9. Moses Merrill quotation: Wishart, 46.

[7]Alfred Sorenson, *History of Omaha from the Pioneer Days to the Present Time*, Omaha: Gibson, Miller & Richardson, Printers, 1889, 58. The grave was dug at the southwest corner of 10th and Howard, in what is today known as the Old Market.

[8]Frank Burkley, *The Faded Frontier*, 359.

[9]Beadle, 27-28.

[10]Beadle, 41.

[11]Beadle, 43.

Chapter Five

The Claim Club and the
Battle of Gophertown

1850s

S trong hands drew Callahan from the river and stood him
on the ice. It was late winter, 1857, and the ice still lay
thick over the Missouri. Callahan stood soaked and shivering beside the watery hole from which he had just been
pulled.

He was surrounded by a group of men, men who were warm
and dry, and who were prepared to stay out here as long as it
took to accomplish what they had in mind. It was they who had
pulled Callahan from the icy river. It was they who had pushed
him in in the first place.

They had asked him a question earlier, before they'd
"ducked" him. Now they repeated it.

Will you renounce your claim to that piece of land?, they
wanted to know.

Callahan spat out river water, then made his reply: No, he
would not. The land was his and he wasn't giving it up.

A few moments later he was back underwater.

Though the Missouri was frozen solid on top, the current still
flowed strong underneath, and it pulled at Callahan's body, trying to drag him away to a death by drowning under the layer of
ice. But the men held on to him, by means of a rope, perhaps—
held on for now, anyway. What was it that they'd told him? *That*

he would either renounce his claim or be drowned in the Missouri River. That was what they'd said. Now all they had to do was to let go; the current and the ice would do the rest. The river would not only kill him, but would dispose of the body so far downstream that whoever found him in the spring (if he was found at all) would have no idea who he was or where he came from.

Again, the strong hands drew him out, and again the question was posed: *Will you renounce your claim?*

Again, he refused.

And for a third time there was the stinging water, the removal from the water, the standing helpless on the ice while shivering soaking wet in the winter air—and there was the question.

The men were warm and dry, and prepared to stay out here as long as it took . . .

How could one man fight against that? They were either going to drown him or let him freeze to death—and they didn't seem to care which it was. Callahan realized he had no choice. He said he would give up the land.

They brought him into town to sign the document of relinquishment. Upon their arrival, however, they found that poor Callahan was in no condition to sign. Despite the stiffness of his frozen clothing, he could no longer even stand up on his own, much less hold a pen.

Doctors were summoned. The word *hypothermia* would not enter the English language for another three decades, but it wasn't difficult for the doctors to comprehend that Callahan's body temperature was dropping rapidly and that the thing to do was to warm him up. Taking him into a warm room, they stripped off his frozen clothing, wrapped him in blankets, and prescribed three "doses" of whiskey. Revived somewhat, the blanket-wrapped Callahan was handed pen and paper.

Like too much alcohol, hypothermia causes a state of stupor. We don't know Callahan's exact state of mind when he scrawled his name on the paper, but it was no doubt mellow, malleable, and—as far as his captors were concerned—well-suited to the signing of a legal document.

"An obstinate Irishman was ducked in the Missouri River by the Claim Club," read this illustration's original caption.

Such was one day in the life of the Omaha Claim Club.[1]

The Claim Club was a group of local settlers who agreed to protect each other's land claims from being "jumped" by outsiders. Such clubs were common on the frontier. In Omaha City, Callahan was not the first man, nor would he be the last, to run afoul of the Club. As he learned, their version of justice was swift and brutal.

Understanding what happened to Callahan—and how he got into that mess in the first place—requires a brief explanation of the process by which the virgin prairie was divvied up into private holdings.

It started with the staking of "claims." When Nebraska Territory opened in 1854, the government didn't immediately start selling off parcels of land. Instead, settlers came in and staked out claims. In part, this was exactly what it sounds like: you found some land you wanted, drove stakes into the ground to mark off your boundaries, and claimed it as your own.

There was a little more to it than that, of course. There were rules and limitations. Soldiers were issued land warrants, which entitled them to a certain amount of free public domain land, but others had to pay. You could buy a land warrant from a veteran—and often at a discount, if he was in need of quick cash. Or you could acquire land by pre-emption.

Pre-emption was the forerunner of the famous Homestead Laws of 1862. Under pre-emption law, you could claim 160 acres of the public domain, provided you met a few requirements: that you were a man over twenty-one or a widowed woman (wives and spinsters need not apply); that you'd never pre-empted before; that you didn't own 320 acres or more already; that you weren't acquiring the land with the intention of selling it or turning it over to somebody else; and that—to prove your good intentions—you had built a cabin on the land. Upon swearing under oath that you met these requirements, you could then buy your claim from Uncle Sam, usually for only $1.25 an acre.

A quarter-section of the world's finest corn-and-cattle land for $200—even by 1850s standards, that was a steal.

And it was a great temptation, especially in a new territory with little in the way of government or law enforcement, and in which the surveying had not yet been completed or the land office opened. During this early period—which in Nebraska lasted until 1857—settlers held no legal title to their land. They had to rely on their own surveys, settle their own boundary disputes, and guard their own land against those who wanted to take it away.

Enter the claim clubs. The clubs, or settlers' organizations, were a curious mixture of public and private elements. By an act of the Nebraska Legislature, each club was granted quasi-governmental powers within its neighborhood. Each club had its own elected officers, its own constitution and bylaws. A club could hold court, render a verdict, and enforce that verdict on non-members, using whatever means it felt appropriate. Combining into a coherent body the elements of township, old-boy network, and vigilance committee, the claim clubs became a potent, though short-lived, force on the frontier.

Omaha had its own club, as did Bellevue, Florence, and every other area of settlement in the territories. In the absence of local governments and law enforcement, the clubs were necessary. The settlers understood this clearly.

They also understood that a powerful local club could be a profitable undertaking for all involved. If acquiring 160 acres at a low price was a good thing, then acquiring 320 was twice as good. With this much land—half a square mile per man—a settler could sell half his claim and use the money to improve the other half. Or so they argued.

The Nebraska Legislature gave them what they wanted. The law of the United States said that 160 acres was the pre-emption limit. Nebraska Territory, not seeing the relevance of this law to its own situation, negated it with a law of it own. Nebraska's limit was 320 acres.

The difference in laws led to misunderstandings. Around Omaha, land was quickly gobbled up by claimants, a half-section at a time. But when later emigrants arrived, many did so with the outrageous notion that U.S. law somehow carried more weight than Nebraska law. And more than one latecomer tried to carve a quarter-section out of a club member's half-section. [2]

Just what the claim club members thought of this can be gauged from the wording of the following resolution, passed by acclamation at a mass meeting of the claim clubs of Omaha and surrounding communities in February 1857:

> *Resolved, that persons shielding themselves under the act of congress to pre-empt a man's farm under the color of law, shall be no excuse for the offender, but will be treated by us as any other common thief.*[3]

So they threatened, and so they did. During the following weeks, cabins were burned and men confronted at gunpoint. One man was hanged till unconscious, then made to sign away his claim as soon as he came to. Another man was starved into submission. Many others were taken down to the river.

Regarding this last method, our friend Erastus Beadle makes these comments in his April 18, 1857, diary entry:

> *Claim jumpers are being brought up daily Most of them forego their claimed right on the decision of the Club who give them a fair and impartial trial. occasionally however one is found who is stuborn and will not at once yeald. one of this class was tried last evening and this morning but would not abide by the decision of the club which was for him to yield his claim and withdraw his filling. The captain of "the regulators" is our Mayor a man six and a half feet high and well proportioned[4] he took the claim jumper by the collar escorted him down into the street, and with a dozen or fifteen men with loaded muskets they started for the "big Muddy." In general the prisoner comes to terms. What the result is in this case I cannot say. The party returned without the prisoner and no questions asked . . . I think I will be quiet and peacible.*

Hearing more the next day, Beadle adds the following:

> *The claim jumper that was taken off yesterday held out until they threw him into the river three times. They attached a rope to him threw him into the "big Muddy" then pulled him out if he was not ready to forego his claim they would Souse him in again, repeating the dose until he came to terms, which was not until he had been in the third time.[5]*

It's a safe bet that some of the men punished by the claim

club were genuine claim-jumping scoundrels. It's also well-established that many of the claim-jumpers were merely following the U.S. law of 160-acre claims. And a few cases, such as Mr. Callahan's, are clouded in mystery.

One version of Callahan's story is that the "obstinate Irishman" was simply unfortunate enough to claim land already claimed by a club member. Another version involves Thomas Cuming, the man who twice served as Nebraska's acting governor. In this version, Cuming hired Callahan to live on some land that Cuming was trying to pre-empt—so as to secure it by actual possession. Cuming paid Callahan regularly, the story goes, but when the land office opened, Callahan went there and claimed the land for himself.

If true, there's more than a trace of shady dealing in the Cuming story—and not just on Callahan's part. The idea behind pre-emption was that you could only claim land on which you were in the process of *settling*, not land on which you were paying another to live. The whole point of pre-emption was to allow genuine settlers—and not land-speculating politicians—to acquire farms at a bargain price. Did Cuming really intend to settle on the land, or was it just an investment? And was Cuming really involved in the first place? We don't know. All we know for sure is that Callahan died a few years later, and his death was said to have been hastened by the treatment he received at the hands of the Omaha Claim Club.

Common sense tells us that the claim clubs were necessary to guard the settlers' rights. But one can't read very far into their history without getting the sense that one is dealing with a gang of bullies. And the one thing that everyone likes to read about is a bully getting his comeuppance. This very thing happened to the Florence Claim Club, and happened in the streets of Omaha. The Omaha *Nebraskian,* feeling that the incident deserved epic treatment, told the tale in biblical-sounding language:

> *And it came to pass in the first year of the reign of James and in the seventh month, that a difficulty arose between some people from the town of*

Florence and a man who dwelt in Omaha but whose birthplace was an island across the sea which is called Ireland because the ire of its inhabitants is so easily aroused. [6]

And the portion of Omaha in which the man dwelt is called Gophertown because most of the inhabitants thereof dwell in houses made in the ground like unto the burrows of gophers of the prairies. [7]

And the cause of the difficulty was that the man of Gopher, whose name was Dennis surnamed Dee, had bought of the rulers of the country some land the right to possess which was claimed by a dweller in Florence and the inhabitants thereof—having no business to do—assembled en masse and journeyed to Gophertown to take and punish the man Dennis for buying land without their consent.

And they dressed in divers costumes and came in many different conveyances, by different paths, to avoid awakening the suspicion of their intentions.

And the leader of them was one James whose surname is Mitchell who albeit though small in stature was a valiant and terrible man.

And when the male citizens of Gophertown had departed to their daily work they entered into the house of the man Dennis for they had sworn that they would take him vi et armis and try him under their own vine and fig tree, and administer unto him justice according to their own laws; and by their valiant bearing and the terrible oaths they swore, they frightened greatly the women and children that were in the house; albeit they found not the man Dennis.

But runners were sent out and the men whose homes were in Gophertown were called from the roads and the ditches and the fields where they were at work.

And they armed themselves with guns and pistols, and an implement of war in use among them, called in their language a shillalah, which being translated means a short club.

And they drove the invaders from their households, and pursued them through the streets of Omaha.

At noonday hostilities were suspended, but in the evening after the arrival of reinforcements the wanderers from Florence resumed their activities, and again called on the dwellers in Gophertown to enforce their demands, but this simply caused their wrath to burn and they loaded their guns and took fast hold of their shillalahs and made haste to revenge themselves upon the invaders.

Whereupon the wanderers from Florence suddenly recollected that they had some business to transact at their homes and they turned and fled towards Florence, looking neither to the right nor to the left but running with the speed of the wind with the tails of their coats sticking straight out behind them, and the bullets which followed them were not swift enough to catch them.

And to this day all that is necessary to arouse the anger of a man from Florence is to mention the fourth letter of the alphabet.[8]

Chapter 5 notes

[1]Callahan and the claim club: Sorenson, *History of Omaha*, 108-109. The italicized questions (*Will you renounce your claim*) are not quotations.

[2]Pre-emption law and claim clubs: Dick, *The Sod House Frontier*, 19-20. The main difference between pre-emption and the 1862 Homestead laws was this: Under pre-emption law, the government *sold* the land to the claimant (albeit at a low price) at the time of registration; under homestead law, the government *gave* the land to the claimant after he or she had lived there for five years.

[3]Sorenson, 106.

[4]Jesse Lowe, Omaha's first mayor.

[5]Beadle, 32-33.

[6] "James": James Buchanan, 15th president of the United States. He took office in March, 1857; the incident here told took place in September of that year.

[7]Gophertown, better known as Irishtown, ran along Jones street from 10th to 13th streets. With lumber scarce and expensive, dugouts were an affordable temporary dwelling.

[8]Quoted in Burkley, *The Faded Frontier*, 227-228.

Chapter Six

Parliamentary Procedure

January 1855

Reverend Wood had some bad news for a friend. Since it involved the Territorial Legislature—always a delicate subject—he decided to break the news as gently as possible.

Wood was the chaplain for Nebraska's brand-new House of Representatives, opening the sessions with prayer. But his role was more complicated, for he was not only a chaplain, but also an elected representative. He could not, therefore, stand serenely above the political fray.

And right now it was indeed a fray. A fight was brewing over the location of the territory's capital, and Wood was necessarily part of that fight. He had something to say House Speaker A. J. Hanscom, unofficial leader of the powerful Omaha delegation. Hanscom wasn't going to like it one bit.[1]

It was January 1855, and Nebraska Territory at last had a government. Despite the death of Governor Francis Burt shortly after his arrival in Bellevue, the government's development had gone on without delay. In fact, as far as Omaha was concerned, Burt's illness and death had presented a wonderful opportunity.

Here's how it worked: A territory didn't elect its own governor; he was appointed by the President. If the governor died, the territorial secretary would serve as acting governor until the new man arrived. This could, of course, take months. In this case, it happened that the secretary, a twenty-five-year-old Iowan named Thomas Cuming, was a man friendly to the interests of Omaha and Council Bluffs. And he was not a man afraid to exercise power.

Though Governor Burt had come to Bellevue, and probably would have convened the Legislature there, Cuming announced that the new government would meet in Omaha. Preparing for the election of the legislators, Cuming drew up the electoral districts in such a way as to give Omaha disproportionately high representation. Men from other towns were furious, but the young governor refused to back down.[2]

So the election came and went, and the legislature convened in Omaha. But the fight for the territorial capital wasn't over yet. Reverend Wood's bad news—in fact, his very presence in the Legislature—had something to do with this.

Wood's involvement had begun as soon as he had arrived in Omaha. Both he and another man claimed to have been elected to the same seat. Who was lying? Rather than waste time investigating the matter, the House decided simply to vote on it.

Wood was willing to do whatever it took to get the seat. He talked with Hanscom, the formidable Omaha partisan and newly-elected Speaker. Wood knew that Cuming's choice of Omaha was not final. He knew that there would be a vote in the Legislature, a vote which Omaha—despite Cuming's efforts—was not sure to win. Wood knew, therefore, exactly what Hanscom wanted to hear, and he said it: He promised Hanscom that if he got the disputed House seat, he would vote for Omaha. Hanscom, pleased with the offer, used his influence to garner the necessary votes. Wood won the seat.

Now, several days had passed, and Wood—his election secure—found that circumstances had changed. He tried explaining it to Hanscom as gently as he could.

"Mr. Hanscom," he said, "I am very sorry, indeed, to be obliged to inform you that I shall, owing to the force of circumstances, be compelled to vote against Omaha."

Hanscom was astonished. He knew politics was a dirty business, but he hadn't expected to be double-crossed by a preacher.

Nebraska's first territorial capitol was on Ninth Street, south of Harney. Built in 1854, it was Omaha's first brick building.

"The devil you say!" he exploded. "You're a —— —— infernal lying old hypocrite!"

"Those are hard words, my dear Mr. Hanscom, but—"

"I reiterate it, that you are an infernal lying old hypocrite. You're a wolf in sheep's clothing. And, by gracious! you've said your last prayer before this legislature. If there is any more praying to be done I will do it myself. That's the kind of man I am."

Wood was fortunate to receive only a tongue-lashing. Andrew Jackson Hanscom was not a man to be trifled with; even the fiery lawyer's friends admitted that he would "as soon fight as eat." As his prior history shows, Hanscom was a restless, ambitious, and determined man. A native of Michigan, he left home at age fourteen to seek his fortune. For four years, he clerked in a general store and attended school during the winter. By age eighteen he was studying law. When war broke out with Mexico in 1846, he got himself a lieutenant's commission in the First Michigan Infantry. Hanscom profited from the experience of leadership; he also made a contact whose importance became apparent years later: among the men under his command was a future territorial governor named Thomas Cuming.

After the war, Hanscom returned to his legal studies, becom-

ing a practicing lawyer at age twenty-one. His youth and restlessness, however, were still apparent; that fall, he came down
with a bad case of gold fever. Dropping his legal practice, he
headed for California.

The would-be Forty-Niner got only as far as Council Bluffs,
Iowa. Deciding against the long westward trek, Hanscom
resolved to make his fortune there on the banks of the Missouri
River. Over the next several years he built a mill, established
himself in the mercantile business, and practiced law on the
side.

He also got involved in the plot to build a new town across
the river. When Omaha City's first Fourth of July revelers got
spooked by Indians, Hanscom and his wife were among the little group hustling back to the ferry. That fall, they and their
three children moved to the new town, where Hanscom was
soon elected to the Legislature. With optimism and relentless
energy, he tied his personal fortunes to those of Nebraska's
would-be capital city. He was twenty-six years old.[3]

Hanscom's energy was sorely needed. By acquiring the capital, Omaha had also acquired a host of enemies who wanted to
take it away. Nebraska's first day of legislative government,
January 16, 1855, began with a mob scene calculated to end
Omaha's reign as capital city before it even began. Coming in
from Nebraska's other "cities," an anti-Omaha mob descended
on Omaha's "State House." Wearing red blankets (to look like
Indians), the angry out-of-towners came in boasting that they
would break up the Legislature by force. Soon, the halls were
filled with what an observer described as "excited and desperate men."[4]

Acting Governor Cuming was not so easily frightened.
Sensing a bluff, he chose to ignore the mob—and got away with
it. The Legislature was seated and Hanscom elected Speaker of
the House.

With Hanscom in the speaker's chair and Omaha over-rep-
resented on the floor, petty scoundrels like Wood found themselves no match for the torrent of skulduggery thrown their way
by the Omaha men. True to his promise, Hanscom got Wood
fired as chaplain, and managed—with the help of friends—to

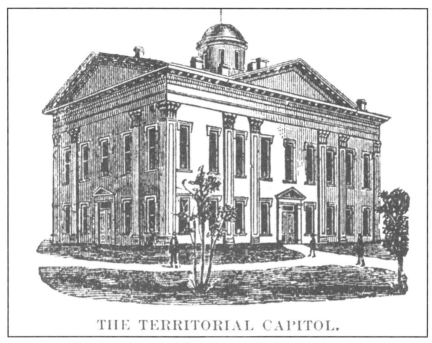

THE TERRITORIAL CAPITOL.

The second territorial capitol was built in 1857 on the
present site of Central High School.

make Wood's life as a legislator as miserable as possible for the
rest of the term.

The Omahans tried a softer touch with many of the other legislators. Many a man became friendlier to the capital city after
his pockets were lined with dollars and with Omaha town lot
certificates. The bribery was as extensive as it was brazen. So as
to have more land to give away, the Omaha men surveyed a
half-mile-wide strip which they then annexed to the city. It was
soon known as "Scrip Town," because most of the certificates of
ownership ("scrip") were given away as legislative bribes.[5]

Meanwhile, on the floor of the House, Hanscom and his
friend and co-conspirator Andrew Jackson Poppleton kept
things running smoothly. The House was governed by the rules
of parliamentary order that Thomas Jefferson had developed for
the U.S. Congress. Hanscom and Poppleton had their own take
on parliamentary procedure. Dr. George L. Miller, another

Omaha politician who would later found the *Omaha Herald*, admiringly described the pair in action:

> *Speaker Hanscom was a great power in that struggle, upon which the existence of Omaha actually depended. Poppleton on the floor was more than a match for all comers; this was certainly so in debate and parliamentary fence and skill. He was eloquent of speech and masterful in both attack and defense.*
>
> *But as a presiding officer in a legislature Hanscom was simply a genius. He could murder Jefferson's manual and then mutilate the corpse when any exigency demanded it with an audacity that appalled the opposition. Speaker Hanscom would rule in support of Poppleton on occasion with a banging of gavels that must have startled the gophers of the surrounding prairies from their subterranean abodes. But the speaker was always insistent upon parliamentary order.[6]*

Dr. Miller noted that Hanscom had some peculiar methods of keeping order. A legislator who was out of order (i.e., speaking against Omaha) would be ordered by Hanscom to sit down and be quiet. If the legislator failed to take his seat, he "was emphatically notified that if he didn't sit down he would get knocked down."

The result, Dr. Miller reported casually, "was usually satisfactory to the speaker."

Such was democracy, Omaha style. It was loud, combative, corrupt, potentially violent, and generally a little sour from the odor of alcohol. One of the best descriptions of the early legislature comes to us from J. W. Pattison, editor of the *Omaha Arrow*:

> *It is a decidedly rich treat to visit the General Assembly of Nebraska. You see a motley crowd inside of a railing in a small room crowded to overflowing, some behind their little schoolboy*

desks, some seated on the top of desks, some with their feet perched on the top of their neighbor's chair or desk, some whittling—half a dozen walking about in what little space there is left.

The fireman, doorkeeper, sergeant-at-arms, last year's members [he was describing the 1856 session], *and almost anyone else become principal characters inside the bar, selecting good seats and making themselves generally at home, no matter how much they may discommode the members. The clerk, if he chooses, jumps up and explains the whys and hows of his journal. A lobby member stalks inside the bar, and from one to the other he goes talking about the advantages of his bill.*

A row starts up in the secretary's room, or somewhere about the building, and away goes the honorable body to see the fun . . . then a thirsty member moves an adjournment and in a few minutes the drinking saloons are well patronized . . . .

Although both bodies [the upper and lower houses of the legislature] *have about seven more days to sit, only four bills have been passed. It is one continued personal and local fight—a constant attempt at bargain, sale and argument.*[7]

Omaha's first years were boom years. The town may not have looked like much, but people were eager to invest in it. Consider, for instance, the case of a German immigrant traveling by steamboat in 1855. Before arriving in Omaha, he bought a town lot for $400, a considerable sum. Arriving at "Omaha City," he was appalled by what he saw—or rather by what he *didn't* see, which was anything resembling a city. He realized, to his dismay, that he'd been swindled out of roughly a year's wages in exchange for a 66-foot x 132-foot patch of dirt (a "hole in the ground," he called it) located amidst a motley assortment of rude cabins and dugouts, and accessible only by one of those muddy paths of which the locals had the effrontery to call *streets.*

He soon sold the lot for $800.[8]

And he'd have done even better to hold onto it for a year: by the summer of 1856, Omaha men were refusing offers of $3,000 per town lot. That summer, Omaha's population grew from 800 in June to 1,500 by October. By the fall of 1857, the town boasted 2,000 inhabitants.[9]

Then came the collapse.

A national economy built on speculation and financial recklessness came crashing down in the fall of 1857. The panic spread across the country east to west, collapsing inflated stock and land prices, and bankrupting banks and businesses. In the aftermath of the panic (one of the worst in U.S. history), many frontier boom towns suddenly found themselves destitute.

Omaha was hit hard. By the winter of 1857-58, it was on its way to becoming a ghost town. By one estimate, the town's population declined from 2,000 to about 500 during the following year. Those who stayed ate from their gardens and made do in what was now mostly a barter economy. One early politician estimated that by January 1858, there was not, on average, $2.50 cash to each resident of Nebraska Territory.[10]

This meant, of course, that the other Nebraska towns were in dire straits as well. Many withered away entirely. But Omaha had an advantage, one thing which ensured its survival: it still had the territorial capital.

January 1858

The news came quietly on January 6—quiet, but as ominous as a death sentence. Eight days remained before the end of the Legislature's forty-day annual session. Tomorrow, Omaha's enemies would introduce a bill which would move the territorial capital to a new, as yet non-existent town.[11]

In a way, this was nothing new—the fight over the capital's location had recurred every year since 1855—but this time, Omaha did not have the votes to stop it. Once introduced, the bill would surely pass, and by a veto-proof majority. After that, Omaha would still have the stately white edifice on the hill, but the former capitol would stand as empty as the cabins of Omaha's former settlers. The main—and perhaps the only—

Legislators "debate" the location of the Nebraska capital.

good reason in favor of the town's continued existence would be gone.

That night, Omaha's representatives met privately. The bill must be stopped, but how?

They had been trying to head it off all session. Weeks earlier, they had discussed paying the usual bribes. This had been effective before, but was getting harder and harder. A. J. Hanscom, out of office but still recognized as the leader of Omaha's defense, wanted no part of it. Angrily, he complained that he'd been paying out money long enough, and proposed instead to "whale" somebody.[12]

By the sixth it was clear that Hanscom's modest proposal was not exactly a winning strategy either. Nebraska City's James Decker, the thirty-one-year-old Speaker of the House and staunch anti-Omaha man, was reputed to have armed himself with a revolver. Rumor had it that his friends were likewise prepared for trouble.

Omaha, then, had but one more card to play, and that would involve a bit of parliamentary procedure. The trick would be getting Decker out of the speaker's chair and an Omaha man into it. There would be only one chance to do this, but if it worked, the capital—and with it the city of Omaha—might still be saved.

The next day's legislative session began quietly enough. The House's first order of business was to consider some matters regarding government printing. The House went into something called "Committee of the Whole," with a man named

Strickland in the speaker's chair. The speaker's job was not to participate in the debate, but to maintain order and enforce parliamentary rules. Strickland, however, soon decided that he wanted to join in the discussion. So he called J. Sterling Morton of Nebraska City to take his place.

That was the fatal mistake. It gave the Omaha men the opening they needed, for Strickland was an anti-Omaha man, but Morton was an ally.

How could Omaha turn an ordinary discussion of printing to its advantage? *By dragging it out for the rest of the term.* The plan was to "talk against time," what today we would call a *filibuster*. Morton had the chair; A. J. Poppleton had the floor. Poppleton would talk until exhausted, at which time Morton would give the floor to another Omaha man, and so on, all day long till they adjourned. Then they would come back in the morning and pick up where they left off—and keep it up for eight days. Then the legislative session would end, and Omaha would be safe for another year.

According to his enemies, the twenty-seven-year-old Poppleton "spoke of all conceivable subjects except public printing, beginning as far back as Gulliver's famous history of the Lilliputian War. The lobbies were crowded and Mr. Poppleton was loudly applauded by the Omaha lobby members."[13]

The anti-Omaha men began to realize that they'd been had. Led by Decker, they withdrew from the capitol to talk things over in private.

Decker was frustrated. Despite Omaha's bribery and other shenanigans, he and his allies had a twenty-four to eleven majority in the House and a nine to four majority in the Council.[14] Yet the majority couldn't get anything done. Time and again, the Omaha legislators reached into their bag of parliamentary tricks and derailed measures unfavorable to them. As an implied threat, they had "a mob" of friends waiting in the lobby and the one-man mob of A. J. Hanscom waiting near the speaker's chair.

Omaha had even shown the audacity—as was recently discovered—to secretly retain title to the capitol and its grounds. Though built partly with federal money, Nebraska's capitol was, amazingly, legally owned by the city of Omaha, which had used the building as collateral on a local bond issue, even while putting a lien on the building for every cent of the money that Omaha had contributed to its construction.[15]

It was too much, and Decker, for one, had had enough. He wanted a new capital city. To get it, he needed to be in control, just once more, in the speaker's chair. He vowed to "have it this afternoon or die trying."[16]

When Decker and company returned to the capitol that afternoon, they found an Omaha man named William Thrall, a twenty-eight-year-old physician, in the speaker's chair. Another Omahan had the floor. On cue from Decker, the sergeant-at-arms interrupted and announced that he had a message from the Council. Decker approached the speaker's chair to receive the message. According to parliamentary rules, Decker needed to resume his role as speaker, then call the House out of committee and back into full session before they could receive the message.

It was a formality, but in this case an important one. For Decker to resume the speaker's chair, and thus to regain control of the proceedings, was the whole idea. Once back in control, Decker wasn't going to be tricked out of it again, not until the capital was safely voted out of Omaha. The plan was for the House to adjourn temporarily to Florence, Omaha's rival to the north. Once in Florence and away from any Omaha mob that might threaten the proceedings, the capital removal vote could safely take place.

By now the back of the room was packed with an anxious crowd of onlookers. They watched as Omaha's future faded with each step Decker took toward the front. But before Decker reached the chair, Poppleton sprang to his feet and raised a point of order. He asked the clerk if the Council was presently in session. When told that it was not, Poppleton triumphantly opened Jefferson's manual and read aloud a rule which prohibited the House from receiving messages from the Council *unless both were session*. Since this was not the case, Decker would have to sit down.

Decker was livid. Poppleton's response, even for his lawyerly mind, had been too quick to be spontaneous. Someone had tipped him off. But Decker had no time to discover the identity of the rat. Outmaneuvered or not, he wasn't about to sit down and be quiet. Advancing to the rostrum, he announced that he would "have that message or die right here." Then, reaching for the gavel, he tried prying it from Thrall's hands.

A. J. Hanscom, sitting nearby, offered Thrall a piece of truly Hanscom-esque advice:

"Hit the rascal over the head with the gavel!"[17]

By now, Decker was trying to tip Thrall out of the chair. Hanscom sprung to his feet and grabbed hold of Thrall from the other side. Soon Decker and Hanscom were engaged in a bitter tug-of-war, with the unfortunate Thrall as the rope. What with the little schoolboy desks at which the legislators sat, the scene might have been mistaken for a classroom—only with bigger boys, more swearing, and no teacher in sight.

Events followed rapidly. Two Omaha men charged and dragged Decker away from the chair. Decker wrestled on the floor with one of them. Hanscom, still on his feet, grabbed Decker by the back of the neck and the seat of the pants and threw him under a table. Thrall, having lost the gavel (but fortunately not his arms), grabbed a heavy statute book and began pounding the rostrum and shouting for order. A man who was addressing the House continued his oration as though nothing out of the ordinary was happing. Decker, emerging from the under the table, declared the committee dissolved and the House adjourned.

At some point, this chain reaction of events reached a critical mass; in the back of the room, about fifty onlookers—Omaha men—sprang to their feet and charged into the area where the House members sat.

What followed was bedlam, and the anti-Omaha men got the worst of it. As an early-day Omaha historian told it, "All was excitement and uproar, and when it gradually subsided it was found that several persons had been badly used up. Bloody noses and black eyes were too numerous to mention. It was hard to tell which were in the majority—the ayes or the noes."[18]

With the anti-Omaha men "cleaned out" and order restored, it appeared that Omaha was safe for another year. But Decker and company weren't ready to give up yet. On the morning after the disturbance, they sprang their own surprise. Immediately after the Legislature's opening prayer, one of the men sprang to his feet and moved that the House adjourn to meet in Florence the next day. The motion was seconded and carried before the Omaha men knew what hit them.

For the next several days, Nebraska found itself in a bizarre legislative predicament. The Omaha men, considering the adjournment to Florence illegal, stayed behind; the anti-Omaha men met in Florence and demanded to be recognized by the governor as Nebraska's real Legislature. For several days, these two rival governments denounced each other from afar.[19]

The Florence Legislature, led by Decker, issued a manifesto to the people of the territory. "Omaha still retains the capital," one paragraph admitted, "bought with such an infamous past of corruption[,] violence and crime[,] but the sceptre of legislation has departed from the ill-fated city, and the law givers from its riotous halls forever."[20]

The Omaha *Nebraskian* saw it differently. Comparing Nebraska's fractured political situation to that of "Bloody Kansas" to the south, a headline screamed:

BORDER RUFFIANISM IN NEBRASKA!
KANSAS OUTDONE!!
BOLD ATTEMPT AT REVOLUTION!!!
SPEAKER DECKER HEADING THE REVOLUTION!!!!
**REVOLUTIONISTS TO ORGANIZE ANOTHER **
GOVERNMENT AT FLORENCE UNDER
THE PROTECTION OF BRIGHAM YOUNG!!!!![21]

Since Florence had been built on the site of the winter quarters of the Salt Lake-bound Mormons, it stood to reason (at least to the *Nebraskian's* editors) that the new Legislature was somehow a Mormon plot.

The *Nebraskian* also took issue with its rivals' reporting. Certainly, the other towns had reason to exaggerate the violence, for it helped to show that Omaha was unfit to be the capital. But likewise, Omaha had reason to minimize the incident. However, in an extra devoted to coverage of the crisis, the *Nebraskian* could not resist admitting—with obvious pride— that "a pretty general melee ensued, creating a nice scene of confusion, which, in the expressive language of an eye witness, would 'almost make one think that H-ll had given a holiday and turned all the devils loose in the Nebraska Legislature.'"

This aside, the *Nebraskian* vented its wrath on a Cuming City paper which claimed that Bowie knives and pistols had been drawn during the fight. Referring to the paper's editor as "an ignoramus who murders the Queen's english," the *Nebraskian* said that his "statement is so glaringly false that it bears upon its face the only refutation so imbecile a production demands."

The Cuming City editor claimed to have been an eye-witness of the brawl, but the *Nebraskian* berated the notion: "If he was in the House at the time of the disturbance, he must be a more practiced liar than we had even supposed—and his reputation in that line is by no means small—or his imagination at least very lively, for he is the only person of about one hundred who were present who even pretends to *think* that any weapons were drawn, except the gavel with which Decker attempted to strike Thrall."

For all its fulmination, the *Nebraskian* nevertheless displayed big-hearted tolerance toward the erring editor, saying gently, "But we do not wish to be severe on our whiffet contemporary. His position in newspaperdom is very much like a certain substance that is usually found in the vicinity of horse stables. . . ."

Before long, the snide remarks were all that remained of the crisis. Not only did Acting Governor Cuming refuse to recognize the Florence legislature, but the new governor, William Richardson, proclaimed that even a majority of the Legislature had no legal right to relocate the government without his approval, which he refused to grant.

In short, Omaha's enemies had failed again. They would not succeed in prying the capital from Omaha's grasp until 1867, the year of Nebraska statehood.

Like the city itself, several of Omaha's young defenders went on to positions of prominence. A. J. Poppleton, the shrewd parliamentary manipulator, was elected mayor that year. Later, the Union Pacific Railroad—perhaps recognizing the wily lawyer as a kindred spirit—made him the railroad's general attorney. Meanwhile, Omaha ally J. Sterling Morton made a fortune from his business ventures (such as Morton Salt), but is best remembered as the founder of Arbor Day. And A. J. Hanscom—a man who embodied the violently partisan spirit of Omaha—eventually grew wealthy from dealing in Omaha real estate and securities. In 1872, he donated some of his land to the city for a park. It is known as Hanscom Park to this day.[22]

Chapter 6 notes

[1]Wood and Hanscom: Sorenson, *History of Omaha*, 80-81.

[2]Sorenson, *History*, 69-78.

[3]J. Sterling Morton (ed.), *Illustrated History of Nebraska*, Vol. I, Lincoln: Jacob North & Co., 1905, 293-296.

[4]Sorenson, 73.

[5]Sorenson, *History*, 78-80.

[6]Morton, 297.

[7]Quoted in James P. Olson and Ronald C. Naugle, *History of Nebraska*, 3rd Ed., Lincoln: University of Nebraska Press, 1997, 84.

[8]Burkley, *The Faded Frontier*, 71. Town lot size: *Omaha Arrow*, July 28, 1854.

[9]Dick, *The Sod House Frontier*, 46.

[10]Burkley, 104-105.

[11]Morton, 327-328 (quoting a 1904 letter from participant W. R. Thrall).

[12]Sorenson, *History*, 93.

[13]James Savage and John Bell, *History of the City of Omaha Nebraska and South Omaha*, New York: Munsell & Co., 1894, 71-72, quoting the *Nebraska Pioneer*. The account of this day's legislative session is based on: Sorenson, *History*, 93-97; Savage and Bell, 64-68; Morton, 327-328.

[14]The Council was the upper house of the legislature, the territorial equivalent of a state senate.

[15]James B. Potts, "The Nebraska Capital Controversy, 1854-59," *Great Plains Quarterly*, 8 (Summer 1988), 178-179.

[16]Savage and Bell, 68 (quoting the sworn testimony of eyewitness Daniel Nelson).

[17]Sorenson, *History*, 94.

[18]Sorenson, *History*, 95.

[19]Savage, 68-72.

[20]Quoted in the *Omaha Nebraskian*, January 13, 1858.

[21]*Nebraskian*, January 8, 1858 extra, reprinted in January 13, 1858, issue.

[22]Biographical information on Poppleton, Morton, and Hanscom: Morton, *Illustrated History*, 324 (Poppleton); 710 (Morton); 293, 296 (Hanscom).

Chapter Seven

The Coming Dictator

1863-1873

Newspaper headline, December 4, 1863:

"A PROUD DAY FOR OMAHA!

Formal Opening of the Union Pacific Railroad.

FIRST 'BREAKING OF THE GROUND.'"[1]

The bloodiest year America had ever seen was finally staggering to a close. More than two-and-a-half years had passed since the Civil War had begun—a war that most people had thought would be over in a month or so—and the conflict was showing Americans carnage on an incomprehensible scale. From July alone, the numbers were staggering: 50,000 casualties at Gettysburg; a forty-eight-day siege at Vicksburg, Mississippi—the residents hiding in caves to survive the bombardment, and reduced, by the siege's end, to living on mule meat; anti-draft riots in New York City, three days of anarchy, U.S. troops called in to fire upon rioting civilians, casualty estimates ranging from 300 to more than 1,000.[2]

But there was hope. Gettysburg and Vicksburg had both been decisive Union victories, while New York City had managed to survive its riots, though the draft was still highly unpopular there, as elsewhere. But there was hope that the terrible war would finally end, and that America would soon get back to its real line of work: westward expansion.

And so it was an act of great faith—right there in the middle of a bloody civil war—to begin the most ambitious and expensive building project the country had ever attempted. It began in Omaha on December 3, 1863. It was a day, as the Omaha *Nebraskian* put it, "to thank God and take courage."

The groundbreaking took place near the ferry landing. Less than ten years earlier, a small group of Fourth of July revelers had landed on that same spot, talking big and boasting of the great city they were going to build. On this day, despite the chilly weather, it seemed again like the Fourth of July, with "the booming of cannon, the waving of flags, and the enthusiastic demonstrations of a large concourse of people."[3]

And the usual dignitaries were there—the governor, the mayor, and the prominent local citizens—and speeches were called for. The speakers brought out their gaudiest adjectives and no doubt covered much of the same ground as did Omaha's original Fourth of July orator back in '54—with the advantage that this scene didn't end with a panicked race for the river.

But one of the speakers outdid them all. His name was George Francis Train, and he was a remarkable man. Just thirty-four years old, Train was one of the big Union Pacific men, and was the only one of the big shots to come all the way out from New York City for the ceremony.

Orphaned at age four, by his early twenties Train had made a fortune in shipping. He then traveled around the world, wrote books, introduced street-railways (the horse-drawn kind) to England, and—while still in England after the Civil War broke out—risked his business interests to speak out boldly in the United States' behalf.[4]

When George Francis Train spoke out boldly on a subject (and he spoke in no other way), he got attention. In an age of great orators, Train was among the finest, a man with such strong personal charisma that his effect on a crowd can scarcely be understood by reading in cold print the text of his speeches. And as far as Train was concerned, Britain was past its prime, played out. America was the new empire.

"Before the first century of the nation's birth," he told the Omaha crowd, "we may see in the New York depot some strange Pacific railway notice: 'European passengers for Japan will please take the night train. Passengers for China this way.'" This was outrageous stuff for the time—he might as well have said that men would walk on the moon—but the crowd applauded, dreaming along with him.

"Down with England and up with America!" Train cried, and everyone

History of Omaha, Nebraska, 1894
George Francis Train

cheered. Could anyone but Americans undertake such a work as the transcontinental railroad? True, it would cost an unimaginable fortune to build, but what of that?

"When they [the English] spoke of our national debt I asked them what right England has to monopolize the entire national debt of the world. (Laughter.) I told them . . . that one of these days we would roll up a national debt that would make them ashamed of themselves. (Loud laughter and applause.)"

It was simply a matter of history, Train told the crowd, launching into a breathtaking dismissal of the world's great civilizations. What follows is nothing less than the history of the world—according to George Francis Train:

> *Here are a few stock points with which I have always interlarded my Fourth of July speeches:*
> *. . . That humanity, a puking babe in Asia, a lazy school-boy in Europe, came here to America*

> *to air its magnificent manhood. (Applause.) That*
> *industry came out of Egypt—then a tidal wave of*
> *time giving Law from Rome; more centuries, and*
> *Art springs from France, commerce sails from*
> *England; while America was reserved to combine*
> *all the good of the past—Industry, Law, Art,*
> *Commerce, with the grand Pacific Railway idea of*
> *Progress. (Applause.)*[5]

There you have it. What was happening that December day in Omaha was not merely an act of hope or ambition. It was nothing less than the culmination of all human history.

"It was the raciest, liveliest, best-natured and most tip-top speech ever delivered west of the Missouri River," the *Nebraskian* gushed, though it added, "The Train of ideas sometimes lacks the coupling-chains."[6]

There was something to that last observation. Just what it was would grow clearer as the years passed.

Though Train had more talent for promotion than he had discipline for the tedious work of railroad-building, his involvement with the Union Pacific—and with Omaha—didn't end there. Despite the hoopla, railroad construction made little headway until after the war. The biggest obstacle was money. Incessantly, Train lobbied for government funding, even as he cajoled wealthy investors into risking their fortunes on the grand scheme. He even helped organize something called the Crédit Mobilier, a construction and finance company designed to fund the building of the railroad. In a sense, it worked—the railroad *did* get built—but meanwhile Crédit Mobilier became ridiculously corrupt and led to what was perhaps the greatest financial scandal of the nineteenth century. Train was not implicated; before the dirty-dealing began, the mercurial promoter had long since moved on to other interests.

Such as Omaha real estate.

In 1865, Train bought 500 acres of land just south of Omaha, a tract that extended (more or less) from Pierce Street south to Deer Park (now I-80), and from Second Street west to 20th. Or, to put it more simply, Train's purchase extended roughly twenty city blocks north and south and twenty east and west.[7]

Which pretty much equaled the dimensions of Omaha at that time. An 1868 lithograph shows the city extending from Pierce Street north to Izard, and from the river west to about 20th. Simply put, Train believed that the railroad was going to make a big city of Omaha, and he was positioning himself to be a major player. The new area was known as "Train Town" for many years.

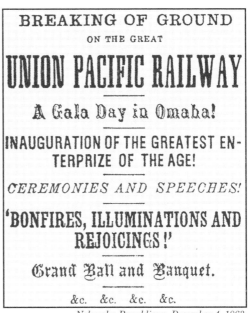

BREAKING OF GROUND
ON THE GREAT
UNION PACIFIC RAILWAY
A Gala Day in Omaha!
INAUGURATION OF THE GREATEST EN-TERPRIZE OF THE AGE!
CEREMONIES AND SPEECHES!
'BONFIRES, ILLUMINATIONS AND REJOICINGS!'
Grand Ball and Banquet.
&c.   &c.   &c.   &c.

Nebraska Republican, December 4, 1863

To get some idea of how Train did business, consider the following story from 1867, told by Train himself many years later. For some reason, Train's stories of himself always seem to take on a larger-than-life quality, but this one—if you can believe it—does not seem to have been stretched much:

> *When I went out to Omaha there was only one real hotel in that town. This was the Herndon, a respectable affair. I was astonished that men of energy, enterprise and means had not seized the opportunity to erect a large hotel at this point, which had already given promise of rapid and immediate growth. But what directly suggested to me the building of such a hotel on my own account was a little incident at a breakfast that I happened to be giving. I had invited a number of prominent men—representatives in congress, and others—as I desired to present to them some of my plans. The breakfast was a characteristic western meal, with prairie chicken and Nebraska trout.*

While we were seated one of those sudden and always unexpected cyclones on the plains came up. Our table was very near a window in which were large panes of glass which I feared could not withstand the tremendous force of the wind. I called to a negro waiter to stand with his broad back against the window. This proved a security against the storm; but it precipitated a storm within.

Allan, manager of the Herndon—and a man with a political turn of mind—saw in the incident an assault on the rights of the negroes. He hurried over to the table and protested against this act as an outrage. I could not afford to enter into any quarrel with him at the time, so I merely said: "I am about the size of the negro; I will take his place." I then ordered the fellow away from the window, took his post, and stayed there until the fury of the storm abated. Then I was ready for Allan.

I walked out in front of the house and, pointing to a large vacant square facing it, I asked who owned it. I was told the owner's name and immediately sent a messenger for him. He soon arrived and I asked his price. It was $5,000. I wrote out and handed him a check for the amount, and took from him, on the spot, a deed for the property.

Then I asked for a contractor who could build a hotel. A man named Richmond was brought to me. "Can you build a three-story hotel in sixty days on this lot?" asked I. After some hesitation he said it would be merely a question of money. "How much?" I asked. "One thousand dollars a day," he replied. "Show me that you are worth $60,000," I demanded. He did so, and I took out an envelope and sketched on the back of it a rough plan of the hotel. "I am going to the mountains," I said, "and shall want this hotel, with 120 rooms, complete, when I return in sixty days."

Durham Western Heritage Museum

Cozzen's Hotel

> *When I got back the hotel was finished. I imme-*
> *diately rented it to Cozzens of West Point, New*
> *York, for $10,000 a year. The Cozzens was more*
> *written about than almost any other hotel ever*
> *built in the United States. It was the show place of*
> *Omaha.*[8]

Now *that* was a man who made things happen.

But, alas, some stretch marks do appear in the closing words of the story. Was the Cozzens really the "show place of Omaha"? Let us consider that claim in light of the following letter, written in 1901 by a man named Dewitt Weld, a traveling business-man, in which he describes one truly unforgettable night at the Cozzens Hotel:

> *It is a great many years ago since I was in*
> *Omaha. It was then very much on the border. This*
> *was in the spring of 1869. It was then just when*
> *the Union Pacific had come through to connect*
> *with the Iowa roads. Among the passengers in our*
> *car was the French ambassador, Baron Baudice*

Boileau, going to the Pacific coast, who caused his valet to sit up all night to wake him when we crossed the Missouri.

We got into Omaha on a Saturday. Rain was falling in bucketfuls. When the stage got up the hill to the Cozzens hotel I volunteered to go to the post office to get the baron's mail as well as my own. Walking along the plank sidewalk in front of the hotel, I reached the end to find a canal almost, and stepping on what I took to be a plank I landed waist deep in mud and water. However, I managed to get to the post office all the same. Having but one suit of clothes I paid the penalty. I had to dry and clean my trousers before going to dinner. Meantime I had to remain in my room clad only in my underwear. The baron in recognition of my services braced me with some champagne.

Omaha was a terror in those days. After the storm all was motion. Saturday night the town was alive with open carriages occupied by questionable women—the gamblers urging you to go into their shanties and take a hand—the stray Indian with a squaw and papoose begging for money and drink—these and other sights interested me extremely. But the worst was to come.

About 2 o'clock in the morning I was awakened by loud curses, the clinking of glasses, shouts and hurrahs, and finally bullets coming through my door panels and making their exit through the window, smashing the glass. I hugged the wall pretty close, as my bed was almost in line of the shots. So it went on in the hotel until daybreak. When I demanded an explanation at the office I was told the racket was caused by a party of gamblers who had been drinking and had killed the editor of a paper, and were running the hotel to suit themselves. I think the editor's name was Miller. The clerk said the only hope to quiet the boisterous gamblers was to get them so drunk that they would be harmless. Meanwhile they had been shooting at a hat held by a darkey hall-boy in fear of his life.

These incidents, with cigars at $1 apiece, make up my experience in Omaha in 1869. Now we do a nice business there.[9]

One wonders: If the Cozzens was indeed Omaha's "show place" as Train said it was, what were the rowdy places like?

It seems that perhaps Mr. Train was stretching a bit in his memoir—though not as much as the hotel clerk did in the preceding excerpt. Dr. George L. Miller, editor of the Omaha *Herald*, had not been killed, nor had anyone else. As historian Alfred Sorenson put it, "it is quite evident that the hotel clerk amused himself by 'stringing' an eastern tenderfoot."[10] But perhaps we can forgive our traveling businessman for believing the tale. The bullets that crashed through his door and window that night were real enough.

George Francis Train probably never knew about the goings on at his hotel. He was not a man to worry about such trifles, nor even to stay put long enough to hear about them. For the rest of his life, Omaha would occupy his attention only intermittently, though he is linked to the city in one other important way—which will be revealed shortly.

In 1870-71, Train traveled around the globe in a record eighty days—or would have, had he not stopped for a month to support the Paris Commune during the chaotic aftermath of the Franco-German War. Two years later, when Jules Verne published his novel *Around the World in Eighty Days*, it was believed to have been inspired, at least in part, by Train's journey.

By 1872, Train was a presidential candidate, though not a mainstream one. His recent association with the French "Communards," as well as with Irish nationalist groups, was giving him a reputation as a dangerous radical.

"The majority of people incline to think that Train is but one remove from a madman," wrote an observer. Though he had no clear party affiliation, no experience in public office, and no coherent political philosophy, Train—who by now was signing his name "George Francis Train, N.P.A." (for "Next President of America")—seemed convinced that in November he would defeat both Republican incumbent U.S. Grant and Democratic challenger Horace Greeley.[11]

"The Coming President," Train's campaign literature announced in his characteristic telegraphic style, "The Man of Destiny. First Campaign Gun. Victory, 1872; Six million votes, Nov. 12, for the Child of Fate. Train and the People Against Grant and the Thieves! Associated with Mr. Train in the Credit Foncier of America [another of Train's financial schemes] are 100 of the wealthiest men in the country, which is the nucleus of the White House Pool to form the People's Ring that elects the President in 1872."[12]

But, of course, Train lost the election—and not only lost, but doesn't appear to have received any votes. The enthusiastic crowds all over the country who had been coming to hear him speak (and paying admission to do so) had been coming, not to seek a leader, but merely to be entertained.

And things were about to get even more entertaining, as Train—his presidential hopes dashed—injected himself into one of the most bizarre scandals of the nineteenth century.

In those days, not only did women lack the right to vote, but the idea of women's suffrage was one of those wild-eyed, radical causes espoused by only a brave few. Train, of course, had spoken out in its favor. But even as Train was mounting his hopeless presidential campaign, an even more hopeless, even weirder campaign was under way.

Victoria Clafin Woodhull was a radical even among suffragettes. Mainstream feminists like Susan B. Anthony and Elizabeth Cady Stanton wanted nothing to do with her, and you can hardly blame them: Woodhull was a divorcee, a wearer of short skirts (just touching the tops of her shoes) and "bob" haircut (a sure mark of the hussy), a spiritualist and ardent believer in astrology and magnetic healing, and an advocate of what was even then called "free love." With her sister, Tennessee Clafin, she ran a stock brokerage in New York City, while publishing a radical newspaper called the *Woodhull & Clafin Weekly*, which, among other things, is credited with the first

U. S. publication in English of *The Communist Manifesto*. With these credits to her name, Woodhull decided to run for president.

All this made for great copy in the papers, but it soon led to trouble. When Henry Ward Beecher, the best-known and most highly-respected minister in the country, condemned Woodhull's behavior, she replied by printing in her paper a lengthy and detailed accusation that Beecher had been having an affair with a married woman. Woodhull commented that while she didn't object to the affair, she wished Beecher would drop the hypocrisy, and come out in favor of free love. In the ensuing explosion of publicity, Woodhull and Clafin were arrested on obscenity charges for printing the sordid accusation.[13]

Enter George Francis Train. Not only did Train come to the defense of the sisters, but he also managed to get himself imprisoned in the process. In his own newspaper, *The Train Ligue*, he reprinted the Beecher story, adding 'scandalous' stories from the Bible (such as David and Bathsheba) under sensational headlines. Near the top of the front page was the following inscription: "Suppressed by the Government in Omaha; now published by George Francis Train in New York."[14]

This doesn't seem to have been the case. Train was not a resident of Omaha, nor had he spent much time there in recent years. But his personal secretary, one George P. Bemis, was an Omaha resident, at least when he was not traveling with Train. At any rate, the inscription, like the rest of the later issues of the *Train Ligue*, seemed calculated solely to draw attention—and prosecution—to the paper's publisher.

The plan succeeded; Train's irreverence landed him in jail. Though the whole scenario seems impossible to modern readers, in those days the First Amendment was not interpreted as strongly as it would be in later years; the states had much more latitude in the matter of censorship. And that was what Train was attacking. Once he was arrested, the state of New York was in the awkward position of prosecuting a man mainly for printing "sophisticated" Bible stories in an irreverent manner. Soon, the state realized the predicament they were in, and tried to let the case go without formally dropping the charges. Train would have none of it. Refusing bail, he remained in jail for months.

Finally, despite Train's protests, he was declared insane, and the charges were dropped. By then, Train's business interests had fallen into ruin, his reputation had been permanently tarnished, and his presidential ambitions . . . well, by then he had ceased using the title "Next President of America" in favor of "The Coming Dictator." For many years afterward, he made the rounds of the lecture circuit "Psychologizing the World!" and "Organizing Prosperity through Absolute Dictatorship."[15]

Not until November 1874, a year and a half after the insanity hearings, did George Bemis end his services as Train's private secretary. Bemis had worked for Train twelve years—since he was a young man of twenty-four—and had gone along with one outrageous scheme after another, had gone around the world with Train, to the barricades in the streets of Paris, to the hopeless campaign of '72, to the New York City courtroom in '73, testifying that Train was as sane as he had ever been. During this time, Bemis was paid only intermittently, receiving four years' wages for twelve years' service. In 1876, he sued Train for the difference, but by then his former boss's fortunes had evaporated. The Omaha land, the Cozzens Hotel, had long since been seized by creditors. Bemis got nothing.

Except perhaps an education. Now settled down in Omaha, Bemis went into the "real estate and loan business" and made a fortune. Eventually, he was elected mayor. He held no grudge against Train, and kept in contact with the would-be dictator for years.[16]

Train continued to lecture and write, though in later years he mostly spent his days on his favorite park bench in New York City, where he became a favorite of the local children. In 1902 he wrote his autobiography, *My Life in Many States and In Foreign Lands*, from which you have already read an excerpt—which was Train's version of the Cozzens Hotel story. Rather good for an insane man, don't you think?

Omaha didn't think him insane, not completely, anyway. In 1894, James Savage and John Bell published a thick volume titled, *History of the City of Omaha Nebraska*. In their biographical sketch of Train they admit, "It is true that his mind frequently wanders into the 'voids of space,' but it has, nevertheless, an orbit (eccentric though it is.) And that mind, on its return into the 'full glare of the sun,' such is its brightness, it fairly blinds the average intellect of men with its flashes."[17]

In fact, the first illustration in Savage and Bell's *History*, located just inside the front cover and facing the title page, is a full-page engraving of George Francis Train. You see, Omaha couldn't get over the fact that Train had—in his own inimitable way—helped to found the Union Pacific Railroad, the railroad that made Omaha into a city. Train had predicted great things for Omaha, and had thrown his support behind making them happen. What did it matter that he turned out to be something of a madman?

Nebraska Republican, December 4, 1863

Chapter 7 notes

[1] Omaha *Nebraskian*, December 4, 1863.

[2] Shelby Foote, *The Civil War: A Narrative*, Vol. 2, New York: Random House, 1963, 427, 578, 637.

[3] *Nebraskian*, December 4, 1863.

[4] Willis Thornton, *The Nine Lives of Citizen Train*, New York: Greenberg, 1948.

[5] *Nebraskian*, December 11, 1863.

[6] December 4, 1863.

[7] James W. Savage and John T. Bell, *History of the City of Omaha Nebraska*, New York: Munsell & Co., 1894, 101.

[8] George Francis Train, *My Life in Many States and in Foreign* Lands (1902), quoted in Sorenson, *The Story of Omaha from the Pioneer Days to the Present Time*, Omaha: National Printing Co., 1923, 227-28. The Cozzens Hotel was located on the southeast corner of Ninth and Harney. Despite the hastiness of its construction, the building stood for 35 years, being torn down in 1902. The Herndon House, built in 1857-58, was located on the northeast corner of Ninth and Farnam. See Federal Writers' Project, 106-107.

[9] Sorenson, *Story*, 232-33 (I have inserted some paragraph breaks).

[10] Sorenson, *Story*, 233.

[11] Thornton, 221.

[12] Thornton, 223.

[13] The charges against Beecher were never proved one way or the other. Beecher was the brother of novelist Harriet Beecher Stowe, author of *Uncle Tom's Cabin*.

[14] Omaha *Daily Bee* (evening), November 23, 1873. Train and Woodhull, Thornton, 228-232.

[15] Thornton, 220.

[16] Savage and Bell, 524.

[17] Savage and Bell, 581-82.

EXTRA! EXTRA!
Omaha Quotations

OMAHA!!

As many of our foreign friends will be unable to pronounce this word, we will from our Indian Dictionary assist them. The proper pronunciation is O-maw-haw, accenting the middle syllable.

—*Omaha Arrow, July 28, 1854*

* * *

The town is situated upon a point of high bottom land and a position commanding a view of the high variation of the Bluffs to the East. It contains 2 stores, 2 public houses, and is steadily on the march of improvement, and some 20 buildings.

—*Omaha Arrow, July 28, 1854*
(A ridiculously exaggerated report.)

* * *

One thing Omaha cannot boast of and that is good looking women.

—*Erastus Beadle, June 18, 1857*

* * *

We suggest . . . that there are no . . . girls now-a-days; they are either babies or young ladies, progressing immediately from the cradle into hooped skirts with a beau on each arm.

—*Omaha Nebraskian, July 8, 1857*

* * *

It may not be generally known that, about seven miles north of Omaha, on the Missouri River, there is a small hamlet, yeleped Florence, the proprietors of which have been, for months, laboring assiduously to delude strangers that it was a city.

—*Omaha Nebraskian, January 7, 1857*

* * *

We learn that the Otoe Indians have suffered severely this winter with cold. Many of them have frozen to death; and they have lost nearly all of their horses.
—Omaha Nebraskian, February 11, 1857

* * *

Another of Father's ventures that first winter [1858-59] after his return was the wood business. Wood was the only fuel available in Omaha at that time, and the most prolific source of it was north of Florence among the hills in that wooded district. Accordingly, he bought a lot of it and had it piled along the north end of our lots, where he retailed it.

The presence of a large quantity of good hard wood in Omaha afforded quite an attraction to some of the early residents of that neighborhood, and it was not long until it began to disappear on dark cold nights.

Father then employed a trusty Irishman to watch it and things went along very satisfactorily for a while. As the nights got colder the job was not overly attractive to the Irishman, so he decided on a labor saving device to allow him to put in more time at home where he was more comfortable. Accordingly, he made the long pile of wood which extended east and west much higher and left the east end of it lower so that it could be easily appropriated.

Then he took about twenty pieces, bored holes in them and filled them with [gun]powder, after which he plugged up the holes and left the wood where it could readily be taken.

It was not long after that until the cook stoves of some of the neighboring residents mysteriously blew up, and the designs upon our woodpile were correspondingly curtailed . . . .
—Frank Burkley, The Faded Frontier (1935)

* * *

OMAHA CITY, NEBRASKA TERRITORY.

. . . The site of Omaha was first known as "Lone Tree Ferry,"

where, for several years, W. D. Brown ran a flat-boat across the river with California emigrants; and the place was an old camping-ground, where the Indian war-dance and other wild extravaganzas were practised without restraint. . . . Omaha, being one of the places earliest settled, has been the theatre of many scenes of interest, excitement and border collision, the pique and jealousy of other rival towns being brought constantly against "the capital."
—*Frank Leslie's Illustrated Newspaper, November 6, 1858.*

* * *

40 CASES
OF OLD BOURBON WHISKEY
Just Received and for Sale at
DAWKIN'S SALOON,
FARNHAM STREET.
—*Omaha Nebraskian, December 13, 1859.*

* * *

The Anti-Slavery Bill.
The bill introduced in the Council, for the abolition of slavery in this Territory, was called up yesterday, and its further consideration postponed for two weeks. A strong effort will be made among the Republicans to secure its passage; we think, however, it will fail. The farce certainly cannot be enacted if the Democrats do their duty.
—*Omaha Nebraskian, December 14, 1859.*

* * *

A nice young man has lost a daguerreotype likeness of himself. If any gentleman has found it, he will confer a favor upon the loser by leaving it at this office. If a lady has picked up the said likeness, she will please leave her address with us, and the original of the picture will call for it.
—*Omaha Nebraskian, December 30, 1859*

* * *

Presidential Election.

By reference to our telegraphic despatches of a day or two past, it will be seen that Lincoln has probably carried Northern States enough to secure his election by the electoral college. . . . New Jersey appears to be the only Northern State that has declared against the irrepressible nigger, although it is possible that Illinois may give her vote to Douglas. This, however, cannot change the result. If the bluster of the South about secession meant any thing, an opportunity is afforded them of putting their threats into execution. The ubiquitous nigger has prevailed.
—*Omaha Nebraskian, November 9, 1860.*

* * *

The latest dispatches by telegraph bring us the most startling news of war and rumors of war. We have never doubted the intention of Mr. Lincoln to maintain the integrity of the Union, but we cannot yet believe that we must have war. We have hoped, and still trust that it may be indefinitely postponed. Until the rumors are confirmed we must doubt the reports.
—*Nebraska Republican, April 10, 1861, two days before the*
Confederate attack on Fort Sumter.

* * *

KOUNTZE BROTHERS,
BANKERS AND COLLECTORS
DEALERS IN
Gold Dust and Land Warrants,
Omaha, Nebraska.
—*(Omaha) Nebraska Republican, June 5, 1861*
The Kountze brothers' bank was the
First National Bank of Omaha.
* * *

Telegraphic News.
Reported in Omaha by the Pacific Telegraph Company.
———
BATTLE IN PENNSYLVANIA!

Gen. Meade and Reynolds Command the Federals Against Longstreet and Hill.

THE REBELS REPULSED.

Maj. General Reynolds Killed.

Gen. Foster Moving on Richmond.

—Omaha Nebraskian, July 10, 1863.

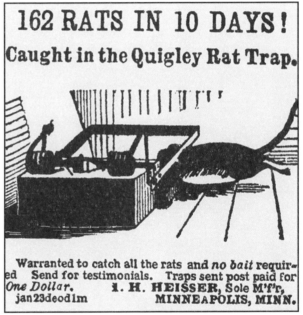

Omaha Daily Herald, February 10, 1883

Chapter Eight

A DIRTY TOWN

1850s-1880s

If you've read this far, I'm guessing that you're the sort of person who'd like to travel back in time (if only it were possible!) and walk the streets of nineteenth century Omaha, to take in its sights and sounds, and to experience the character and Old West charm of the place. In fact, the purpose of this book is to do something like that, to use words and stories to rebuild old Omaha in your imagination.

But in order for you to see clearly the Omaha that is growing before your eyes in these pages, you must abandon certain modern notions of city life. Consider the following story:

One day in 1874, a 300-pound hog died in the street at Nineteenth and Cass. At the time, this did not seem particularly important to anyone. The hog was left where it lay. However, after two days under a hot August sun, the carcass became bloated and stinking. A group of local residents went to the city board of health, asking that it be removed. It was *already* being removed, of course—bit by bit—by the rats and vermin that swarmed over it, but the citizens seemed to take little comfort in this knowledge. So the city marshal was dispatched. He went to see the carcass, then returned to the board of health to ask for help in removing it. Eventually, the hog was removed, but not before a number of Omahans tried to make it somebody's else's responsibility.[1]

Today, we take for granted certain basic notions of sanitation and cleanliness. We recognize, for instance, that a *city*, a *barnyard*, and a *dump* are three distinct places, not to be confused with each other.

It was not always so obvious.

Prior to the twentieth century, most people were rural people, and when they came to the city, they brought rural practices with them. They kept chickens and hogs and milk cows, they threw their garbage out wherever it suited them, and they drew their drinking water from wells dug into the same backyards as their outhouses. This was how things had always been done. Cities were, by their very nature, dirty and foul-smelling. Only as cities began growing ever-larger following the Industrial Revolution, and only as scientists began understanding the spread of disease, did the old ways of city life begin to seem unacceptable. But the change did not happen overnight.

This chapter, therefore, will introduce you to six different kinds of urban uncleanliness, Omaha style. For your convenience, the categories are as follows: Mud; Dust; Stray Animals (Alive); Stray Animals (Dead); Garbage and Sewage.

Enjoy.

Mud
Some towns are famed for beauty,
And others for deeds of blood,
But say what you may of Omaha,
It beats them all for mud.
—*Omaha Daily Herald, March 13, 1868*

At first, all of Omaha's streets were covered with native prairie grass. Quickly worn away by horses' hooves and wagon wheels, the streets remained bare dirt for years. The city made its first attempt at pavement in 1877, when a few blocks of Farnam were covered with a crushed-rock surface called "macadam." Other surfaces were tried—cedar blocks, granite blocks, and brick—and the paving of existing streets seems to have been more-or-less complete by the late 1880s.[2]

Until then, it was a mess. "There was mud, mud every-

Farnam Street, from 16th Street east, 1866.

where," recalled Emily Doane, the 1850s pioneer we met a few chapters ago.[3] Grant Marsh, later a famous steamboat captain, saw Omaha for the first time in 1857. He was not impressed. "It was a veritable mudhole," wrote Marsh's biographer, "consisting of two wretched streets straggling along the river bank and lined with the flimsy frame and log structures of a people too eagerly bent upon the pursuit of success to squander time or expense on the niceties of civilization."[4]

This condition was acceptable in the early days, at least to those "bent upon the pursuit of success," but as the years passed and Omaha maintained its reputation as a mudhole (even by the loose standards of the nineteenth century), many began to feel embarrassment.

"There is not a citizen of Omaha who does not feel ashamed of the condition of our streets," wrote a *Herald* editor in 1869. "From the deluges of the passing season for weeks together they have been well nigh impassable for teams and most uncomfortable for pedestrians. Ditches, holes and unfathomable mud have been the rule, an eyesore to ourselves as well as to strangers, and an expensive inconvenience to business men."[5]

According to pioneer Frank Burkley, the worst time was during "the spring when the frost was coming out of the ground." Conditions then "made walking or hauling almost out of the question." He cites the following 1868 news clippings as evidence:

> *Yesterday afternoon an express wagon containing the driver and a lady sitting in it and a horse hitched to it were going at a rapid rate down Farnam street when suddenly the horse plunged*

into deep mire near Eleventh street. He became detached from the wagon and at once made a break for the stable, leaving the wagon, lady and driver in the mud to paddle their own canoe.

* * *

Near the corner of Twelfth and Douglas streets yesterday there stood in the mud hole a white-washed barrel upon which was painted in large letters, "No bottom! Trains leave daily for China and intermediate points."

* * *

We saw a dray[6] laden with groceries sink into three feet of mud on Eleventh street near the northwest corner of Douglas street yesterday morning. Its freight had to be taken off and put on an express wagon before it could be moved from that slough of despond.[7]

As late as 1880, Farnam Street was said to have had mud-holes that could sink a horse belly-deep.[8]

Dust

Of course it was only muddy in wet weather. In dry weather, the wind swept the bare dirt away as dust. In 1867, Henry Stanley—later a famous explorer in Africa—complained in his diary that "no town on the Missouri River is more annoyed by moving clouds of dust and sand—when the wind is up—than Omaha. It is absolutely terrific. The lower terrace along the river is a waste of fine sand, which is blown about in drifts, and banked up against the houses like snow in a wintry storm. For two or three days, people have been obliged to shut themselves up in their houses for protection from the sand."[9]

Strangely, the potential for dust storms grew more, and not less, severe as the years passed. Consider this 1880 story from the *Bee*:

About six o'clock yesterday morning an

immense cloud of dust was seen sweeping up from the south, and a few moments later it struck the city, enveloping everything in a perfect whirlwind of sand and dirt. The velocity of the wind was terrific and the streets were soon filled with whirling eddies of sand, dirt, pebbles and rubbish, which dashed in showers against the window panes and rushed into the doors and windows, covering every object with dust.

Walking the streets was almost impossible. The eddies of sand and dirt struck the faces of the foot passengers like hail stones, even the goggles which were generally worn, proving of little protection to the eyes. An immense cloud of dirt through which the sun vainly endeavored to struggle, hung over the city and obscured the heavens.

Many of our oldest citizens declared that in an experience of twenty years they had never experienced anything to equal the force of the wind and the dirt. Windows were broken, blinds dashed from their hinges, and houses and stores deluged with the sifting sand which permeated every crack and crevice, and rendered life a burden and existence a bore.[10]

Thomas Tibbles—whom we will meet in "The Trial of Standing Bear"—had just returned to Omaha when the storm hit. He describes hearing an "ominous rumbling" and seeing "a dense black mass rise up as if the prairies had been ground into fine powder and then spouted out by volcanic force. The mass moved up toward Omaha with terrifying velocity. It hid the sun, and then almost total darkness closed down upon the city."

He found no escape from the dust. "All windows were closed," he recalled, "all blinds shut, all window shades pulled down. The taste of it flavored every particle of food . . . Dust piled up inside the closed window on the sill. It sifted into the air of the room through countless invisible crevices in the walls and doors."

This was something on a far larger scale than what Stanley had observed in '67. What was happening? Tibbles, an advocate of Indian rights just returning from a lecture tour, understood clearly why a dust storm of this magnitude was happening now and why it had not happened before.

The frontier was coming to a close, and the land was being changed. Though the plains had seen drought before, this time a prolonged drought had fallen on vast areas of *cultivated* plains soil. Stripped bare of its grass covering, the dry earth was swept up into enormous clouds of dust.[11]

"In this era of transition," Tibbles wrote, "even the soil was passing from the plains with the buffalo and the roving tribes. The unchanging grassland days were gone forever."[12]

Stray Animals (Alive)

A *Herald* editorial, 1876:

> *Men and women of Omaha: Your dearest liberties are being taken from you! Unless you rise up in honest indignation and kill off a few thousand dogs, the blessed privilege of going out at night without a corporal's guard will be taken from you. When the fire alarm sounded yesterday morning, and the clattering engines rushed to the fire, five thousand dogs rushed out and pursued, and came very near eating up everybody who rushed out on the street to see whose house was on fire. Constantinople obtained a world-wide reputation on account of the number and worthlessness of her dogs. Omaha, in proportion to her population, has more dogs than Constantinople.*[13]

As Omaha's human population increased, so did its population of dogs. Though the city passed ordinances requiring the fencing or muzzling of dogs, these were generally ignored. In time, countless stray dogs—often moving in packs—roamed the streets and alleys at will, fighting, eating, excreting, and reproducing. By the 1870s, dog overpopulation led to food shortages for the strays, resulting in brutal competition and attacks on sheep, cattle, and sometimes people.[14]

For dogs that were unused to fighting, the streets could be terrifying. Clement Chase, later the editor of the *Excelsior*, Omaha's society weekly, told this story of how a local livery stable owner protected his pets:

> *Clark* [the stable owner] *had a pack of fancy coach dogs, the spotted variety* [i.e., Dalmatians], *which frequently accompanied these carriages about the city, and almost as frequently suffered from the attacks of the city dogs, which were a nuisance at the time. Wondering how he could protect his cherished pets Clark hit upon the idea of sending with them one day a white bulldog* [i.e., a pit bull] *which one of the coachmen had decorated with black spots in true imitation of the pretty but pusillanimous coach dogs. It was a complete surprise to the city dogs to find their vicious attacks unexpectedly repulsed and they retreated tumultuously and in disorder and from that time on the mild-mannered stable dogs were permitted to pass through the streets unmolested.*[15]

During the spring of 1874, someone began anonymously poisoning the "city dogs" with strychnine. Said the *Bee*, "it is hoped that the good work will go on until there is a noticeable decrease in the canine population of Omaha." A few days later, the *Bee* noted that though an unusual number of canine corpses were still appearing on the streets, "the dogs appear to be as thick as ever."[16]

To the modern reader, perhaps the most shocking thing about this treatment of dogs is that it *wasn't* shocking to the people of the time. Consider this: The autumn previous to the poisonings saw a bizarre execution of a dog that had bitten two mail carriers. The dog was taken outside the city in a wagon, tied to a tree, and shot at with a revolver. A post office clerk fired four shots, hitting the dog three times, but failing to kill it. After the revolver misfired, the clerk then tried to kill the dog with a fence rail. This was also unsuccessful. Undaunted, the group headed back to town—leaving the shot and battered dog tied to the tree—and, procuring two more loaded revolvers, returned to finish the job. The *Bee* reported the story without comment.[17]

Incidentally, the presence of stray cats does not seem to have been an issue. They were present, no doubt, but since cats do not run in packs, they would not have attracted as much attention as the dogs. And of course, cruelty toward cats was considered so un-newsworthy as to fail to receive even the brief mention given the unfortunate dog in the previous paragraph.[18]

As we have seen, rats were ubiquitous—as were mice—but they seem not to have generated much publicity other than frequent newspaper advertisements for mouse traps and rat poison.

Other than the dogs, it was the farm animals, particularly hogs and milk cows, that caused the most consternation for Omaha residents. In May 1872, for instance, the *Bee* reported that people in north Omaha were complaining of "numerous hogs running at large." The hogs' owners had to be threatened with arrest in order to get them to pen up the animals.[19]

Cows, too, were often turned loose to graze. In those pre-refrigeration days, if you wanted milk, you probably had to keep a cow. Even into the 1880s, by which time Omaha had outgrown its frontier-town status, complaints about stray cows continued. In 1886, the city government ordered Jefferson Square (Omaha's original city park) to be fenced in order to prevent stray cows from grazing there.[20]

The main problem with stray animals, however, wasn't that they wandered and made pests of themselves. It was that sometimes they died.

Stray Animals (Dead)

It was a common thing for packs of hogs to roam the city, feeding on garbage. There was no shortage of that article in the streets. But in the winter, some of these hogs took shelter underneath Omaha's wooden sidewalks. And some of them died there. Come spring, the result was . . . unpleasant.

As we have already seen, the main problem with dead animals is that, while everybody wanted them taken away, nobody wanted to take them away. The city government did not solve this dilemma till 1881, when it created the job of City Scavenger. The scavenger's job was to remove dead animals from public property (i.e., if a 300-pound hog expired under your front porch, that was your own problem). The scavenger was paid $1 for each horse, mule, cow, or other large animal removed. Pigs, goats, and calves brought 25¢, while chickens, ducks, dogs, and the like brought a dime apiece.[21]

In those days, most non-elected city jobs were given as political spoils to the supporters of the winning party. I am guessing that this job was not one of them.

Garbage and Sewage

During the first few decades of its existence, Omaha had no garbage collection and no sewer system. Garbage was simply thrown out wherever was convenient, and the streets were often very convenient for this purpose. The original city garbage collectors were, of course, hogs.

Without a sewer system, Omahans relied on the time-honored tradition of the outdoor privy—essentially, a hole in the ground with a little shack built over it for privacy. Trouble was, a privy eventually filled up and had to be cleaned out. Until the late 1870s, most Omahans avoided doing this. "To avoid cleaning privies," writes historian Michael Harkins, "Omahans usually provided openings in the rear of the outhouse and allowed waste to freely run out. The fecal matter found its way into alleys, streets, and eventually into the local water supply."[22]

Hotels added to the mess. When the privies collapsed at the Grand Central Hotel,[23] employees began emptying waste into a nearby cesspool. Eventually, the cesspool backed up into adjacent streets. When, in the spring of 1876, area residents complained to the city council, theirs was one of about a hundred petitions and complaints regarding open privies and backed up cesspools throughout the city.

Two years later, the city council proposed a sewer system. Though soon underway, it was not fully developed till 1895. And not for another fifty years—1945—did the city finally outlaw privies and cesspools. They continued to exist, illegally, in some parts of the city into the 1970s.[24]

The real wonder of the situation is that Omaha did not experience any major epidemics. Though the city had occasional outbreaks of typhoid fever, dysentery, diarrhea, and the like, these were normal and acceptable by the standards of the day. That it never got more severe than that is most fortunate indeed.

Chapter 8 notes

[1]Michael J. Harkins, "Public Health Nuisances in Omaha, 1870-1900," *Nebraska History*, 56:4 (Winter, 1975), 471.

[2]Richard Orr, *O & CB: Streetcars of Omaha and Council Bluffs,* Richard Orr, 1996, 23, 47.

[3]"Reminscences of Early Omaha, Series of Articles Printed by Clement Chase in 1916," *Nebraska History*, 17:3 (Summer, 1936), 209.

[4]Joseph Mills Hanson, *The Conquest of the Missouri, Being the Story of the Life and Exploits of Captain Grant Marsh*, New York: Murray Hill, 1946 (originally published in 1909), 24.

[5]*Herald*, September 17, 1869.

[6]Dray: a flatbed wagon used for heavy-duty hauling.

[7]Burkley, *The Faded Frontier*, 298-300.

[8]Federal Writer's Project, 105.

[9]Quoted in Federal Writer's Project, 26.

[10]*Bee* (evening), April 19, 1880.

[11]This phenomenon would be seen again on the Plains during the "Dust Bowl" years of 1930s.

[12]Thomas H. Tibbles, *Buckskin and Blanket Days: Memoirs of a Friend of the Indians*, Garden City, New York: Doubleday & Co., 1957 (written in 1905), 222-223.

[13]*Herald*, August 5, 1876.

[14]Harkins, 473.

[15]"Reminiscences of Early Omaha," *Nebraska History*, 201.

[16]*Bee* (evening), May 22, 25, 1874.

[17]*Bee* (evening), September 27, 1873.

[18]You would think that modern domestic cats would be grateful for their improved status, but it is not so. Your typical housecat cares nothing for history, only for the process of writing history, which—as it involves large books lying open on the floor and authors' laps available for long stretches at a time—provides convenient napping opportunities for lazy and ungrateful cats.

[19]*Bee* (evening), May 3, 1872.

[20]Orr, 31, 47. Jefferson Square was the city block bordered by Chicago, Cass, 15th and 16th Streets. The area is now covered by I-480.

[21]Harkins, 475.

[22]Harkins, 478.

[23]Grand Central Hotel: southwest corner of 14th and Farnam, present site of Paxton Manor.

[24]Harkins, 478-480.

Chapter Nine

HARD-HITTING JOURNALISM

July 1873

B y the early 1870s, Omaha had three daily newspapers, the *Herald*, the *Republican*, and the *Bee*, and they hated each other with a warmth and sincerity which the modern reader can only regard with misty-eyed nostalgia.

Of the three, the *Bee* was the upstart, having been founded in 1871 by a cantankerous thirty-year-old smart-aleck named Edward Rosewater. Nominally a Republican paper, the *Bee* was primarily dedicated to the proclamation of Rosewater's opinions, and this frequently put it at odds with both the *Herald* and the *Republican*.

Born Edward Rossenwasser in Czechoslovakia, Rosewater came to America with his parents and nine younger siblings when he was thirteen. As a young man, he became a telegrapher, and during the Civil War worked at the War Department telegraph office in Washington. He was in the thick of things there, for the office was the nerve center of Union Army communications. President Lincoln himself was a frequent visitor.

Sometimes the dispatches made history: On January 1, 1863, the twenty-one-year-old Rosewater was handed a message, signed by Lincoln, to send out over the nation's telegraph lines. It was the Emancipation Proclamation.[1]

Later that year, Rosewater moved to the city where he was

to live the rest of his life. Drawn by a job offer from Edward Creighton, Rosewater got his start in Omaha by working for the new transcontinental telegraph line. With the political education he received in Washington, it's no surprise that he soon became involved in Nebraska public affairs. And being as he was free of such encumbering traits as tact, prudence, and unwavering accuracy, he also made an effective journalist.

Like its editor, the *Bee* exuded energy, approaching the news like a cavalryman charging into battle. "Another foul libel upon the fair fame of this city has been placed in circulation by a Chicago newspaper," one issue of the *Bee* complained, and quoted the story as follows:

> *A woman in Omaha has sued a man for $1,000 for living with him three years as his wife. She thought she was married to him. He says she isn't.*

The *Bee* felt there was no basis to the story, and thoughtfully pointed this out to the Chicago paper:

> *It's no such thing, as you may find out to your sorrow at the expense of your scalp, if you ever show your face in Omaha.*[2]

The *Bee* could also be pleasant and lighthearted, as it often was in the "Omaha Brevities" column:

> *An excited gambler was seen rushing frantically around on Farnam Street yesterday afternoon to find a brick with which to put a head on a brother sport. Cause of the breeze—an unliquidated four dollar debt.*[3]

In the *Bee*, the stories of drunks, gamblers, and domestic violence were presented as lighthearted fare, and were not allowed to distract the paper from its more important mission of sniping at the *Herald* and the *Republican*. Granted, sometimes they started it, as in this item from the *Herald*:

> *The* Bee *proposes to discuss the question of public improvements with the* Herald. *Its editor is*

*referred to by one of Esop's fables, 'The frog and
the bull.''*

In Aesop's fable of self-conceit, the frog is convinced that the
bull is really no bigger than himself. To prove his point, he
swells himself up with air, bigger and bigger, till he bursts. The
Herald saw itself as the mighty bull which the little croaking
Rosewater was trying vainly to match. Rosewater had his own
interpretation:

> *The insufferable egotism that constantly
> exudes from every pore of the* Herald, *and causes
> its elastic epidermis to swell out to unnatural pro-
> portions, renders the reference to Esop's frog and
> bull fable strikingly appropriate. Everybody will
> recognize that "bull frog at a glance."*[4]

All this brings us to a little incident in July 1873 which
caused quite a stir in its day. It started on Independence Day,
when a man and a woman were politely refused a marriage
license by Probate Judge Robert Townsend. The would-be groom
was black. This was no problem, but his sweetheart was white,
and therein lay the difficulty: In Nebraska, such a union was
illegal.

A man of progressive ideas, Townsend wrote a lengthy apology on the back of their application, then saw to it that the note
was published in the *Herald*. After explaining the legal precedents, Townsend complained that:

> *the recent legislature of Nebraska were asked to
> repeal the law forbidding the consummation of
> happiness between male Negro and elegant white
> women and between a white man and a lady of
> dark complexion; but the God and Equality
> Legislature killed the bill.*
>
> *I trust the time will soon come when "Equality"
> will mean equality in all things, politically, civil-
> ly, religiously, (no African M.E. Church,) socially,
> and especially matrimonially.*
>
> *My advice is, cross over into Iowa, where a*

negro can marry the Governor's daughter, if she is
willing, as she ought to be.[5]

That isn't the sort of thing that you expect a public man in
1873 to sign his name to, let alone to have printed in a newspaper. But Townsend did it, and the *Herald*, though not in sympathy with Townsend's views—let it go without comment.

Rosewater was not so lenient. On Monday, July 7, the day
after Townsend's article appeared, the *Bee* ran the following
item:

If any public man wants to make a "commodious ass" . . . of himself in a public journal, he always ought to be accorded that glorious privilege. For this reason we interpose no objection to the publication by the Herald *of Judge Townsend's witty and weighty endorsement on that rejected application for a miscegenated marriage license.*

To this, the *Herald* didn't reply, probably because the editors
didn't feel personally involved in the squabble. Then came an
unexpected salvo from the *Republican*:

When Edward Rosewater presents himself at the probate office for a marriage license, he need have no fears that he and his "wench" will be referred over to Iowa. Differences of race will, in his case, be made up by entire compatibility in other respects save that the wench would get the worst of the bargain.[6]

I don't know what Rosewater said when he read this, and am
not sure I'd care to print it if I did. Rosewater was already married—to a white woman—and he took the article as a direct
insult not only against himself, but against his family. And he
knew just who to blame. We can imagine him sitting at his desk
at the *Bee* that Tuesday morning, red-faced and ruminating on
a single word: Balcome . . . *Balcome* . . . BALCOME!

Major St. Ambrose Durant Balcome—called "Balky" by his

friends—tall, lean, and long-bearded, Lincoln-esque in his stove-pipe hat, was managing editor and part-owner of the *Republican*.[7] Rosewater despised him, of course. Though the article was unsigned, Rosewater knew immediately that Balcome was behind it.

Reaching for pen and paper, Rosewater began composing a letter, which he then arranged to be hand-delivered to Balcome. In the letter, Rosewater reminded Balcome of his oft-repeated intention to hold Balcome "individually responsible" for "every

Edward Rosewater

article derogatory to my private character" printed in the *Republican*. He demanded that the *Republican* print a full apology, and failing this, closed with a thinly veiled threat to "seek reparation and redress in such a manner as in my judgment I may deem proper under the circumstances."[8]

Receiving such a letter, a modern editor might call the company attorney with a warning of a possible libel suit, and the paper would play it safe after that. Balcome, living in an earlier, more direct age, merely told the bearer of the letter that he would "see the local about it."[9] This was relayed back to Rosewater, giving the fiery owner of the *Bee* reason to expect that an apology would be forthcoming.

Which of course it was not. Next morning's *Republican*:

> *If E. Rosewater will apply to the proper person, he will get his fill of satisfaction for the article that appeared in these columns yesterday morning.*[10]

Omaha Daily Herald cartoon of the fight.

The gauntlet was thrown. When an angry gentleman spoke of *satisfaction*, he was saying that he was ready for a fight. The next move was Rosewater's.

About noon, Balcome was walking along a wooden sidewalk when the diminutive Rosewater came tearing after him, overtaking the tall man at the southwest corner of Fourteenth and Douglas. Rosewater was carrying a cowhide whip—such as one would use for horseback riding—and had the handle tied to his wrist so it could not easily be taken away from him.[11] What happened next . . .

ah, but let the *Herald* tell it:

G O R E.
Terrific Hand-to-Hand Combat Between Two Bloodthirsty Journalists in Douglas Street Yesterday—Detailed Account of the Mill,

Two eminent journalists had a terrific encounter on Douglas street yesterday. It is our painful duty to describe the scene as it actually occurred, but deference to our feelings will require that no names shall be mentioned. As sufficiently suggestive substitutes we will use Shorty and Lengthy. According to our most reliable reports it appears that the fearful conflict began in a preliminary skirmish for position, in which Shorty with a strategic skill worthy of a better result, met Lengthy on the corner of Douglas and Fourteenth streets, where he seized a stepladder, and, climbing halfway up his back, landed a stinger with a small rawhide whip on the neck of Lengthy. Shorty preferred to climb up the back of Lengthy for reasons which will be apparent to most people, and from considerations of safety. The feat was performed with a great deal of artistic dexterity, and had a tendency to arrest the attention of Lengthy, who immediately coiled himself into position for the fight. It was evident that the first movement of Lengthy was to play the boa constrictor game with Shorty, but he changed his tactics for a square stand-up fight. It came very near being a fall-down fight, when Lengthy let fly both arms at the elbow in the direction of Shorty's eyes, but, recovering himself according to the rules of the journalistic ring, the belligerents threw themselves into the London prize position, and then began

THE MILL.

First Round—Shorty sailed in without any preliminary sparring, much to the astonishment of Lengthy, who evidently anticipated some fancy maneuvers previous to the more solid work, landing his cocoanut in the bread-basket of his opponent, which elicited a most vehement and heartfelt grunt and which doubled him up in the shape of a half opened jack-knife. Then reaching out his left flipper he seized the goat-like appendage of Lengthy, and, shutting both eyes, handed him one on the bugle in handsome style, drawing the claret copiously.[12]

First round for Shorty. Time 40 seconds. Betting lively and two to one on Shorty.

Second Round—By this time Lengthy seemed to have become thoroughly roused. His eyes dilated and his nostrils quivered. He had smelt blood and trembled in eagerness for the fray. Shorty seemed somewhat groggy with the shock he had received when he landed in the empty bread basket of his elongated and emaciated adversary, for instead of a cushioned adipose pad, he had struck against a consolidated mass of bone and gristle.

After a little scientific sparring the exasperated Lengthy, put in a sockdollager on Shorty's left optic leaving a gory gash ghastly to gaze upon.

The latter made an excellent attempt to ward off the impending blow but his proboscis intervening between him and Lengthy, he did not see the direction of the stroke until too late. Quick as lightning, he put in a counter, striking Lengthy on the left shoulder a blow which sent him gyrating a half dozen feet up the street. The attenuated combatant quickly recovered his equilibrium and came thundering down on Shorty with blows dealt in rapid succession with the grace and effect of a windmill under full headway that our truthful and on-the-spot artist is obliged to own that he could not tell where they fell. The arms of Lengthy, far-reaching and strictly moral, moved with the rapidity of lightning, and crushed poor Shorty ignominiously to grass. The accomplished Lengthy made

ONE TERRIFIC LEAP

into the air, and landed on all fours upon the body of his prostrate foe.

In this position, with his face to the sky and his back to the earth, Shorty held his antagonist, John Phoenix-like, to his work. He kept the hands of Lengthy busily occupied with his countenance and his hair, and with twisting his neck-handkerchief, until time was called, and thus ended the second and last round.

Time one minute fifteen seconds.

Our special artist who had been eminently successful in obtaining a sketch of the first round, failed on the second. This was owing to the effect of the terrible encounter upon his nervous system, and the more embarrassing fact that in the latter part of this sanguinary set-to, arms and legs flew about so thick that it was difficult to see daylight between them.

The mill terminated in favor of Lengthy, although Shorty was at first the favorite. Perhaps had be been in better training and condition he might have been the conqueror. His friends removed him from the field as the bluebottles began to gather thick. It is thought that as soon as these masters of the noble art recover from their injuries another match will be on the tapis.

THE SCENE OF THE ENCOUNTER presented at this time a terrible picture. The pavement was torn up, pieces of clothing were scattered about, and bloody hair hung in gory ringlets from the rough edges of the stones. Some of the friends of the participants tried to create the impression that a portion of the gore was made of raspberry juice from a grocery box that had been thrown over in the scuffle. We scorn the insinuation. We know blood when we see it.[13]

The *Herald*'s sober and understated report wasn't the only account of the incident. The *Bee* and the *Republican* each had their own version of the story. The *Republican* complained that:

Any gentleman is liable to personal assaults from loafers on the streets, and it was Mr. Balcome's fate yesterday to have an insignificant, worthless, two-legged puppy, named E. Rosewater, attempt to rawhide him in the streets by crawling up behind him in a stealthy, cowardly manner. . .

In the *Republican*'s version, Balcome threw Rosewater to the ground and sat on him, pounding the *Bee* editor's face "evidently with a view toward converting it into another shape" before bystanders intervened.[14]

As usual, Rosewater saw things quite differently. The *Bee*'s version ran under the headline "DISGRACED," referring to Balcome. Rosewater, the *Bee* explained, used the cowhide because he "wished to disgrace and degrade, in the most public manner" the man who had insulted him. While Rosewater was applying the lash, Balcome:

> *attempted to gouge Mr. Rosewater's eyes and scratch his face; but the lash was playing so lively about his neck and face, that he soon gave up this style of defense, and being at least a foot taller, suddenly leaped upon Mr. Rosewater, and both came to the ground together. Maj. Balcome, with his feline nature, renewed the scratching process. . .*

The *Bee* article ended with Rosewater defiant and supported by the crowd:

> *The street talk, from what we can hear, is that Mr. Rosewater pursued exactly the right course, and many expressed their regrets that he did not use a club, or even a deadlier weapon.*[15]

Soon after the fight, both editors were arrested. In court, Rosewater pleaded guilty to disturbance of the peace, and paid a $10 fine. Balcome's case was dismissed. It was all over but the talking, and there was plenty of that. According to the *Republican*, hundreds of Omahans visited the "battle ground" later that day.[16]

The *Republican* revealed another detail, one which Rosewater may not have been inclined to believe: Balcome did not write the "Rosewater and his wench" article; hadn't even known about it, in fact. The editor of the *Republican*'s city desk, a young man whom the *Bee* had publicly branded a "dead beat" and a "bummer," had inserted the article without Balcome's knowledge. This editor had been given the article by its author—*Judge Townsend*.[17]

Rosewater never tried to cowhide either Townsend or the city desk editor, but we can forgive him the oversight. He was a busy man. One day, a police captain started to whip him, but bystanders intervened. On another occasion, he was attacked by James Creighton—member of the prominent Creighton family, and who had recently been arrested for choking a city councilman during a barroom quarrel. Creighton was a tougher character than Balcome, but Rosewater was prepared. Having lost his faith in cowhides, he drew a gun. Creighton backed off. Still

This illustration of the Rosewater-Balcombe fight appeared in *The Day's doings,* a sensationalist New York City newspaper.

itching for a fight, however, Creighton then suggested a duel with shotguns. For once in life showing some discretion, Rosewater declined the challenge.

And that was just 1873. Three years later, Rosewater was clubbed nearly to death by an irate reader wielding a "lead-loaded slingshot." Amazingly, the hard-headed editor lived to be 65. He died in 1906, apparently of natural causes.[18]

Chapter 9 notes

[1]Orville D. Menard, *Political Bossism in Mid-America: Tom Dennison's Omaha, 1900-1933*.
New York: University Press of America, 1989, 66-75 (Dennison was Rosewater's political protegé).

[2]*Bee* (evening), March 12, 1873.

[3]*Bee* (evening), March 13, 1873.

[4]*Herald* quotation and *Bee* reply: *Bee* (evening) June 16, 1873.

[5]*Omaha Daily Herald*, July 6, 1873.

[6]*Omaha Republican,* July 8, 1873.

[7]Dorothy Devereux Dustin, *Omaha & Douglas County: A Panoramic History*.
Sponsored by the Douglas County Historical Society. Woodland Hills, CA:
Windsor Publications, 1980, 60.

[8]*Bee*, July 8, 1873.

[9]*Bee*, July 8, 1873.

[10]*Republican*, July 8, 1873.

[11]*Bee,* July 8, 1873.

[12]*Translation*: Rosewater grabbed Balcome by the beard, punched him on the nose, and
drew blood (claret is a dark red wine).

[13]*Herald*, July 10, 1873.

[14]*Republican*, July 8, 1873.

[15]*Bee*, July 8, 1873.

[16]*Republican*, July 10, 1873; also, *Herald*, July 10, 1873.

[17]*Republican*, July 10, 1873.

[18]Lawrence H. Larsen and Barbara J. Cottrell, *The Gate City: A History of Omaha*. Pruett
Publishing Co., 1983, 98-99; Menard, 72-73; Sorenson, *Story*, 440.

Chapter Ten

THE DELICATE ART OF BUNCO

1873

There's a certain magic in the rhythm of steel wheels on steel rails. There's music in it, and it's part of the romance and the mystique of the railroad. That rhythm has inspired countless songs, and it may have been inspiring one of them on December 7, 1873, as a westbound passenger train made its way toward Omaha.

Inside one of the cars sat a young man strumming a guitar. We can only guess at the song that was flowing out from his brain to his fingertips. It may have been a song he knew, or one he was writing. It might have been a song of love gained, or of love lost, or a song about heading West, about possibilities and ambitions and *dreams* . . . but whatever it was, it is lost to us. It was lost to him as well, for (predictably) he was interrupted by an idiot. Another passenger—a man who had just boarded the train at the last stop—sat down opposite the young man and asked,

"Say, stranger, what's that instrument you're drumming on?"

"That's a guitar," the young man replied patiently, and probably hoped that that would be the end of it. It wasn't.

"No it isn't," the stranger replied. "That's a *banjo*."

The young man's misery was complete. He was not merely afflicted with an idiot, but with an idiot of the worst (though the most common) variety: an idiot *who thinks he knows what he's talking about.*

They argued. Both men being stubborn—the one stubborn in his knowledge and the other equally stubborn in his ignorance—they soon got all worked up about the matter.

And then a most unexpected and wonderful thing happened. The idiot offered to bet $25 that the instrument was indeed a banjo. They would ask a neutral party, and that would settle it.

The musician was overjoyed. Here, in the midst of a pointless and frustrating argument with this bullheaded moron, he had suddenly been handed a three-flower bouquet of sweet-smelling opportunity: the chance to prove the other man a blockhead, to take his money, and to *shut him up.*

"All right, put up your money," the musician said.

The idiot then called to another passenger sitting nearby,

"Stranger, come here and hold the stakes." Both the idiot and the musician handed him $25, after which the idiot suggested,

"Now then, let that man sitting behind us—reading that blood-and-thunder novel[1]—decide the bet." The musician agreed.

Meanwhile, the train had come to a stop at a tiny western Iowa station. For a short time, the car sat motionless, no longer swaying to the magical rhythm of the rails. Both rails and guitar were silent when the instrument was shown to the blood-and-thunder reader, who thereupon delivered his verdict:

He said it was a banjo.

And then everything happened in rapid succession. The musician uttered we-can-only-guess-what oaths of astonishment and incredulity; the stakeholder handed the $50 to the idiot; the train lurched forward and began to leave the station; and finally—and most important—the idiot, the stakeholder, and the blood-and-thunder reader all together made for the door and jumped off the car.

For of course the three men were not strangers to each other, nor were they strangers to the type of man with whom they preferred *doing business*. They'd spotted the musician as their kind of man, and they'd played him as skillfully as ever he had played a guitar. And then, having made a quick $8.33 per man, they left the musician to complete his ride to Omaha in a most

Union Pacific Museum Collection
Union Pacific Depot, 1868.

profound and reflective solitude.

I don't know if he ever got back to that tune he'd been play-ing. If he played anything at all for those last few miles, I'm guessing it was a sad, sad song, a heartfelt lament of loss and betrayal.[2]

It is well that our young musician was headed for Omaha, for he was coming to a great center of the arts, a thriving commu-nity of ambitious, clever, creative men. Omaha's music and the-ater may have been unspectacular, but in another medium Omaha built a national reputation. That medium was the time-hallowed, delicate art of *bunco*, the craft of separating a fool from his money by the use of one's wits. A man of this profession was known as a *confidence man*, for his first task was to gain the confidence of his victim. We have since shortened it to *con man* or even *con artist*—thus revealing our grudging admira-tion for the skills involved.

It was no accident that so many confidence men chose Omaha as a home base. They came with the railroad. By the 1870s, seven railroad lines either started from or ended in Omaha. Every day the trains arrived, disgorged their passen-gers, and filled the dirty streets of the city with travelers and with travelers' dollars. The field was ripe unto harvest.

There was the small matter of law enforcement, of course, for Omaha's city government was in the able hands of energetic and ambitious men. But this was no obstacle. A political man of energy and ambition was just the sort of man to find himself too busy lining his own pockets to worry much about the emptying of someone else's—especially when that someone else was an out-of-towner with no voice in local affairs.

In those cases in which the wheels of justice broke down and prosecuted a swindler, the Missouri River—which doubled as the state line—provided an easy escape hatch for those wishing to avoid the laws of either Nebraska or Iowa.

In short, the situation was perfect, and it did not take long for the word to spread. Soon it seemed that every lying, cheating, four-flushing, double-dealing, card-sharping, counterfeiting scoundrel who did not already hold high public office was setting up shop in the streets of Omaha. [3] A letter printed in the *Republican*, signed "ORDER" and complaining of the city government's inaction, gives us this picture of Omaha's gambling scene in April 1873:

> *Within the past ten days traveling people have been victimized in this city to a terrible degree. Sums of money ranging from $50 to $2,000 have been taken from parties here by these pests of society, gamblers. But yesterday a party was taken for $1,800 . . .*
>
> *Go down Farnham [sic] street any nice day, between Tenth and Twelfth street, nearly every other man you meet will be a representative of the gambling fraternity. From thence go on Douglas street, between Twelfth and Thirteenth, and you will find from ten to twenty of them assembled along there. From thence to the U.P. depot. This place seems to be the grand assembling place for all the gamblers in the city.[4]*

Bunco came in many flavors, but the most popular was a game called three-card monte, described here by the *Bee*:

The game of three-card monte, for the informa-tion of those who do not know much about it, is, as its name indicates, played with three cards. One man throws them, one after the other, in rapid succession, and at the conclusion of the operation, any person, who may have been roped in for the occasion, bets, if he can be induced to do so, that he can pick out a certain card, which has been pre-viously shown. There is one chance out of three in a square game for a man to win.

The professional throwers of three-card monte attain such dexterity in their sleight-of-hand per-formances—for they can be called nothing else—that they have what may be called a dead-sure thing. An expert thrower will show the victim the card which is to be picked out, and while han-dling it he will turn up a corner, or crimp it, as if by accident, so that the "sucker" can follow it with his eye, or at least is led to believe that he can, and so he thinks that he has got it sure; but when he turns it over he finds that he is mistaken, and that the error has cost him something—generally all the money and jewerly that he has with him. The thrower, of course, while manipulating the cards, bends back the turned up corner, and turns up the corner of another card in a similar manner. The successful operations of three-card monte throw-ers is all owing to one single principle—that the action of the hand is quicker than the movement of the eye.

The victim is generally allowed to win several times in succession, until the bets run up to large amounts, when he is sure to lose every time. The trick appears so simple to him, that he is willing to risk everything he possesses on it.[5]

Clearly, this was more than sleight-of-hand. Much more. Playing a crooked game of monte was one thing, but getting a man to bet against the game was quite another. The usual method was to approach a man on the street, engage him in friendly conversation, invite him for drinks at a local saloon, and then—as the alcohol and personal charm began taking effect—introduce a "friendly" game. But not every man could be led so gently into the trap. As important as the game itself was the choice of prey. A comment in the *Bee* is revealing:

> *These cappers[6] are bold and shrewd men, of vast experience in the ways of the world, and their knowledge of the human character, acquired by constant contact with men in every station of life, enables them generally to "spot" the right kind of man for their victim.[7]*

Who was the right kind of man? Travelers were targeted because they often carried large amounts of money, were usually ignorant of the local bunco scene, and were generally on their way to someplace else—meaning that they would be hard-pressed to stick around long enough to press charges. But not every traveler made a good sucker.

What was it that made a man a sucker?

Stupidity is the easy answer, but most victims seem to have been reasonably successful men, and therefore reasonably intelligent. Gullibility—that by-product of a trusting nature—certainly played a part, but there was something else about a confidence game that observers generally missed. Consider the *Bee*'s description of monte and of the "accidentally" turned up edges on the cards. Consider the story of the guitarist and the "idiot" who offered to bet that a guitar was a banjo. In both cases the victim was led to believe not only that he could get something for nothing, but that he could do so by taking advantage of a lesser man. In other words, a bunco victim not only had to be trusting and naive enough to believe in the con's performance, but he also had to be sinister enough to try to take an innocent stranger for a lot of money. The perfect sucker, therefore, was something of a capper himself.

Conversely, the capper was usually something of a sucker. Most of the three-card monte men consistently gambled away their hard-swindled money at the local faro tables.[8]

His name—apparently—was William Jones, but he was better known as Canada Bill. He was one of those shadowy figures who arrived unannounced on the stage of Omaha history, origins shrouded in mystery. Supposedly he had been born in Canada. Supposedly he had come to Omaha from the Mississippi River, having long infested the steamboats of that great waterway with his card-playing, greenhorn-swindling presence.

Arriving in Omaha in late 1871, Canada Bill began introducing the city to three-card monte. Gathering around him a gang of cappers and assorted scoundrels, he soon became known as the "king of the monte men."[9]

Like all great con men, Bill was a gifted actor. He had several stock roles, but his favorite was "that of an unsophisticated farmer, with a squeaky voice, a slouch hat, and with one trouser leg stuffed in the top of his boot." Day after day the show went on, the street serving as a stage, the cappers serving as extras, and unwary travelers serving as audience members. A man who saw a Canada Bill performance tended to pay handsomely for the privilege.[10]

His work did not go unnoticed. By April 1873, the local newspapers were growing increasingly shrill in their demands for a crackdown. The *Republican*, noting city hall's lack of vigor in prosecuting the swindlers, suggested a cause, saying, "we are almost constrained to believe that more money is made by not interfering in these cases than would be made if the guilty ones were promptly arrested."[11] Granted, the *Republican*'s righteousness was new-found: Major Balcome and company discovered monte shortly after a Democratic mayor replaced an equally lackadaisical Republican incumbent. Even so, it was becoming clear to everyone that something had to be done. Within the week, Canada Bill was arrested.

Charged with bilking a man out of $800, Bill wasted no time in going over to the offensive. On April 22, he appeared in police court with his two attorneys, who promptly filed a motion to dismiss the charges. They cited two grounds for dismissal: first, that the charges against William Jones were too vague; and second, that the police court had no jurisdiction over this type of case—meaning that the city would have to seek a grand jury indictment.

Judge Dudley—a newly-elected Democrat—was unimpressed. Denying the motion, he ordered the trial to begin. Dudley would decide the case himself; this being the police court, there would be no jury.

Despite the failed motion for dismissal, Canada Bill was already a step ahead of his enemies. The *Republican* reported that the "plaintiffs were not ready, alleging that the defendant had spirited away witnesses and that it was impossible to proceed."[12]

But proceed they must. Next day, the trial began in earnest. Canada Bill, appearing "cool, self-possessed, and assured," arrived in the courtroom with attorneys in tow.[13]

He called character witnesses.

To hear these honest citizens tell it, Canada Bill was not a man who was known to cheat. Of the "witnesses" at the saloon where Bill had acquired the stranger's $800, none said that they were aware of any cheating, and most testified—with straight faces—that they didn't even know that a card-game had been played.

Ignoring the testimony, Judge Dudley found Canada Bill guilty as charged, and fined him $65 or $70—the reporter didn't remember the exact amount. Even the *Republican* didn't believe that the evidence warranted conviction, but Dudley said he was determined to rid the city of the monte men. Canada Bill left town the next day.

"That's right, William," taunted the *Republican*, "inflict some other more classical community with the shining light of your serene countenance . . . Open a little game for them. We won't miss you much."[14]

And they didn't. Even without Canada Bill, and despite Judge Dudley's stated determination, the con games went on. Bill lay low for a while, like an actor waiting offstage for his next scene. He was a showman, and his conviction and departure became part of the show, the scene in which the audience is led to believe that the monster is dead.

In fact, the game of monte—and the associated con games— would wax and wane in Omaha for years. For most victims, the police and courts were of little help. Most often, the wronged traveler:

> *becoming tired and disgusted . . . proceeds on his*
> *way to his destination, bearing with him no pleas-*
> *ant remembrance of Omaha, but considering it a*
> *place above all others to be shunned by the travel-*
> *ing public. It is thus that Omaha has gained a*
> *most unenviable reputation abroad, and is now*
> *looked upon as one of the most demoralized cities*
> *in the Union.*[15]

Omaha's bad reputation is a subject in itself; we will look into it shortly. But we are not yet finished with that great, gambling, brawling year of 1873. Right now we have a prizefight to attend.

Chapter 10 notes

[1] *Blood-and-thunder novel* - a cheap, sensationalistic novel. It may have been one of the ubiquitous "Beadle's Dime Novels," published by our friend Erastus Beadle, now of New York City.

[2] *Bee* (evening), December 9, 1873.

[3] *Bee* (morning), April 15, 1873.

[4] *Republican*, April 11, 1873.

[5] *Bee* (morning), April 15, 1873.

[6] *Capper:* a man who chooses the victim and leads him to the game. Also known as a *bunco steerer.*

[7] *Bee* (morning), April 15, 1873.

[8] Sorenson, *The Story of Omaha*, 463.

[9] *Bee* (morning), April 15, 1873.

[10] Sorenson, *The Story of Omaha*, 463.

[11] *Republican*, April 18, 1873.

[12] *Republican*, April 23, 1873.

[13] *Republican*, April 24, 1873.

[14] *Republican*, April 25, 1877.

[15] *Bee* (morning), April 15, 1873.

Chapter Eleven

THE PRIZEFIGHT

November 1873

The news was just too outrageous to be true. It had to be a hoax, somehow. A con. A bit of misdirection, perhaps. So felt many Omahans in early November 1873, after a strange announcement came in over the telegraph wires.

For weeks, sporting men across the country had been talking about the great prizefight that was brewing. Heavyweight champion Tom Allen had accepted a challenge from his personal enemy Ben Hogan; their managers made plans for them to settle their differences in Illinois.

But the fight hadn't come off. A small matter interfered—the law—and Allen and Hogan and their handlers had to flee from the wrath of the governor of Illinois. In that state, as in the rest of the country, prizefighting was illegal.

Then came the surprising announcement. The championship fight was on again. It would take place in Omaha, Nebraska.

It isn't clear why Omaha was chosen. Prizefighting was no more legal in Nebraska than it was in Illinois. (In fact, Nebraska law prescribed one to ten years' imprisonment for the crime.) But Omaha had several advantages which the promoters may have considered: It was surrounded by sparsely-populated prairies, which were well-suited for a semi-clandestine gathering of sporting men. It was located just across the river from Iowa—and not far from Missouri—which opened up many possibilities for confounding state authorities. And, of course, Omaha had a bit of a reputation as a "wide-open town," a town that might welcome such amusement. Heck, even Omaha newspaper editors duked it out sometimes.

In the Omaha press, reactions were mixed. The *Republican* announced the fight under the headline, "The Next Sensation," while the *Bee* boasted of its reporters' determination to witness the fight and flaunt the law which could land them in jail for doing so. The *Herald*, meanwhile, was more cautious: as late as November 14—just four days before the scheduled date of the fight—it warned its readers that the truth of the announcement was "not yet believed by us." [1]

Skepticism aside, the growing excitement could not be suppressed. Even foes of the *noble art* of pugilism admitted as much. "It is useless to say that man is not almost as much of an animal in his combative instincts as a bull, deny it as men may," a writer for the *Herald* lamented, ". . . When men say they abhor pugilism, whilst they tell the truth, they do not tell the whole truth. We have never seen a man who has seen a dog fight that did not have his choice of dog." [2]

In comparing a prizefight to a dogfight, the *Herald* was not just trying to be colorful. In those days, professional fights were not governed by the modern Queensberry rules, but by the older rules of the London Prize Ring. The differences were, well, *striking*: The boxers fought bare-knuckles, and they fought as many rounds as it took to settle the issue. The rounds were untimed, and ended when a man fell. When that happened, both fighters had thirty seconds to "come to scratch," a line drawn in the center of the ring. It didn't matter how a fighter got back to scratch—his seconds could carry him there if they needed to— just so long as he was on his feet, toeing the line, at the half-minute mark. The fight continued until one or both fighters were unable to come to scratch. Eye-gouging, rabbit-punches, or anything below the belt was prohibited, and such a foul ended the fight in the favor of the one fouled. Wrestling, on the other hand—even throwing one's opponent to the ground—

Durham Western Heritage Museum
Douglas Street, 1870. Looking east fron Nineteenth.

was allowed.

What were such fights like? Boxing aficionado Gerald Suster gives us this description of boxing's bare-knuckle days:

> *The contests of those days were usually fought at a much slower pace. Knuckles can be surprisingly fragile, fingers fracture easily, and so a pugilist had to take precise care in planting his punches. The thirty-second recovery period meant that dazed, exhausted men could be sent back to the battle time and time again by the gamblers who were backing them. Bernard Shaw, a good amateur middleweight and relatively astute boxing commentator, deplored the bare-knuckle days when a contest usually ended with two bloodied, dizzy, damaged and exhausted men merely trying to outlast one another and protect their brutally damaged hands for the sake of the livelihoods they owed to their backers.*[3]

Such was the trade of Tom Allen and Ben Hogan.

"I am seeing what this blower says," said Tom Allen to the *Herald* reporter. Sitting in his room at Omaha's Wyoming Hotel, Allen put down the newspaper he had been reading. It was a copy of the *Herald*—the reporter duly noted this—and moreover was the issue that featured an interview with Ben Hogan. Allen continued his commentary in his Cockney accent. He was calm, polite, supremely confident, and utterly disdainful of his opponent.

"You have got a good report of it," he said of the interview, "Better than he deserves. He is a blower, sir—only a blower." As Allen told it, Hogan was even worse than that: he accused Hogan of approaching Allen's manager and offering "half of the excursion money just to make a draw of it."[4]

Such charges couldn't be verified, of course, but Allen was a man who seemed to know what he was talking about. Squarely-built, a little above medium height, and wearing a short, gray-flecked mustache, the thirty-three-year-old Allen appeared "a splendid specimen of physical manhood." Despite his eighteen professional fights, he retained "a pleasant face which does not at all remind one of the prize ring"—a testimony to his fistic skill.[5]

Not that he hadn't been beaten. Of his eighteen fights since entering the prize ring in 1861, Allen had won thirteen, lost four, and drawn one. Of his four losses, he had avenged two. One loss which he had not avenged was an 1864 defeat at the hands of a fighter named Bob "the Black" Smith. In this two-hour, forty-seven-minute marathon, a young Allen had succumbed after 102 rounds.

Allen came to America from his native England in 1867. Though he lost to English champion "Gypsy" Jem Mace, in 1870, he twice defeated American champion Mike McCoole. When Mace retired from the ring, Allen reckoned himself the world's heavyweight champion. In America, at least, no one disputed his claim.[6]

And now came Ben Hogan—the "blower," as Allen styled him. Based on Allen's remarks, one would expect Hogan to have been full of bravado in his interview. But it was not so.

A day before the Allen interview, a neatly-dressed and handsome Ben Hogan had met reporters in his room at the Grand Central Hotel. A native of New York City, the thirty-year-old Hogan possessed "broad shoulders, long arms and large hands and feet."[7] Even so, the *Bee* noted that he was "a much smaller man than Allen, and if he wins the coming fight it will be by pure science and pluck, and not by prowess or muscular strength."[8]

Those wondering whether Hogan possessed the necessary "science and pluck" may have looked to his fight record for evidence. To put it bluntly, what fighting credentials did Hogan possess when he arrived in St. Louis—Tom Allen's adopted hometown—to challenge the champion?

"I came to St. Louis a novice," Hogan admitted, "And do not claim any record. Maybe I had one or two scrub fights, just a quick knock down or so, but that counts for nothing."

A novice? Hogan's own words cast doubt on this. Though he claimed no fight record, he mentioned that he had trained other boxers. Did these boxers let themselves be trained by a *novice?*

The interview grew stranger still. Hogan complained that he had been ill recently, that he was not yet up to full strength, that because of illness he had not even been training for the fight and that, in fact, he did not even have a trainer at present. He even mentioned that Tom Allen outweighed him by twenty pounds.

Hogan portrayed the fight as the result of a personal quarrel, "an old matter between me and Allen . . . we had some words." He didn't explain further, but the personal animosity was clear enough, especially on Tom Allen's side. This didn't, however, explain how Hogan proposed to gain any satisfaction by stepping into the ring with the champion. In Allen's most recent fight, he had destroyed the hulking Mike McCoole in just twenty minutes. McCoole had been a champion—what would Allen do to a "novice"?[9]

Overall, Ben Hogan sounded like a man who knew he was going to receive a beating. Or like a man who wanted others to think so.[10]

Since prizefighting was illegal, the fight could not be held in town, nor could its location be made public. Nor were any fight tickets available.

None of this was a problem to any man who wished to attend. On November 15, some rather bizarre railroad tickets went on

sale in Omaha. Each ticket read, "From Omaha to ——— and
return," which, as the *Herald* playfully pointed out, "might lead
one to suspect that the projectors of this bit of pleasure travel
must be of a vacillating turn of mind. Or, perhaps, they are
preparing a gentle surprise for their guests." In case anyone
still didn't get the joke, the *Herald* added that:

> *it may not be out of place to mention that Mr. T.*
> *Allen and Mr. B. Hogan are not wholly uncon-*
> *nected with this pic nic. Indeed, it is supposed that*
> *they will be there themselves, dressed, it may be, in*
> *a somewhat primitive manner, and that a little*
> *ring will be formed in order that these distin-*
> *guished men may stand and gaze upon each other*
> *. . .*[11]

With a nod and a wink, preparations for the illegal fight
went on. Out-of-town visitors converged on Omaha from all
directions; mostly they were sporting men (i.e., men who liked
to drink and gamble) and reporters (men who liked to drink and
write). Meanwhile, both fighters gave sparring exhibitions in
crowded halls . . . and the Omaha public ate it all up. By the day
of the fight, the *Herald* reported that "the interest in the coming mill is very general. There is an eager desire to witness it on
the part of many who would not, on general principles, be sus-
pected of caring much for a fight of this kind . . ."[12]

Across the river, a different mood reigned. "Our people do not
care much about witnessing the bruising," sniffed the Council
Bluffs *Nonpareil* on November 14 (not that anyone in Omaha
would have believed it). But then came the news that the "———
———" on the "from Omaha to ———" train tickets would be an
Iowa location. The great gathering of *sporting men*—which
included one "Canada Bill" Jones and his associates—was planning to cross the river to hold its little *pic nic* in Council Bluffs'
backyard. Quickly, disdain turned to concern, and concern to
fear, and fear . . . to something suspiciously resembling panic.
Consider the following telegram:

Council Bluffs, November 17.
Gov. C. C. Carpenter:
Dear Sir: — The Hogan Allen prize fight is to
take place Tuesday in Iowa, and near here. We are
powerless to prevent it, and we ask your authority
and military force to stop it.
[signed by many prominent citizens]

If that didn't get the Iowa governor's attention, perhaps the next telegram—received about an hour later—did:

Council Bluffs, November 17.
Gov. C. C. Carpenter:
Dear Sir: — Can't something be done to prevent
the Allen-Hogan prize fight in Iowa tomorrow?
Fifteen hundred roughs in Omaha. The local
authorities are powerless. Can't you send military
company from Des Moines to prevent them from
coming into the State?
[signed by many citizens][13]

In the end, Governor Carpenter yielded to the demands and dispatched two companies of militia, seventy-five men in all. Traveling by rail, the troops arrived at Council Bluffs at about eleven o'clock that night. There they stacked arms and bivouacked under the cold November sky, awaiting the confrontation that was to come in the morning.[14]

November 18, 1873, dawned cold and blustery. At 6 a.m., a crowded train departed from Omaha's Union Station and began making its way over the bridge into Iowa. Its immediate destination was the junction with the Kansas City, St. Joseph, and Council Bluffs Railroad, on which the train would head south for an unknown distance. At that junction, under the command of Pottawattamie County Sheriff George Doughty, waited the militia.

Sheriff Doughty had requested the authority to stop the train and arrest the passengers, or at least to send them back across the Missouri. Legally, however, no one had committed a crime as yet. Doughty was apparently instructed to use the troops only to prevent what the *Nonpareil* had called the "heathenish and barbarous programme" from taking place on Iowa soil. If the *sporting men* wanted to continue on into Missouri, or re-cross the river at Nebraska City, that wasn't his problem. Accordingly, when the train pulled up at the Council Bluffs station, Sheriff Doughty had in mind to board it, and take his troops along for the ride.[15]

The train eased to stop beside a platform lined with armed and uniformed men. Inside the eight passenger cars, a jolly and well-lubricated crowd of about 450 men looked out at the troops; outside, the rows of troops looked back at the men inside. It might have been an ominous moment.

Might have been—but wasn't. A *Herald* reporter wrote smugly of the "brave militia" lined up outside, "exposed to a raking wind, as cold as ever blows . . . there they stood and shook, while their victims . . . sat quietly inside by the most comfortable of fires."[16]

While the passenger cars waited for a new engine to take them south along the St. Joe Road, Sheriff Doughty boarded and began a futile search for Allen and Hogan, both of whom were secretly traveling by carriage.

Unable to make any arrests as yet, the sheriff had one more card to play—his trump. He and his troops would ride along.

Without argument, the "excursion" managers agreed. The troops were more than welcome. As soon as they paid five dollars apiece for tickets, they could all come aboard.

Sheriff Doughty was taken aback. This hadn't been part of his calculations. He would need $375 to cover the cost, and that was a lot of money. The sheriff replied that he was certain that the government of the State of Iowa was good for it. To this, the managers replied that they didn't wish to deal with the state at this time. And Sheriff George Doughty, the man who had, a day earlier, proposed to arrest the whole lot of Omaha "roughs," and who now had seventy-five armed troops backing him, didn't know what to do.

So he did nothing. As the train pulled away from the platform, the passengers gazed out their windows at seventy-five shivering militiamen and one befuddled sheriff who stood helpless, watching them go. "For aught we know, they are there yet," chuckled the *Herald* the next day. In Council Bluffs, the *Nonpareil* could only sputter indignantly that the "attempt to stop the fight came to a most lame and impotent conclusion."[17]

A little after noon, the train stopped at Pacific Junction, a hamlet about fifteen miles south of Council Bluffs. Tom Allen and Ben Hogan were waiting.

Stakes and ropes were brought out, and a ring constructed on the grass—twenty-four feet square—outside of which a larger ring was built, to mark off a special-admission, ringside area. The fighters then named their "seconds" (their ringside assistants, who would actually stand inside the ring), and argued over who was to be the referee.

The fighters entered the ring. Going to their corners, each stripped down to a pair of belted tights and shoes. They would fight bare-chested in the raw November air. A slight breach of etiquette occurred when Hogan failed to throw his cap into the center of the ring, as Allen had done. "Why the bloody hell don't you pitch your cap in, man?" asked one of Allen's seconds. Hogan, looking like a novice, smiled and threw the cap.[18]

Just then a voice rang out, a "hear ye" voice, as a reporter described it. It was the Mills County sheriff, come to read the riot act. He gave each fighter his little speech, informing them of the illegality of what they were about to do, and then—his duty discharged—paid two dollars for ringside admission and settled in to enjoy the fight.

It was time to begin. The fighters came to the center of the ring and shook hands. It was the first time the crowd had seen the two men next to each other, and Allen's superior height and bulk were plain to all. But the crowd cheered loudest for the challenger.

"Are you ready, Ben?" Allen asked.

Hogan's only reply was to assume the sparring position, standing with his left shoulder toward Allen, leading with his left fist, guarding with his right—the classic, upright stance of the bare-knuckles pugilist.

They began. Studiously, the men advanced and gave way,

advanced and gave way, jabbing tentatively, guarding, each man looking for an opening. The crowd was silent.

Suddenly, without warning, Allen struck hard, but Hogan parried the blow and immediately threw a counterpunch at Allen's head. It missed. Allen then struck again, but could not get the better of his opponent. A murmur of applause rippled through the crowd. Hogan may have called himself a novice, but so far he wasn't fighting like one.

The sparring continued. Hogan feinted with his left hand, then threw a hard right against Allen's forehead. The champion fell, landing doubled-up on the grass near the edge of the ring. While Allen's seconds carried him back to his corner, the crowd erupted in cheering, and money exchanged hands. First knock-down to Hogan.

But the fight was not over. Thirty seconds later, Allen was on his feet again, facing Hogan in the center of the ring.

The second round grew more serious. The fighters spent less time studying the situation, and more time throwing and blocking punches. Defense dominated. "They both strike blows that would knock a common man senseless," wrote a reporter, "and they are resolutely met and parried." But some got through. Allen struck Hogan in the chest; Hogan smashed Allen on the nose and upper lip, drawing blood.

First blood for Hogan. Outside the ring, more money exchanged hands.

For a moment, the two fighters backed away from each other, then came together again, fighting close now, fighting hard. In the struggle, Allen's head passed for a moment under Hogan's arm. Hogan struck. The crowd heard the thump of fist on flesh and saw the spatter of Allen's blood, saw Hogan standing so close to Allen that he got blood on himself as well.

The bloodied champion struck back, and struck low. "It hits Hogan's body so low down that it breaks his breath," reported the *Herald*. In those days, fighters wore no protection; Hogan therefore felt the full weight of the blow to his groin, and instinctively put one hand there. His guard was down. In the next instant, Allen smashed him under the left eye. Hogan fell.

"Foul! Foul!" came the cries from the crowd. As far as they were concerned—and as far as the rules of the London Prize

Ring were concerned—the fight was over. Hogan had won on a foul.

But within the ring, confusion reigned. John Sweeney, one of Hogan's seconds, gave the following version of events: After carrying Hogan back to his corner, Sweeney went to the referee and protested. The referee admitted that a foul blow had been struck, but instead of stopping the fight, merely went over to Tom Allen and warned him not to do it again. At that moment— with the referee still in Allen's corner, and before the thirty-second rest period expired—someone called time, and the fighters came out for the third round. That someone, said Sweeney, was Tom Allen's manager, Jack Looney. Looney was one of the two umpires for the fight, but had no authority to call time.

Whether Looney really interfered or not is unclear. Other witnesses said that the referee, standing with watch in hand, called time. With several men milling about inside the ring, and many more howling in protest outside of it, it was difficult to know just what was happening.

With the call of *Time!* the two fighters arose and came together again, "both bleeding, both desperate," in the words of a reporter. Hogan's left eye was rapidly swelling shut, while his expression spoke "of a grief that can never be put into words." He had been hurt, and badly.

Several things happened at once. At the ring's center, Allen and Hogan fired away at each other, striking at face and body. In Hogan's corner, Sweeney tried to make himself heard, still protesting the foul. Outside the ring, many of the spectators echoed Sweeney with shouted protests.

"Foul! Foul!"

"Hogan has won!"

"Give the fight to Hogan!"

At some point, according to most witnesses, Allen struck a second foul blow. This was not as harmful to Hogan as the first foul, but created a furor in the crowd. Pistols and knives were drawn, and men pressed forward against the ropes. At about this time, Allen threw a hard left to Hogan's cheek, following it instantly with a right to the jaw. The one-two combination dropped Hogan like a side of beef.

By then the ropes were cut and the ring was flooded with a

swarm of angry men. Though most of them backed Hogan, not all of them did—and the threat of violent confrontation hung in the air. The men cursed, they threatened, they shook their fists in other men's faces and brandished revolvers and bowie knives. They insisted that Hogan was the winner, or that Allen was the winner, and they told each other to go to hell.

Tom Allen and Ben Hogan, meanwhile, returned to their corners, got dressed, and left the ring. As far as they were concerned, the fight was over.

As indeed it was. The argument inside the ring, though heated and well-armed, never grew into a real fight. Truth be told, the men inside the ring weren't like the fighters who had just left it: none of them were willing to strike the first blow. They may have argued over what the rules specified, argued over who was the winner, and argued over which of them ought to seek out a new home in the fiery pit . . . but eventually they argued themselves back aboard the train, and set out for home. Somewhere between Pacific Junction and Omaha, the referee ruled the fight a draw. Tom Allen retained his title.[19]

"The battle was short," said the *Herald,* "and in the case of Allen, disgraceful and cowardly." Echoing the opinions of the *Bee* and the *Republican*, as well as the St. Louis and Chicago papers—all of which had sent reporters to the fight—the *Herald* declared that Allen was a "boastful braggart," who was "fully matched and out-fought" before striking foul. The St. Louis *Globe* began referring to Ben Hogan as the "Champion of America."[20]

Tom Allen did not take the abuse quietly. Marching down to the *Herald*'s office (located conveniently above the billiard saloon at Fourteenth and Douglas), Allen made his case in person. He denied striking foul, and claimed that the referee had been forced to decide the fight with pistols to his head. Later, writing to the St. Louis *Democrat*, Allen issued a public challenge to Ben Hogan, offering to fight him "anywhere in Canada." He argued that "no man can be Champion of America . . . who gives all his portion of the stake money to a gang of murderers, who not only broke up the fight, but threatened to kill me and my friends."[21]

Funny thing, that last accusation. Alfred Sorenson, an early-day Omaha historian, claimed that the fight ended after the second foul when "the three-card monte men, who had bet heavily on Hogan, cut the ropes and entered the ring with drawn revolvers . . . ." Sorenson specifically identifies one *Canada Bill*—along with his gang of thugs and swindlers—as one who "figured prominently" in the fight.[22]

Might this explain Hogan's self-effacing words before the fight? Was Hogan trying to drive the betting odds in favor of Allen even higher, so that he and his *associates* could clean up after an upset victory?

Allen may have something there. But his trouble is this: everyone but Allen agrees that he struck foul. That should have cost him the championship, but didn't—Hogan's "gang of murderers" notwithstanding.

Allen and Hogan never did fight a rematch. In 1876, Allen fought a rematch with another old opponent, middleweight Joe Goss, a fellow Englishman with whom Allen had fought a two-hour draw in 1865. By the time of their 1876 fight, both men were overweight and past their prime. After pounding on Goss for twenty-one rounds, Allen smashed him in the face after Goss had fallen to his knees. That was a blatant foul, and this time it cost Allen the fight—and with it the heavyweight title. The aging Goss went on to lose to veteran bar-room brawler Paddy Ryan, who in turn lost—in 1882—to one John L. Sullivan, the last of the bare-knuckles champions and the first boxing superstar.[23]

Ben Hogan, meanwhile, went back to the saloon and dance hall he operated in Pennsylvania. But within a few years, his life changed completely. According to Sorenson:

> *He became a reformed man and evoluted into an evangelist. He was sincere in his reformation, and in evangelising work on the Pacific coast he succeeded in doing a great deal of good among the down-and-outers, many of whom he helped financially so far as his then limited purse would permit.*

Canada Bill, the king of the monte men, continued to haunt the streets of Omaha until 1876, when he was finally run out of town for good. Like most of his "cappers," Bill was as much sucker as swindler, and his ill-gotten wealth slipped through his fingers. He ended his days in a Pennsylvania poorhouse.[24]

And what of Omaha, the fight's strategic headquarters? As far as the *Herald* was concerned, the "picnic" was "the best advertisement for Omaha that it has had in many years." And as for rival Council Bluffs, "the performance of the 'milish' was farcical beyond even the *Herald*'s power to describe." What more could Omaha ask for?[25]

Chapter 11 notes

[1] *Republican*, November 1, 1873; *Bee* (evening), November 5, 1873; *Omaha Weekly Herald*, November 14, 1873.

[2] *Omaha Weekly Herald*, November 14, 1873.

[3] Gerald Suster, *Champions of the Ring: The Lives and Times of Boxing's Heavyweight Heroes*, London: Robson Books, 1992, 1994, 3.

[4] *Daily Herald*, November 13, 1873.

[5] *Daily Herald*, November 11, 1873.

[6] *Daily Herald*, November 13, 1873.

[7] *Daily Herald*, November 12, 1873.

[8] *Bee* (evening), November 11, 1873.

[9] *Daily Herald*, November 12, 1873.

[10] *Note on the locations*: The Wyoming Hotel, at which Tom Allen stayed, was located on the southeast corner of Ninth and Farnam (the present site of the ConAgra headquarters). The Grand Central Hotel, at which Ben Hogan stayed, was located on the southwest corner of 14th and Farnam (the present site of Paxton Manor).

[11] *Daily Herald*, November 15, 1873.

[12] *Daily Herald*, November 18, 1873.

[13] *Nonpareil*, November 20, 1873.

[14] *Nonpareil*, November 20, 1873; *Herald*, November 19, 1873. (The *Nonpareil* reported that 63 militiamen were coming; reports from the day of the fight state that 75 were present.)

[15] *Nonpareil*, November 18, 1873.

[16] *Daily Herald*, November 19, 1873.

[17] *Daily Herald*, November 19, 1873; *Nonpareil*, November 19, 1873.

[18] *Daily Herald*, November 19, 1873.

[19] This account of the fight is based on the following reports: *Daily Herald*, November 19, 20, 1873; *Nonpareil*, November 19, 1873; *Bee* (evening), November 18, 19, 1873. The *Bee* report seems a little confused on the chronology of the fight.

[20] *Daily Herald*, November 19, 1873; *Weekly Herald*, November 28, 1873.

[21] Reprinted in the *Weekly Herald*, December 5, 1873.

[22] Sorenson, *The Story of Omaha*, 467-468.

[23] Michael T. Isenberg, *John L. Sullivan and His America*, University of Illinois Press, 1988, 34.

[24] Sorenson, *The Story of Omaha*, 468.

[25] *Weekly Herald*, November 21, 1873.

Chapter Twelve

Go Around It

1869-1873

May 10, 1869, ranks as one of the great days in American history. It marked the official completion of the transcontinental railroad. On that day, at Promontory, Utah, the rails advancing eastward from San Francisco met the rails advancing westward from Omaha. The United States, a nation lately divided North and South by civil war, was now joined East and West by a road of iron.

Omaha thus found itself at a great national crossroads. Now, it not only lay beside the mighty Missouri River—that great steamboat highway from St. Louis to the gold fields of Montana—but it also lay at a major ferry crossing along the route of the transcontinental railroad, and at the terminus of Union Pacific portion of that road. It appeared to many people that Omaha was on its way to becoming one of America's great cities, and that it would soon acquire reputation and prestige commensurate with its coming greatness. And indeed, before the year 1869 had ended, Omahans could say in truth that theirs was a city that inspired poetry.

Not that they were likely to boast on that point. Although the masterpiece which follows is truly a sparkling gem of poetic craftsmanship, and although it was published in the prestigious *Harper's Magazine* in September 1869, and although no book of

Omaha history would be complete without it, the poem is . . . but you will have to judge it for yourself:

> *Hast ever been in Omaha,*
>   *Where rolls the dark Missouri down,*
> *And four strong horses scarce can draw*
>   *An empty wagon through the town?*
> *Where sand is blown from every mound*
>   *To fill the eyes and ears and throat—*
> *Where all the steamers are aground*
>   *And all the shanties are afloat?*
> *Where whisky shops the livelong night*
>   *Are vending out their poison juice;*
> *Where men are often very tight,*
>   *And women deemed a trifle loose?*
> *Where taverns have an anxious guest*
>   *For every corner, shelf and crack;*
> *With half the people going west,*
>   *And all the others going back?*
> *Where theaters are all the run,*
>   *And bloody scalpers come to trade;*
> *Where everything is overdone*
>   *And everybody underpaid?*
> *If not, take heed to what I say:*
>   *You'll find it just as I have found it;*
> *And if it lies upon your way,*
>   *For God's sake, reader, go around it!*[1]

For Omaha, the really uncomfortable part about the poem was its accuracy. "There was more truth than fiction" in it, admitted historian Alfred Sorenson, who moved to Omaha in 1871 and who would later write with easy familiarity about the muddy streets, the rowdy saloons, the "immoral women," and the crime.[2]

But there is one other thing about the poem, something about the advice contained in the closing line. Consider the following item from the *Herald*, which appeared shortly after the Allen-Hogan fight in 1873. Complaining about a Farnam Street gambling house, the *Herald* noted that two recent visitors—a couple of sporting men in town for the fight—had lost $1,700 of what was probably not their own money. Implying that a rigged roulette wheel was to blame, the *Herald* commented:

> *It was similar outrages, when monte was played here which turned travel away from this city and induced railroad men in the East to sell tickets by routes which would enable travelers to proceed West and avoid Omaha. They held our city responsible for the robberies which were committed here and they were not far from right.*[3]

One can only guess if any of those Easterners who opted to "go around it" did so after reading the *Harper's* poem. But truth be told, too many people "found it just as I have found it" for Omaha's bad reputation to require the assistance of any highbrow Eastern magazine.

Omaha's reputation didn't need the help of the Kansas City press, either, but that didn't stop the editors of that city from excoriating Omaha after the Allen-Hogan debacle. "We are not certain that Omaha is a fit subject for an editorial," said one paper, "But this we know, no better subject for the prayers of a nation can be found." Warming to his theme, the editor continued:

> *It requires but little, if any, stretch of the imagination to regard Omaha as a cesspool of iniquity, for it is given up to lawlessness and is overrun with a horde of fugitives from justice and dangerous men of all kinds who carry things with a high hand and a loose rein . . . Curses are wafted on every breeze, wickedness abounds everywhere, and after learning the true state of affairs the visitor's impulse is to fly from the place as though it were a terrible scourge . . . Mobs of monte men, pickpockets, brace faro dealers, criminal fugitives of every class find congenial companions in Omaha, and a compartive safe retreat from the*

*officers of the law . . . If you want to find a rogue's
rookery, go to Omaha.*[4]

We don't know whether the writer of the preceding passage
knew Omaha by experience or merely by reputation. Perhaps he
had heard stories from those who had gone to see the prizefight.
Perhaps he had gone himself and had been outraged by what he
had seen and heard.

Or perhaps he had recently lost a good deal of money at an
Omaha roulette wheel.

Chapter 12 notes

[1]Sorenson, *The Story of Omaha*, 460.
[2]Sorenson, *The Story of Omaha*, 461.
[3]*Daily Herald*, November 27, 1873.
[4]Quoted in Sorenson, *The Story of Omaha*, 469.

Chapter Thirteen

Mr. Rosewater and the Great Balloon

1872-1875

John Steiner may have been a reckless fool, but he was also a painstakingly well-prepared fool. His preparedness "was shown by his rigid examination of every cord, knot and fibre" of his hydrogen-filled balloon. His foolishness was shown by his intention to go up in the thing at all. Ten thousand people, by the *Bee*'s enthusiastic estimate, waited anxiously to see if he could do it.[1]

It was the Fourth of July, 1872, and "the Professor" was performing his fussy pre-flight inspection before the largest crowd Omaha had ever seen. At Eleventh and Farnam, "all the windows were filled, the roofs of all the buildings for blocks around were covered, the streets were jammed with pedestrians and persons in carriages, all anxiously waiting to witness the ascension."

Slowly, the snow-white balloon took shape. Inflated, it would stand seventy feet tall and hold 20,000 cubic feet of gas.[2] Everyone in the crowd had heard of the great, manned balloons, but few, if any, had ever seen one. From time to time, as the ascension drew nearer, the crowd broke into spontaneous cheering. Flight was a mysterious and wonderful thing.

It had started in France in 1783. As with the early space

flights of the twentieth century, animals were sent aloft first, and for the same reason—to see if they could survive in the strange environment. The first hydrogen balloon was also tested that year. When the unmanned balloon landed several miles outside Paris, terrified peasants attacked it with pitchforks, "killed" it, and dragged it triumphantly through the streets of their village. Fortunately for the human aeronauts who were to follow, the King of France soon issued a proclamation assuring everyone that, despite rumors to the contrary, balloons were *not* man-eating monsters.[3]

Nearly ninety years had passed since those pioneer flights, and no one was going to mistake Steiner's balloon for a monster. Neither would they mistake Steiner for a completely sane man. A German by birth, he had come to America in the 1850s, and within a few years had earned a national reputation as an aeronaut of exceptional daring. His 1857 attempt to fly across Lake Erie is the stuff of legend. Floating placidly among brewing thunderclouds, Steiner nearly reached the Canadian shore before the wind shifted and blew him back out over the lake. Desperate, he descended toward a passing ship far below. He missed the mark by three miles. Splashing down into the white-capped water, the partly-deflated balloon was dragged along by the wind, bouncing its way toward the ship. When it drew near, Steiner leapt overboard and swam to safety.

During the next several years, Steiner won a balloon race against another famous aeronaut, flew observation balloons for the Union Army during the Civil War, and gave exhibitions and passenger flights in various cities.[4] He was also a balloon builder. The craft he proposed to fly in Omaha was his own design, and had been constructed under his supervision.[5]

Not that his balloon was particularly original. In many ways, balloons had changed very little over the years. The main part of a gas balloon was, of course, the fabric envelope, the "balloon" itself. At the top of the envelope was a valve to let out gas in order to descend. Near the valve was a "rip panel," a portion of the fabric that could be torn open if the valve stuck. Both valve and rip panel were operated by ropes that ran down inside the balloon to the basket below.

On the outside, the envelope was covered with netting, which was tied to a "suspension hoop," a large ring from which hung the wicker basket in which the aeronaut would ride. A typical basket was equipped with a map board, an instrument box, a drag rope (for someone on the ground to catch hold of during a landing), and a number of sand bags. The balloon was piloted by dropping sand bags in order to rise, and by pulling the valve rope in order to descend. For guidance, most aeronauts carried map, compass, and a barometer metered to show the altitude. Beyond that, they went wherever the wind carried them.[6]

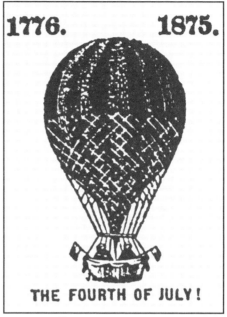

Bee Balloon version one. From the Omaha *Daily Bee*, June 21, 1875.

Fifteen men held the balloon down as Steiner climbed aboard at seven o'clock.

"Let her go," he said.

At once, the balloon "shot upwards amid the deafening cheers and waving of hands, hats and handkerchiefs of the assembled thousands. The Professor boldly stood upon the edge of the frail looking basket, grasping hold of the rigging above, and waving his hand in answer to the unbounded enthusiasm below."

For the next half hour, the crowd watched spellbound as the balloon soared ever higher and ever farther south in the yellow light of the setting sun. And then they could see it no more, and could only wonder where the Professor was now, and what he was experiencing.

From an altitude of 12,000 feet—a little more than two miles above the Missouri Valley floor—Steiner gazed out over the endless expanse of prairie that lay below him. He breathed deeply in the thin air, and his breath was as frosty as on a winter's day. The thermometer read thirty-one degrees. Steiner was wearing his overcoat. His ears hurt with the cold.

But it was a good flight. As the *Bee* described it,

> *He looked with delight upon the enthusiastic assemblage below, and took in the magnifcent proportions of Omaha with the naked eye, while he was obliged to discover the whereabouts of the insignificant village of Council Bluffs by means of a telescope. He saw the Missouri for over fifty miles each way, and came to the conclusion that it was more crooked than the ways of the evildoer. He traced the Platte for a distance of about sixty-five miles. As the sun shone on it, it resembled a streak of silver . . .*

He landed about fifteen minutes after sunset, having been in the air about an hour and a quarter. He "struck in a swamp fifteen miles south of Council Bluffs," and near the Kansas City, St. Joe, and Council Bluffs Railroad. (He was probably within shouting distance of the spot where Allen and Hogan would fight their battle a year and a half later.) Found by a wide-eyed local man, Steiner and balloon were soon aboard a farm wagon and on their way back to Omaha. Next morning, Steiner had the satisfaction of strolling into the Metropolitan Hotel to tell his story to a surprised and admiring audience.

Soon, "the Professor" went on his way to other cities and other flights. But in Omaha, a seed of an idea had been planted. It would spring to life three years later.[7]

Gold was the watchword of the mid-1870s. In the midst of a severe economic depression, rumors of gold in the Black Hills of Dakota Territory could hardly have been more strategically timed. When an 1874 military expedition led by George Armstrong Custer confirmed the rumors, the rush was on. Who cared if the Black Hills had been guaranteed to the Sioux by a treaty? Who cared that the Sioux, or *Lakota*, had earned a rep-

utation as the hardest-fight-
ing natives of the Plains,
and that such an invasion of
their sacred hills was likely
to start a war? The mighty
Custer didn't care—though
he would, in due time.

At the Omaha *Bee*, Ed
Rosewater followed the
news of the gold rush with
keen interest. Ever ambi-
tious, he wanted to send a
reporter to the Black Hills,
and wanted, in doing so, to
draw as much attention as
possible to the *Bee*. Just four
years after the *Bee*'s founding, Rosewater was already
promoting it as "the leading
newspaper in the west," and
he was willing to consider

Bee Balloon, version two, June 26, 1875.

any idea that would enhance its prestige.[8]

Strange opportunities can come to those who are watching
for them. In June 1875, Rosewater learned that no one in
Omaha was planning a citywide Fourth of July celebration for
the nation's ninety-ninth birthday. Further, he learned of the
availability for purchase of a large gas balloon. Suddenly, the
fiery editor's ambitions converged into a single, outrageous
scheme.

Readers of the *Bee* could not have missed the announcement
that appeared in the June 21, 1875, issue. Under the heading,
"1776. 1875.," an engraving of a balloon was displayed proudly
over the words, "THE FOURTH OF JULY!"

What the *Bee* was proposing was a grand Independence Day
celebration featuring a balloon ascension—but that was only
the beginning. The ascension, to take place at the Fair
Grounds,[9] would be nothing less than the departure of an aerial expedition to the Black Hills, a flight of 450 miles west-north-
west to the gold fields of Harney Peak. The balloonist, "Ranger"

John H. Pierce—a former tightrope walker—would be accompanied by his wife and by Andrew Rosewater (brother of Ed) of the *Bee*.

The *Bee* spared no expense, and made sure that its readers appreciated the magnitude of the undertaking. In the weeks following the first announcement, the *Bee* boasted of the "great expense" of the "Bee Balloon" and of the veritable circus that would surround its departure. Indeed, the numbers were impressive: 5,000 pounds of iron, 18,000 pounds of water, plus sulfuric acid and a large battery—just to manufacture enough hydrogen to fill the balloon; 30,000 handbills distributed along various railroads, 5,000 postcard invitations mailed to every part of the state, plus "mammoth red, white, and blue posters," and several small balloons in which to send up live animals such as "hogs, cats, dogs, &c." There would be music from one, maybe two full bands, plus dancing, horse races, foot races, sack races, a greased pole climb, a greased pig, a "base ball match," a fine picnic, and fireworks. In short, it was going to be the grandest thing Omaha had ever seen. And it was being put on solely by the *Bee*.[10]

If any of this impressed *Republican* editor Major St. Ambrose Durant Balcome, he was careful not to show it. In fact, he soon had the dirt on the Bee Balloon, and gleefully spread it all over the June 22 issue of the *Republican*. The balloon, the *Republican* claimed, had been mouldering in a local warehouse for three years before it was bought cheaply by the *Bee*. It was none other than Steiner's balloon from '72, which the Professor had left with a local merchant as payment for a debt. Said the *Republican*, "The *Bee*'s large 'balloon at a great expense,' has been 'in soak' so long that, it will probably be as rotten as the concern that sends it to the Black Hills (?)"

Rosewater, of course, responded in kind:

> *No one, except the* Republican, *has attempted to throw cold water on the celebration. The spite of that decaying sheet is easily accounted for by the fact that it cannot bear to see anything succeed that is undertaken by the* BEE. *Its venomous mal-*

ice does not hurt the Bee *balloon in the least, but reflects upon its own head, and shows to the public the selfish nature which controls its every action.*[11]

On July 3, the day of the planned ascension (the Fourth itself fell on a Sunday that year), the *Republican* stated its case in more detail. Citing an unnamed source, it claimed that Rosewater had paid all of $7.50 for Steiner's old balloon, which had been "stored in a warehouse on the bottoms, and has been accessible to the rats and the vermin that are peculiar to warehouses."

"An aerial voyage in a new and stout balloon is a perilous undertaking," the *Republican* warned, "But it is as near suicide as it can be for a man to attempt to start skyward in an old and rotten balloon as this one is."

However spiteful these charges were, they appear to have had substance. As the *Bee* later admitted, the balloon needed repairs before its flight date. Its netting "was not strong enough for an extended trip," and its basket "was in poor condition."[12] The *Bee* boasted that it had purchased a Steiner balloon—did Rosewater expect anyone to believe that a *new* balloon built by the meticulous Professor would have such defects?

And was he really going to send his own brother up in such a decrepit contraption?

"When will the balloon start?" was the question on everyone's lips. The Third of July was growing old, and a crowd of two to three thousand people milled impatiently about the Fair Grounds. The music and games and picnic had gone well enough, but these had been merely the sideshows. The main event everyone had come to see—had paid admission to see— was a balloon launch. But even as its shadow grew long in the late-afternoon sun, the Bee Balloon still hung from a pole in a shapeless mass. Pierce and both of the Rosewater brothers were scurrying about, working "like Turks," but their iron-and-sulfuric-acid brew was not making hydrogen quickly enough to fill the envelope. Things started to get ugly.[13]

"So they pressed up around the balloon," reported the

Republican next day, "and one man offered ten dollars that the balloon wouldn't rise ten feet from the ground. He was accused of working in the interest of this paper in talking down the balloon, but the sympathies of the crowd were with him, and Pierce got out his two 'pops' and held the crowd at bay at the muzzle of his revolvers."[14]

By nightfall, even Pierce and the Rosewater brothers admitted it was hopeless. Promising a launch next day, they arranged for the balloon to be taken by wagon down to Jefferson Square, a city park near a gas main.[15] Though earlier issues of the *Bee* had ridiculed the use of "coal gas" as an amateur's way of ballooning, right now it didn't look like such a bad idea.

But there was no launch the next day, or the day after that, or the day after that. The *Bee* Balloon refused to become buoyant enough to rise. Among Omahans, impatience and disappointment began turning to scorn and ridicule. Consider the *Republican*'s report of the events of July 4:

> *Pierce had a "small circus" of his own on Jefferson Square on Sunday with the balloon . . . About two hundred small boys gathered around Pierce and the balloon and they . . . advised him to go home, to sell his balloon, and gave him a great quantity of advice that they considered sound. They also entrusted him with hundreds of messages to their friends in the Black Hills to be delivered when he arrived there. The sarcasm and sharp wit of the boys goaded Pierce to a frenzy. He went raving mad, and tore around the premises, charging the boys back, and making just such fun as the boys wanted. He declared that he hadn't had any sleep or food for two days, on account of that balloon, and he really didn't believe that the boys appreciated the balloon anyway.*[16]

Day by day, the failures mounted. By July 8, a taunting *Republican* headline proclaimed:

FRAUD, FIZZLE, FAILURE.

and gleefully detailed each of the six failed attempts to send the balloon skyward. The seventh, the *Republican* noted, was to take place that morning, in case anyone was foolish enough to want to go out and watch it. "An Aerial Elephant on Rosewater's Hands," noted part of a headline, and it was the truth. Instead of launching a balloon, Edward Rosewater had launched the worst public relations disaster in the *Bee*'s short history.

No one had said that the seventh attempt would be the last, but you had to wonder how long it could go on. The gas was hooked up at four a.m., an hour before sunrise. By six, when much of Omaha was still in bed, a small gathering looked on as the basket was attached and Pierce gave the word to let her go. He stood alone in the basket, the idea of three passengers having been abandoned days earlier.

The men let go, but the balloon would not rise. It was filled full—as much as it could hold without bursting—but still it would not rise.

But even then, Pierce was not beaten. Ordering the basket untied, he climbed up into the balloon's netting, sat on the suspension hoop, and held onto the ropes. And with a boost from the onlookers, the balloon slowly began to rise.

And so, at the very time the *Republican*'s newsboys were hitting the streets with the "FRAUD, FIZZLE, FAILURE" issue, a small crowd at Jefferson Square was cheering the madman hanging in the netting of a large white balloon as it floated serenely over the city.

Pierce was heading north, soon leaving Omaha behind. There was no hope of the Black Hills now, not without a basket. He was flying for pride now, out of sheer, mad determination, flying with a tenacity that a man like Ed Rosewater could surely appreciate. After a slow start, he rose steadily into the sky, topping out somewhere between a quarter and a half mile up. He could see the Omaha & Northwestern Railroad track below, the town of Florence up ahead, and the Missouri River to his right.

The wind began carrying him a little to the east, out over the wide Missouri. On the other side of the river, fifteen miles of swamps and sloughs lay between him and the loess hills of

Iowa.[17] Pierce realized that he had forgotten his life preserver, and "at this time he wished for it more than any other thing in the world." There was only one thing to do now, and that was to try to get back down quickly, and on dry land. The river twisted this way and that, and Florence, Nebraska lay about a mile ahead. Opening up the gas valve, Pierce began descending toward it.

Seeing a farmer below, Pierce called out for help. He meant, of course, that he would need help with the balloon once he landed, but the farmer, a German immigrant, did not understand this.

"Vat in hell's de matter, ony how?" the farmer shouted back. "You takes me for a tam fool, as Ieh kann nicht do noddings mit you up dere."

By now, the balloon was slowly collapsing above Pierce, "toppling over on one side owing to the escape of the gas and the inrushing air." He was coming down, all right, but he was headed straight toward Florence Lake. Trying to drop more quickly, Pierce pulled the rip-rope, but it broke without tearing open the balloon. He continued straight for the lake.

Growing desperate, Pierce changed his strategy. Taking off his boots, he let them drop, sending his pistol and other possessions after them. If he could reduce his weight, he thought, maybe he could float past the lake to the other side.

He was in the process of taking off his pants when he hit the water. The *Bee* described what followed:

> It [the balloon] *gave a sudden lurch forward, and dragged him up out of the water for fifteen feet. It then struck the water and dragged him along the surface. The cloth flapped and then filled with wind like a sail, making the water fly in every direction. He was approaching a clump of willows on the opposite shore, and could see no opening except near the top of the trees, and a very small cover them* [sic] *in one place, just wide enough for the balloon to pass through. Sticking out his left leg, he guided the craft through this narrow place, and thus reached the shore. He was*

then dragged through the mud, weeds and bush-
es, steering along with his legs, arms and shoul-
ders, all the time trying to stop the thing, but it
couldn't be stopped, as no gas was being exhaust-
ed, and he could not get hold of the valve rope. At
length a little lull in the wind came, and then
catching the valve rope, he let the gas escape, and
began yelling for help, the balloon taking ten or
fifteen lively jumps before he could get it under
control.

Two men witnessed the landing, a pair of Winnebago Indians. According to the *Bee*, they "yelled, gesticulated, and danced about in the wildest manner imaginable." Surely the natives were astonished, reasoned the *Bee*.

More likely they were just doubled over with laughter.

Recovering somewhat, the Winnebagos came to Pierce's rescue and helped him recover his battered balloon.[18]

And so it ended. Rosewater, declaring himself vindicated, blamed the repeated failures wholly on the local gas company, railing against the "miserable quality" of gas it supplied him. The *Herald*, noting that the balloon had been "the direct and immediate cause of much profanity," admitted that its flight "was really a fine spectacle." Nevertheless, it added that "as a newspaper enterprise the balloon business was something of a collapse."[19]

The *Republican* couldn't deny that the flight had happened, but it could belittle it, which it did under the headline, "RECK-LESSNESS." Referring to Pierce as a "hair-brained dare-devil fellow laying in the netting," it called the flight a "sickly attempt at an ascension."[20]

Which is about all you can say when your arch-enemy has gotten a crazy idea off the ground, and you haven't.

Chapter 13 notes

[1] *Bee* (evening), July 5, 1872.

[2] *Bee* (evening), June 21, 1875.

[3] Edwin J. Kirschner, *Aerospace Balloons: From Montgolfiere to Space*, Fallbrook, CA: Aero Publishers, Inc., 1985, 11.

[4] In St. Paul in 1863, Steiner took aloft a young German count named Ferdinand von Zeppelin. Zeppelin was thrilled by his flight, but noted the difficulties of navigating such a craft against the wind. Steiner told the young count of his plans for a long, thin balloon with a strong rudder, an idea that Zeppelin later credited with inspiring his great airships of the early 20th century.

[5] Tom D. Crouch, *The Eagle Aloft: Two Centuries of the Balloon in America*, Washington, D.C.: Smithsonian Institution Press, 1983, 230-235, 283-284.

[6] Donald Dale Jackson, *The Aeronauts*, Alexandria, VA: Time-Life Books, 1980, 56.

[7] *Bee* (evening), July 5, 1872.

[8] *Bee* (evening), June 21, 1875.

[9] Fair Grounds: Also known as the Driving Park. Located just northwest of 16th and Sprague.

[10] *Bee* (evening), June 22, 25, 29, 1875.

[11] *Bee* (evening), June 24, 1875.

[12] *Bee* (evening), July 5, 1875.

[13] *Herald*, July 4, 1875.

[14] *Republican*, July 4, 1875.

[15] Jefferson Square: Omaha's first city park, bordered by 15th, 16th, Chicago, and Cass. It is now covered by Interstate 480.

[16] *Republican*, July 6, 1875.

[17] The Missouri Valley is almost all farmland today, but in its natural state it was mostly wetlands.

[18] *Bee* (evening), July 8, 1875.

[19] *Herald*, July 9, 10, 1873.

[20] *Republican*, July 9, 1873.

Extra! Extra!

The mud on the streets yesterday was less than 20 feet deep.
—*Omaha Daily Herald*, March 13, 1868

* * *

Darwin has another book to prove that his grandfather was a monkey, but the public were convinced by his first efforts.
—*Omaha Weekly Herald*, December 11, 1872, commenting on the recent publication of *The Descent of Man*, Darwin's follow-up to *Origin of Species*.

* * *

Yesterday's election may be called the whisky, beer, and money election. Money was scattered freely in every direction; beer, drawn about by four-horse teams, flowed like water, and whisky filled the space that beer did not occupy. The worst passions of men ran riot, and the moral effect will not be wiped out for many a day.
—*Omaha Republican*, April 2, 1873, following a Democratic victory in a city election.

* * *

John Johnson, perpetual member of the society of inebriates, was sent up for the 249th time yesterday.
—*Omaha Republican*, April 10, 1873

* * *

A FEROCIOUS DRUNKEN FEMALE.

—

**She Tries to Make a Square Meal
Off An Officer's Thumb.**
—*Omaha Daily Bee*, December 21, 1873

* * *

It is sincerely hoped that the "adult residents" of Omaha,

who may attend the public exhibition of the High School on Friday evening of this week, will not take "their whisky with them and make a night of it," and thus prove that the New York Herald *of a recent date, slandered the fair fame of this city, when it made the following statement: "One of the most encouraging evidences of advancing civilization in Omaha is the interest manifested in the public school exhibitions by the adult residents, who are in the habit of taking their whisky with them and 'making a night of it.' The only difficulty is that their attendance is sometimes so numerous and enthusiastic as to drive the teachers and pupils altogether out of the room, as has happened two or three times lately in Nemaha county."*
—Omaha Daily Bee, *April 14, 1873*

* * *

STRAYED. — A red cow. There is a little piece of her right horn broken off. She probably has a young calf with her. Any one notifying me of her whereabouts will be suitably rewarded. A. C. Wilson, Cor. 10th & Davenport Sts.
—Omaha Daily Bee, *May 12, 1872*

* * *

TOO MUCH CHAIR-ITY.

James Bassis, a Bohemian, drank too much lager, mixed with something stronger, yesterday, and going home tight, he picked a quarrel with the wedded partner of his bosom. Not liking her style of argument, he picked up a chair, and sent it flying through the air at her. A policeman was called, and he was arrested. This morning he paid a fine of $5.00 and costs.
—Omaha Daily Bee, *March 12, 1873*

* * *

The Grand Jury have just finished the consideration of the case of Whitmore, who chawed off the nose and upper lip of Barker the other day, in a fight about a little difference of ten dollars. They found no indictment against the nose-biter, as it was impossible to do so, owing to a peculiar provision of the law regarding mayhem. The provision is as follows:

"No person shall be found guilty of mayhem, where the fact occurred during a fight had by consent, nor unless it appear that the person accused shall have been the assailant, or that the party maimed had in good faith endeavored to decline further combat."

The finding of the jury was based upon the above, and we understand that the circumstances of the case coincided with the provision.

—*Omaha Daily Bee*, March 14, 1873

* * *

FEARFUL ACCIDENT

A Runaway Horse Kicks a Man's Knee Cap off During a Funeral Procession.

—*Omaha Daily Bee*, June 16, 1873

* * *

Saturday evening, a man, whose name we have been unable to ascertain, was runaway with on Leavenworth street, between Sixth and Seventh streets. He was thrown from his wagon, which was loaded with corn, and fell between the wheels, one of which passed over his breast, near his neck. He was quite severely stunned and injured, and was picked up for dead; but upon being revived, it was found that his injuries were not so of serious nature as at first supposed.

—*Omaha Daily Bee*, June 16, 1873

* * *

MRS. DR. LEONARD'S
Electric Bath Cure

Situated in the commodious building corner of Ramsey and Center streets.

COUNCIL BLUFFS, IOWA,

Is the Invalid's Home, and I wish to call the attention of the suffering, particularly those afflicted with chronic diseases of

long standing, to my mild but effectual treatment.
Board on reasonable terms.

MRS. DR. LEONARD,
Box 772, Council Bluffs

—*Omaha Daily Bee,* June 16, 1873

* * *

MANAGER BALCOME'S *congratulatory address to the*
"Citizens of this Commonwealth," was most reckless waste of
precious rhetoric upon a beggarly array of empty benches.
—*Omaha Daily Bee,* July 8, 1873

* * *

A squabble took place between James Creighton and
Alderman Doyle, at D.C. Sutphens store, this afternoon. Hard
names were passed, followed by choking, Doyle being the vic-
tim. Creighton was arrested by the Marshal.
—*Omaha Daily Bee,* July 8, 1873

* * *

And now scientists claim that the moon, instead of being so
"cold and chaste and pallid," is in reality red hot—so much so
that no living thing known to our world can live on there. This
also knocks the green cheese theory.
—*Omaha Daily Herald,* July 10, 1873

* * *

The grasshoppers have come. They have come numerously.
They have brought their families with them, and their friends,
and their relatives, and their relatives' friends, and they are
legion.
—*Omaha Daily Bee,* June 14, 1875

Chapter Fourteen

THE BRIDGE

1868-1877

March 1868

Damn you, Smith, we will make grass grow in the streets of Omaha!

The speaker, Sidney Dillon—a man thoroughly impressed with his own importance—stood shaking his fist in the face of his listener, Francis Smith. It was a schoolyard gesture with a twist. Rather than a schoolyard or a saloon, the scene was taking place in the posh New York City headquarters of the Union Pacific Railroad. Dillon's fist threatened not a brawl, but a business deal which could destroy Omaha's future.

Smith replied bitterly that "it will take a bigger man than you" to carry out the threat, but he knew that Dillon wasn't bluffing. The reality of the threat—and its potential consequences—was the very thing which had brought Smith and his friends here in the first place.

Just then another railroad executive appeared and diffused the situation by announcing, "We shall have another meeting of the directors tomorrow at 2 o'clock."

So the railroad barons would reconsider the fate of Omaha. Now there was nothing to do but wait.[1]

By the summer of 1868, Union Pacific work crews were advancing rapidly across Wyoming, digging, blasting, grading, and laying track toward their eventual junction with the east-ward-advancing Central Pacific line. Soon, everyone knew, the two railroads would meet and the long dreamed-about transcontinental railroad would be a reality. Railroads would then reach from the Atlantic to the Pacific Ocean, with only a single break. That break was the Missouri River, yet unbridged.

Where would the bridge be built? Several possible locations had been surveyed, of which two appeared best: one in "south" Omaha (between Marcy and Mason streets), and another at Child's Mill near Bellevue. The city which found itself at the end of the great bridge stood to benefit from the jobs, the travelers, the commerce, and the prestige that would come from being at this great junction of the transcontinental railroad. The less-fortunate city would soon find itself relegated to backwater status at the end of a railroad spur line.[2]

Omaha had long had ample reason to believe that it would get the bridge. It was already the working eastern terminus of the Union Pacific Railroad. The railroad's depot and machine shops were there; the miles of track started from there. To build the bridge anywhere else was unthinkable. Or so Omaha believed.

Then came disturbing rumors from New York. Quickly, a delegation of prominent local men—Nebraska Governor Alvin Saunders, businessman Ezra Millard, *Omaha Herald* publisher Dr. George L. Miller, and a few others—traveled to New York to settle the issue face-to-face with the railroad executives.

Such an impressive delegation had probably never before gone forth from this part of the country. These were powerful men who arrived in New York City, accustomed to having their own way, accustomed to the respect to which their social rank entitled them. And these impressive, powerful men spent the next several days cooling their heels in the ante-room of the Union Pacific directors' office, waiting patiently for someone to listen to them.

Finally, after interminable delays, General Grenville Dodge, the railroad's chief engineer, came out and announced the board's decision. It was Bellevue.

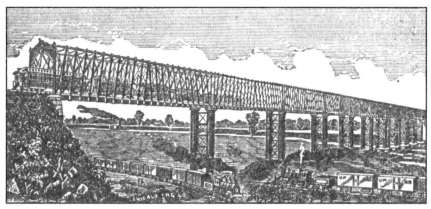

Train crossing the Union Pacific Bridge.

Francis Smith, a New Yorker who was siding with the Omaha delegation, protested that "we have not had a square deal; we are entitled to a hearing." But just then Sidney Dillon appeared—and you know the rest of the scene.[3]

Next day came the crucial meeting for which the Omaha delegation had been so patiently waiting. At stake was the fate of the largest city in the newest state of the Union. Omaha, which in 1860 could claim only 1,800 inhabitants, was on its way to 16,000 by 1870. Everyone knew that this boom was largely due to the transcontinental railroad. Without the railroad, the boom would surely go bust.

The reader will recall that the main reason for Omaha's founding was to help Council Bluffs secure the transcontinental railroad. Back in the 1850s, the Council Bluffs men had felt that a prosperous city directly across the river from them would increase their odds of being located along the railroad's main line. Their money and influence had helped Omaha secure the territorial capitol and defend the prize against rival towns.

The ploy had worked, of course, all too well. By 1868, though it was no longer Nebraska's capital, Omaha had surpassed the Bluffs in size and influence. Despite President Lincoln's 1863 order locating the Union Pacific's eastern terminus in Council Bluffs, Omaha had gotten the offices, the transfer depot, and the machine shops. The railroad directors, preferring to locate west of the Missouri, had—to the consternation of Council Bluffs—"lost" Lincoln's order.[4]

Council Bluffs, then, had ample reason for feelings of jealousy and suspicion toward its daughter city. But for now, the two rivals had to stick together against a common enemy. The bridge *must not* go to Bellevue. Hearkening back to the squabbles over the Nebraska territorial capitol, the Omaha and Council Bluffs men brought out a familiar weapon: money.

"Sound the loud timbrel!" read Governor Saunders' telegraph message later that day, "Bridge located at Omaha!" The delegation had agreed to give to the railroad, free of charge, the necessary land and right-of-ways. To sweeten the deal, Omaha promised to pay the railroad $250,000; Council Bluffs pledged $200,000. [5]

Which may have been the whole point of the exercise. Some have suggested that the railroad directors, never intending to build at Child's Mill, merely used the threat to squeeze half a million dollars out of Omaha and Council Bluffs.[6] Either way, Omaha got the bridge, the railroad got the money, and everyone was happy.

Except Bellevue.

1869

Of the innumerable engineering challenges facing the builders of the Union Pacific, none were more difficult than bridging the Missouri. Plenty of people said it couldn't be done. Even at low water, the Missouri's main channel was 750 feet across; during a flood, the river could spread four miles wide over the valley floor. And distance wasn't the worst of it.

Uncontrolled by dams or levees, the swift current was both powerful and capricious. It was constantly eroding the soft banks and was prone to carving new channels for itself through previously dry ground. The river's bottom, meanwhile, was an unstable layer of mud, sand, and gravel—unsuitable for bridge piers. Bedrock lay anywhere from ten to forty-five feet beneath this submerged layer of goo.[7]

Still, a permanent bridge was needed. Each winter, a temporary wooden trestle bridge was built across the ice, but had to be removed before the spring floods. For the rest of the year, railroad cars stood lined up by the hundreds, filling every side track, waiting their turn to be ferried across by the rickety steamboat *H. C. Nutt.* For passengers, the delay was just one more hardship (along with fatigue, discomfort, and bad food), but for shippers the delay was both infuriating and costly.[8]

Work commenced in 1869. Using a new technology known as the "pneumatic system," cast-iron piers were sunk down to bedrock one cylindrical section at a time. When one of the 20,000 lb. cylinders was in position, a cap was fitted over it and the air pumped out. Atmospheric pressure then drove it down into the earth. Compressed air was pumped in, driving the sand out through a valve; then another cylinder was fitted on top of the first, and the process was repeated. Down and down each pier went, finally hitting bedrock.

It really wasn't that simple. Often, the cylinder would hit gravel or clay and would have to be excavated by hand. Inside the cylinder—a dark, compressed-air world eight feet in diameter—men would dig, filling countless bags and buckets. Your car's tires, if properly inflated, hold air at a pressure of thirty-five pounds per square inch; the men inside the pier worked in an atmosphere of *forty-five* pounds per square inch. It was not pleasant work. One early description of the project reported that "the men say that after leaving work and getting to bed they often felt as if their flesh was being raised from the bone."[9]

What was happening was decompression sickness, what divers today call the "bends." Each time a man left the cylinder, the rapid decompression caused nitrogen bubbles to form in his blood and tissues. As a result, many of the workers endured temporary paralysis. At least one died.

Not surprisingly, it was hard to recruit cylinder men. Even in 1869, men did not line up to work on a project which had to keep doctors and a hospital unit on site. The work stopped for months due to labor difficulties. Pronouncing the whole project "impracticable," the superintendent quit. The chief engineer, apparently desiring laborers who were less contentious and more disposable, tried in vain to get Chinese workers.[10]

Despite the problems, the work went on. At last, after three years and more than two-and-a-half million dollars spent, the bridge was completed in March 1873. "The traveler regards it with an astonishment which would be increased did he know the difficulties overcome in its erection," an observer wrote.

Bearing only a single railroad track sitting high above the water, the bridge's tall and narrow structure emphasized its half-mile length. "At a distance it looks like a fairy fabric, with its slender columns and immense length, but it was well-tested by a pressure of thousands of tons."[11]

In its time, ten years before the Brooklyn Bridge redefined engineering greatness, the Missouri River bridge was an iron wonder, and was seen as an enduring and indestructible symbol of man's triumph over nature.

August 25, 1877, 3 a.m.

Standing in the doorway of his little guardhouse, John Pierson watched the approaching storm. Above, in the black sky, clouds rumbled with thunder and flashed white-hot with lightning. Below, spread out on the valley floor—visible now and again in the flashing light—the city of Council Bluffs lay sleeping.[12]

Pierson was the night watchman at the east end of the Union Pacific bridge. His job was to keep trespassers away. (A walk across the bridge cost fifty cents.) Usually it was a quiet job, just a man and his dog keeping watch up there beside the railroad track. The guardhouse, dwarfed by the massive iron truss beside it, stood atop and near the end of a steep-sided, sixty-foot-tall earthen embankment. Here, earth ended and bridge began.

A harsh wind came roaring out of the northwest. Soon, bridge and guardhouse were enveloped in the storm. Wind whistled through the open framework, making the bridge sing with eerie vibrations. Hail, like hammer-blows from ten thousand blacksmiths, rang furiously on the bridge's iron surfaces. Lightning struck again and again, running in streams of crackling pale fire along the girders and columns.

And for all this the bridge was stable and unharmed.

Waiting for the storm to pass, Pierson and his dog huddled in the guardhouse. After about ten or fifteen minutes, the sky grew calm. He stepped outside. In the cool night air, he felt the wind shifting to the northeast.

He was facing north, looking upstream, when he saw something moving out on the river. It was hard to make out. It was dark and very large, and seemed to be coming downstream. He peered hard into the night's blackness. The thing was roaring like a locomotive, but was unrecognizable. He could see only a tall, dense blackness, "balloon shaped, but tapering at each end," moving quickly toward him.

He turned to duck back into the guardhouse, but never made it. The strange blackness struck the bridge.

Then everything happened at once, as though time had been compressed into a single moment. There was the sound: the explosion of thunder; the roar of swirling wind; the groaning of iron twisting and breaking; the crackling and buzzing of arcing electricity; the splintering of heavy wooden timbers; the snapping of wires—all mingled together into an indistinguishable cacophony.

And there was the sight: a flash of blinding white light; the flickering glare of lightning along the bridge's frame; the bridge itself being lifted off its piers, soaring high into the air, burning as it went; the bridge then falling to earth; one section crumpling and breaking apart as it smashed into the river bank; another section vanishing, swallowed whole by the river.

John Pierson was alive, conscious, and lying on the river bank. Had he really just seen the mighty bridge torn effortlessly from its piers? Had it really been smashed before him like a toy? Or had he just imagined it? "He says that at this moment the situation was appalling to him," a reporter wrote later, "he could scarcely recognize whether he was dead or alive, and he had some idea that the end of the world had come."

Whatever had struck the bridge was gone, roaring away to the southwest. Otherwise, the wind, lightning, and hail continued all about him.

He tried to sit up, but could not move. He was lying amid wreckage from the bridge—trapped—with telegraph wires drawn across his neck. One of his legs hurt from being cut or at lease badly bruised. Somewhere nearby, his dog howled in pain. One of its legs had been cut off.

It had been no illusion. Two of the bridge's eleven spans were gone. The easternmost 500 feet of bridge—weighing about 500 tons—had been swept away before Pierson's eyes. But how?

Battered, soaked, confused, and wired to the ground, John

Pierson knew only a few things for sure: It was about 3:30 a.m. The bridge was out. And at 5:10 a.m., a passenger train was scheduled to depart Omaha's Union Depot and cross that bridge. He had to find a way to stop it.

Pierson struggled to free himself; according to one report, this required a precious half hour. Scrambling to the top of the embankment, he found a red lantern, lit it, and tried to signal the watchman on the other side of the bridge. He received no reply. His signal could not carry far through the stormy air.

If a signal light couldn't penetrate the storm, it stood to reason that neither could the eyesight of an engineer crossing the bridge. As a matter of policy, the trains always crossed the bridge slowly. Would that be enough? No one would be looking for damage from a thunderstorm, however severe. Would anyone in Omaha realize what bizarre accident had occurred on this side? Or would the gap be seen too late, in some awful, helpless moment just before the engine rolled off the rails at pier number nine? A recent sounding—before the rain—had found thirty-eight feet of water at the east end of the bridge, more than enough to swallow a trainload of cars, crew, baggage, and passengers.

He would have to cross the river.

Running to his home nearby, he roused one of his neighbors. Start heading down the track, Pierson said, and be ready to signal any train that might be coming from the east. With that, he returned to the river and found a skiff. Pushing out into the swollen current, he began rowing for the other side.

The storm had not abated. With the wind fighting against him, the current swift, the water choppy and whitecapped, and the sky black and disorienting, Pierson made his way across the main channel. Though his little boat was nearly swept against the piers, he at last reached the large sandbar in the middle of the river. According to the *Herald*, the soggy bar was known to have patches of quicksand that could mire the unwary. Pierson made it across on foot, reaching the river's second channel. Having left the boat behind, he had to swim.

"All aboard!" called the conductor. The passengers of the 5:10 a.m. train climbed aboard and made themselves comfortable. It was half an hour before sunrise. Up ahead in the engine, the

Union Pacific Museum Collection
Union Pacific Missouri River Bridge after the 1877 storm.

firemen stoked the furnaces and let the boilers build up steam.
It was almost time.

Then, unexpectedly, came the word to shut down. In the cars,
the passengers were informed that they'd have to go back out
into the rain and the darkness and return to their hotels.
They'd be going nowhere today. This surprising order came
from the dispatcher's office, where a soaked and battered John
Pierson had just arrived.

By 7 a.m., the word had spread throughout Omaha and Council Bluffs. Rain or no rain, people came out to see the bridge. Those who had witnessed the bridge's slow and laborious construction could hardly believe the wild stories that were circulating. It had to be seen to be believed. Residents from both cities gathered on opposite sides of the river, staring at the damaged bridge and at each other. Everyone was soaked to the skin.

The damage astounded them. One bridge span "lay in a shapeless mass" beside the river, "the strong wrought iron bars being bent into all conceivable shapes" and the cast iron pieces shattered. At pier number nine, where the bridge now ended, the rails of the mighty transcontinental railroad were "twisted like wires," one broken and one dangling in the water.

The force necessary to accomplish such destruction was inconceivable. Many thought that only lightning could have caused such damage. Others, understanding electricity a little better, disputed this. At last, words like *cyclone*, *whirlwind*, and *waterspout* were on everyone's lips.

Three days later, the *Bee* taught its readers what appears to have been a new word, a word so unfamiliar that the *Bee* wasn't even sure how to spell it: "The Union Pacific bridge blow-out should have been called a tor(e)nado," it reported.[13] Thus introduced, Omaha began a relationship with the word *tornado* which in time became intimate, though hardly loving. To the Omahans of 1913 and 1975, it got all too personal.

The bridge was out of commission for several months, during which time ferries came back into use. For pedestrians, canoes and small boats were employed; the railroad even cobbled together a footbridge over the "quagmire" between the channels of the river. This jerry-built structure lasted about a day and a half before collapsing and pitching its travelers into the mud. The *Bee* couldn't resist:

> *Those commercial travelers who were dumped into the mud yesterday afternoon, by the breaking down of the foot-bridge at the Union Pacific bridge, must have played keno some time during their lives, for they all made the same exclamation when they went down. It was—well, no matter, it*

was only an excited reference to the realms of his Satanic majesty.[14]

Union Pacific's poor luck with bridges paid off in another respect: it helped keep the railroad terminus in Omaha. Earlier, the U.S. Supreme Court, citing Lincoln's 1863 order, had ordered the railroad to relocate its terminus in Council Bluffs. The railroad had been dragging its feet. Now, as Omahans saw it, "The four iron columns that stand in the Missouri River . . . are four exclamation points against the removal of the U.P. shops from Omaha." In other words, since the purpose of the U.P. facilities was to service the lines to the west, it was now clear that locating those facilities east of the river would have been a disaster. The Supreme Court decision was doomed. As the *Bee* boasted, "The supreme cyclops of the universe has reversed the decision of the supreme court of the United States and the terminus of the Union Pacific is located in Omaha."[15]

Thus the story draws to a close, happily. In one respect, however, we are left with some loose ends, an important question unresolved. Sure, the passenger train was stopped, the bridge was repaired, and the U.P. terminus was kept in Omaha. I can even add that Pierson was widely praised for his courage and presence of mind. Big deal. What you want to know, and what none of the papers bothered to report, is—*What about the dog?*

Did Pierson's dog bleed to death from its amputated leg? Or was the dog tenacious, like its master, and survive? When Pierson was unable to stop long enough to attend to the dog's needs, did the dog try to follow its master across the river? What kind of dog was it? What was its name? Much as we may find Omaha's old-time journalism amusing, at times we have to mourn its neglect of the important details.

We can, therefore, do no better than to imagine a train passing at twilight, crawling slowly eastward across the Missouri River bridge, reaching at last the embankment on the Iowa side, and gliding past the little white guardhouse. Passengers, seeing through their windows a man and his three-legged dog, smile and wave. The man nods and touches the brim of his hat. The dog wags its tail.

Chapter 14 notes

[1]Sorenson, *The Story of Omaha*, 308.

[2]Maury Klein, *Union Pacific: The Birth of a Railroad: 1862-1893.* Garden City, NY: Doubleday & Co., 1987, 259; Sorenson, *The Story of Omaha*, 307.

[3]Sorenson, *The Story of Omaha*, 308.

[4]Klein, 267.

[5]Sorenson, *Story*, 309.

[6]Lawrence H. Larsen and Barbara J. Cottrell, *The Gate City: A History of Omaha*, Pruett Publishing Co, 1982, 65.

[7]Charles Edgar Ames, *Pioneering the Union Pacific: A Reappraisal of the Builders of the Railroad.* New York: Appleton, Century, Crofts, 1969, 413, 417-418; Klein, 258.

[8]Klein, 268-69; Ames, 418.

[9]J. M. Wolfe, *Omaha Business Directory for 1877.* Omaha: The Republican Steam Book and Job Printing House, 1877, 22. See also: Wolfe, 21-25; Klein, 277-278; Ames, 412.

[10]Klein, 278.

[11]Wolfe, 21.

[12]My version of the story of Pierson and the tornado is based on the reports of four newspapers: *Council Bluffs Nonpareil*, Aug. 26, 1877; *Omaha Daily Herald*, Aug. 26, 1877; *Omaha Bee* (evening), Aug. 27, 1877; *Omaha Republican*, Aug. 26, 1877. Of these, the *Herald*, *Bee*, and *Republican* interviewed Pierson directly. Unless otherwise noted, the quotations are from the *Herald*, Aug. 26, 1877.

[13]*Bee* (evening), Aug. 28, 1877.

[14]*Bee* (evening), Aug. 28, 1877.

[15]*Bee* (evening), Aug. 25, 1877.

Chapter Fifteen

THE TRIAL OF STANDING BEAR

1879

March 29, 1879

It was late, about eleven, but Thomas Tibbles was still hard at work at the office of the Omaha *Herald*. He was an editor, and his work—like that of a woman—was never really done.

A man came to see him at that late hour, bringing strange news. A small band of Ponca Indians, under a chief named Standing Bear, were being held under arrest at Fort Omaha. Their crime? They had left their reservation without permission. The government had recently moved the Poncas from their home in southeast Dakota Territory to a new reservation in Indian Territory.[1] Dissatisfied, some of the Poncas had tried to go home. That, according to the U.S. government, was something they had no right to do.

Tibbles thought otherwise. Though the army had been ordered to take the Poncas back to Indian Territory, Tibbles—an ardent supporter of Indian rights—immediately began trying to think of a way to win the Poncas their freedom.

In fact, the man who brought the news to Tibbles may have been counting on this. Though in 1880, Tibbles would write that the late-night caller had been another *Herald* editor, years later he would identify a different, more prominent man as the caller

A. J. Poppleton

. . . but more about that later.[2]

Next day found Tibbles at Fort Omaha, talking with Standing Bear and some of the other Poncas. Standing Bear, a tall, dignified man, probably in his mid-fifties, spoke no English, so an interpreter was provided.[3] The Chief explained how his people had been living at their old reservation, how they understood that the wild game was gone and that in order to survive they must learn to farm. In 1877, they had been doing just that when, unexpectedly, government men arrived and told them that they must leave their reservation and move to Indian Territory.

The Poncas didn't understand. They had already given up most of their land, and had been guaranteed their reservation by a treaty with the government. How could the government break the treaty without the Poncas' consent?

But the army had orders to make them move, so move they did. Most of their possessions—including the cabins they'd built, their livestock, their crops, their farming implements—had to be left behind. They were told they'd receive compensation at the new reservation.

The Poncas were removed in two groups, both of whom suffered greatly on the journey. For the second, larger group (numbering about 500), the journey south was a fifty-four-day ordeal through incessant rain and mud. Many Native American tribes had their "Trail of Tears," a route of forced migration away from their homeland; for the Poncas, that trail ran south-southeast across Nebraska, starting at Niobrara, passing through Columbus, then into Kansas, through Manhattan and Emporia, and finally arriving at the extreme northeast corner of what is now Oklahoma—roughly 500 miles in all. Along the way, nine Poncas died. Predictably, they were children and old women.[4]

"It was a long and tedious journey," Standing Bear said:

> *When we got there the Agent issued us no rations for a long time. For months we had to beg of the other tribes. We were all half-starved. This was all different from home. There we raised all we needed. Here there was no work to do. We had nothing to work with, and there was no man to hire us. Then we were informed that we were prisoners, and if we attempted to go away we would be punished.*

It got worse. Weakened by hunger, the Poncas were ravaged by influenza, scrofula, dysentery, and malaria. Of these, malaria was the worst. Though it could have been treated effectively with quinine, the new agent had no money for medicine. Standing Bear described the result:

> *There were dead in every family. Those who could walk around were sick. Not one in the whole tribe felt well. I lost all my children but one little girl. A few more weeks and she would have died too. I was in an awful place and I was a prisoner there. I was not a free man . . . I could see nothing ahead, but death for the whole tribe.*[5]

In the first eighteen months following the removal, about one-third of the Poncas died.[6]

Standing Bear knew he could not fight. The Poncas had never gone to war with the U.S., and at any rate they had not the weapons, the numbers, or the health to wage war. But maybe, they thought, they could just go home, home to the land they had never sold. "My boy who died down there," Standing

Bear explained, "As he was dying looked up to me and said, I would like you to take my bones back and bury them there where I was born. I promised him I would. I could not refuse the dying request of my boy."[7]

On the night of January 2, 1879, Standing Bear departed to fulfill his promise. With him were about thirty other Poncas who were willing to undertake the desperate journey. For ten weeks, the Poncas traveled north across the frozen prairie, finally arriving at the Omaha agency (near Decatur, Nebraska) in March. The Omahas, who were related to the Poncas, took them in, gave them food, land, and tools, and asked them to stay permanently on the Omaha reservation.

Soon, however, the Poncas were found out by the Indian agents. The news traveled fast to Washington, and then an order reached Brigadier General George Crook at his headquarters at Fort Omaha. He was to have the Poncas arrested and taken back to Indian Territory.

George Crook was a career officer, a man who could boast that he "had as much experience in the management of Indian affairs as any man in the country."[8] He was a stern man, untalkative, and not much given to military pomp. He wore civilian clothes whenever he could, wore his hair cropped short, and—by way of contrast—let his beard grow long and grizzled. A graduate of West Point and a veteran of the Civil War, Crook was one of the few generals to recognize that the Indian wars were essentially guerrilla wars, requiring different tactics than those used against a traditional army. Not surprisingly, Crook was a clever and resourceful commander in battle, among the most adept of the Old West Indian fighters.[9]

Which may explain why many people have never heard of him. Crook was an intelligent man, but he made a terrible career blunder during the Sioux War of 1876. Following a bloody and unsuccessful encounter with the legendary Crazy Horse, Crook wisely withdrew his battered troops. That was his blunder—not that he failed to win the battle, but that he didn't manage to get himself and all his men gloriously killed in the process. Less than a month later at the Little Bighorn, a pompous, reckless, and not particularly bright officer named George Armstrong Custer succeeded where Crook failed.

Nebraska State Historical Society
Standing Bear and family, circa 1870.

And so George Crook was still alive and well in 1879 when Standing Bear and the Poncas came back to Nebraska. By now, you might be expecting that the hard-fighting Crook was happy to arrest the Poncas and eager to send them south, but it was not so. During his long years of dealing with—and sometimes fighting with—various native peoples, Crook had come to respect them, just as he had grown increasingly vocal in his criticism of federal Indian policy. For a soldier, however, orders are orders, and Crook dutifully had Standing Bear arrested, but he took no pleasure in it.

Incidentally, Crook knew what had led to the Ponca removal, and it would have been little consolation to Standing Bear to learn that it was all just a big mistake. In 1868, the U.S. had made a treaty with the Sioux, creating a large Sioux reservation that happened to include all the land reserved for the Poncas in an 1857 treaty. No one noticed, apparently, until after the treaty was approved by Congress. The government admitted the error, but eventually decided that the easiest solution would be to move the Poncas—by far the smaller and weaker of the two tribes—south to Indian Territory. And of course, once there, it wouldn't do to let the Poncas just pack up and leave if they didn't like it. That would set a dangerous precedent for other tribes.[10]

Tibbles would have none of this reasoning. He was a radical, a crusader, and he felt that an injustice was being perpetrated. But how could one newspaper editor and thirty Indians take on the U.S. Army? It seemed impossible.

But Tibbles had a plan, and it was a plan of such breathtaking audacity that it soon created a national sensation. Standing Bear could challenge the U.S. government after all. He could do it in court.

The modern reader will have difficulty finding any audacity in that last paragraph. In our day, legal challenges to the government are commonplace. But in Tibbles' day, such cases were rare. And never before had a suit against the government been brought on behalf of an Indian.

Tibbles' idea (and it may not have originated with him) was this: that the newly-passed Fourteenth Amendment to the U.S. Constitution guaranteed equal protection under the law to all persons. Since it was clear that the government had no right to hold a white person in captivity unless that person had been convicted of a crime, it therefore had no right to hold the Poncas on a reservation against their will. Standing Bear could therefore petition a judge for a *writ of habeas corpus*, a type of legal order which would require the army either to prove the Poncas guilty of a real crime, or to release them.[11]

The title of this chapter, therefore, is a bit misleading. Though the case *Standing Bear v. Crook* is often called "The Trial of Standing Bear," in fact Standing Bear was, technically, not the one on trial. Rather, it was Standing Bear who was putting the United States government on trial.

The trial opened in Omaha on May 1, 1879, Judge Elmer Dundy presiding. As it was not a criminal case, there was no jury. In essence, there was but one question before the court, and it could be stated simply enough: As a *New York Times* headline put it, "Have Indians Any Rights?"[12]

So the courtroom battle was ready to begin. Though Tibbles had some ideas about the Fourteenth Amendment, he was no lawyer. He needed someone to go up against U.S. District Attorney Genio M. Lambertson, but neither he nor the Poncas had any money to hire a lawyer. Always persuasive, Tibbles talked a young lawyer named John L. Webster into taking the case pro bono. Sensing he was in over his head, Webster sought help from a more experienced attorney, a man whose *parliamentary procedure* had saved Omaha in the territorial days: A. J. Poppleton.

As the trial began, the respective strategies of the lawyers became clear. Webster and Poppleton tried to show that Standing Bear and his followers had severed their ties with the tribe, that Standing Bear was no longer a chief, that they were all trying to live as whites—meaning, of course, that the law ought to treat them as whites. Lambertson, meanwhile, tried to show that Standing Bear and the others were still Indians and ought to be treated as such.[13]

That was what everyone had in mind when Webster called Standing Bear as a witness. Could Standing Bear present himself convincingly as someone who wanted to become white?

But Standing Bear had his own agenda. While most of the Poncas were dressed in the clothing of whites, Standing Bear appeared in court in the full regalia of a Ponca chief. Eagle feather in his hair, bear claw necklace about his shoulders, moccasins on his feet—he looked every inch an Indian. Lambertson wasted no time.

"Does this court think an Indian is a competent witness?" he asked. But the judge replied firmly,

"They are competent for every purpose in both civil and criminal courts. The law makes no distinction on account of race, color, or previous condition."[14]

That wasn't what Lambertson wanted to hear, and Webster took over. Among his questions to the interpreter was the following:

"Ask him what they were doing up there [at their old reservation] to become like white men?"

"What sort of white men?" Judge Dundy interrupted. "You had better limit that a little."

"Well, *civilized*," Webster replied.

To some extent, Standing Bear played the game, saying that he wanted to work, and "become like a white man," but soon, when he had an opportunity to speak at greater length, he changed the subject. Though he was grateful that Webster and Poppleton were trying to help him, he had little understanding of—or use for—the legal niceties that the lawyers were squabbling over. For Standing Bear, the heart of the matter was this:

> *From the time I went down there* [to Indian Territory] *until I left, one hundred and fifty-eight of us died. I thought to myself, God wants me to live, and I think if I come back to my old reservation he will let me live. . . . What have I done? I am brought here, but what have I done? I don't know.*

It was time for closing arguments. Again, the lawyers took over, Webster, then Lambertson, then Poppleton. Poppleton's speech was a wonder of brevity, occupying only four hours in the delivery; Webster had taken six hours and Lambertson five.

For the government, what it boiled down to was this: Lambertson argued that an Indian was *not* a person under the law and had no right to challenge the government. Law is about precedent, and the precedents went against Standing Bear. In 1857, Lambertson pointed out, the U.S. Supreme Court ruled that Dred Scott, a slave, had no right to sue for his freedom—even though the law was otherwise on his side—simply because, as a negro slave, Scott had no rights which a white man was bound to respect. Furthermore, in English law—which long ago produced the idea of *habeas corpus*—the usage of such a writ had always been restricted to certain classes of persons.

There was more to it than that, but essentially Lambertson was arguing that the law had never applied equally to all classes of people, and that therefore, it should not do so in this case.

In reply, Poppleton argued that Lambertson's position, as Tibbles later phrased it, "undermined the very foundations of human liberty."[15]

And so the trial came to a close after two days, leaving Judge Dundy to weigh the arguments and make his decision. But the courtroom drama was not quite over. Standing Bear, though he had gotten in a few licks from the witness stand, wanted to make a speech of his own. Though this was unorthodox in legal proceedings, Judge Dundy allowed it. It was, as Dundy said, the first speech ever given by an Indian before a federal court.

This is the best-known scene of the trial of Standing Bear, described for us by Thomas Tibbles:

> *Standing Bear rose. Half facing the audience, he stretched his right hand out before him, holding it still so long that the audience grew tense. At last, looking up at the judge, he spoke quietly.*
>
> *"That hand is not the color of yours, but if I pierce it, I shall feel pain. If you pierce your hand, you also feel pain. The blood that will flow from mine will be the same color as yours. I am a man. The same God made us both."*

And Standing Bear went on to describe his situation by way of an extended metaphor. He described himself standing at a river bank, flood waters rising, and the way out blocked by high cliffs. He climbs toward a cleft in the rocks, reaches the top, and looks out at the prairie, at safety:

*"But a man bars the passage. He is a thousand
times more powerful than I. Behind him I see soldiers as numerous as the leaves on the trees . . . If
he says I cannot pass, I cannot. The long struggle
will have been in vain . . ."*

*He paused and bowed his head. Then, gazing
up at Judge Dundy's face with an indescribable
look of pathos and suffering, he said in a low,
intense tone:*

"You are that man."[16]

What a speech! That Standing Bear, a man with no formal
education, could deliver such dramatic eloquence, and at such a
crucial moment, is remarkable. As Tibbles describes it, the
scene was one of pure magic.

And pure fiction.

Though it has fooled a number of historians, Standing Bear
never gave that speech, which first appeared in Tibbles' 1905
autobiography *Buckskin and Blanket Days*. Tibbles, though he
meant well, had a weakness for melodrama.

Trouble was, Standing Bear never quite lived up to the
expectations of his white supporters. During the trial, Standing
Bear's lawyers spent two days trying to show that he wanted to
become white; Standing Bear appeared in court in the full
regalia of a Ponca chief. Most white reformers expected the
Indians to adopt American culture wholesale; Standing Bear
was eventually seen as a regressive influence among the Poncas
because, despite his willingness to compromise, he refused to
abandon his culture entirely.[17] And even Thomas Tibbles, whose
genuine respect for native cultures made him a radical even
among the reformers, could not resist putting words in
Standing Bear's mouth.

Standing Bear did give a speech that day, and it was widely
praised and printed in the newspapers. Indian policy was widely debated in those days; many people came out openly against
the Indians, and many claimed to speak on the Indians' behalf.
But rarely was an Indian able to speak for himself in so public
a forum. So it seems appropriate to let Standing Bear have his
say, just as he did before that packed courtroom on May 2, 1879.

This is his real speech, reprinted in full:

> *I see a great many of you here this morning, and I think a great many of you are my friends. You see me here now; you see me standing here; I want you to look at me.*
>
> *Where do you think I came from? Do you think I came out of the ground, or out of the water, or out of some woods, or where did I come from?*
>
> *God made me and he put me on my land. But why was it that all at once I was ordered to stand up and leave my land? There came to me one who did this. Who the man was I don't know; I had never seen him before; but he came and told me that I had got to leave. It was hard for me to go. I did not want to go. I objected to going. I looked around me for some one to help me, but I found no one. I thought, O, if there was only some one to lend a hand to help me! And perhaps I might remain, but I saw no one, neither all the time I was down in the Indian territory until I came back here did I see any one to help me. But I think I have found some one willing to help me, and it makes me glad—it makes my heart glad.*
>
> *When I was taken down to the Indian territory it seemed as though I was taken to a big fire and thrown in there to be burned up, I and my people. And I might say that 158 of us were burned. But now I stand before you this evening. I came away from there, trying to save myself, and to save my wife and children and friends. I look upon you this evening and hope some of you will have sympathy with me and try and help me. I never want to go there again.*
>
> *I want to go back to my old reservation and there I want to die and there I want to be buried in the land of my fathers. If I go back there, I may live some time longer. When I was young when I was a very little boy, I suppose I was sometimes*

very foolish, but when I became a young man so that I could understand the wrongs of our people, I don't think you will ever find—you may ask any one you have a mind to—I don't think you will find I ever did anything that was wrong myself. I never tried to hurt a white man.

When I see men working, I like to look at, I like to watch them work. I like to see farmers work; I like to see the stock they are raising. When I work, I throw off my coat and go to work with a will.

God made me, but I don't know how to write; I don't know how to read. I have not been taught that; I think He made the white people to teach me. When any person is in trouble, he tries to get some friend to help him. If he can't do that, if he is a good man, he will pray to God to help him.

As I stand here this evening, I want you all to have pity on me; I want all of the gentlemen and the ladies, and all in this house to have pity on me this evening, if it is only until we go away.

When I was at my home in Dakota, in travelling one day, I found a man—a soldier. It was winter; he was frozen, his limbs were frozen and he could not walk. I picked him up and took him to my house; I took off his shoes and his socks, and his feet were frozen so badly that the skin all peeled off. I tried to talk with him, but he couldn't understand me and I could not understand him. I said to him, "You may die, but I will give you a bed so that you may die easy." It was when I was out hunting in the woods that I found him. When [I got him back] to the house I went out in the woods and shot a bird and took that bird home and cooked it for him and gave him something to eat. He didn't eat much at first, but kept eating a little more and more, until he could get up and speak.

Down here on the Platte another time I found another man in the same condition. He had wan-

dered off the road and didn't know where he was. I took him home and fed him; I gave him water to drink, and after he had got better I gave him provision enough and showed him the road to his house, where he could go to his house without any further injury.

If I had been a wild, savage Indian, would I have done this? I guess not; I would have been more likely to cut off his head and take his scalp. I think that is two good things I have done, and another good thing is I have tried to work. I have found that the plow was good. I chop wood and have built me a house, and that is another good thing. I had on my land there forty acres of wheat; I had corn, potatoes, cabbage, and onions.

The Great Father (the president) told me to do this—to work on my land, and I did so. I thought I was beginning to get up in the world. I was getting a little higher and a little higher every day, but some kind of a man came and it seems as though he through me down and tied me, and I couldn't do anything more.

Whenever the white men want to do anything they tell their fellow-men their reasons. I asked him what his orders were to remove me. He said he had none. I sent word to the Great Father about it. He said he hadn't ordered any such thing. They didn't know anything about it. Perhaps you don't believe this, but it is all true.

That is all I have to say to you.[18]

And with that, Judge Dundy declared the court adjourned, and withdrew to make his decision.

Ten days passed. Then, on May 12, Dundy re-covened the court. "An Indian is a *person* within the meaning of the *habeas corpus* act," the judge proclaimed, and he ordered General Crook to the release the Poncas, the very thing that Crook was eager to do. In time of peace, the judge explained, the government had no right to move Indians from one place to another against their will, nor to confine them to a particular reservation against their will. Essentially, he agreed with Poppleton that the government's argument threatened the principles of liberty upon which the nation had been founded.[19]

Standing Bear had won—and not just for himself and his small band of Poncas, but for all native peoples. Though the term was not widely used at the time, *Standing Bear v. Crook* was an important *civil rights* case. Government and military officials would try to ignore the ruling, and were careful not to appeal the case to the U.S. Supreme Court—fearing that an even stronger precedent would be set if the nation's highest court upheld Dundy's ruling. In truth, only one thing from this case was clear: for the first time, a U.S. court had ruled that an Indian was, officially, a *person*.

It was a start.

Was an Indian therefore also a U.S. citizen, with voting rights? Judge Dundy made it clear that he was not answering that question. And he made it clear that he was not challenging the authority of government agents to govern the reservations. That was an important point. Indian agents did not usually allow non-Indians on the reservation, and Standing Bear and his followers were now, in a sense, no longer Poncas. Those who left the tribe were free to leave Indian Territory, but they were not free to go back. Nor could they live on the Omaha reservation. Nor was the old Ponca reservation immediately returned to them. In setting Standing Bear free, Judge Dundy had also made him homeless.

Leave it to Standing Bear's allies to find a loophole. An examination of maps and treaties revealed that an island in the Niobrara River had been left out of the treaties. It could serve as a home for Standing Bear and his followers until some better arrangement could be worked out.

Later that year, Tibbles resigned his post at the *Herald* to go East on a speaking tour with Standing Bear. The two of them hoped to raise awareness, create sympathy for the Indians, and see that the Poncas got their land back. Accompanying them was a remarkable young woman named Susette LaFlesche, daughter of the chief of the Omahas. Partly of French ancestry, "Susette LaFlesche" was the woman's "white" name. She had another: *Inshtatheamba*, meaning "Bright Eyes." Beautiful, educated, and highly intelligent, Bright Eyes served not only as Standing Bear's interpreter, but as a powerful speaker in her own right. Eventually, she and Tibbles were married.[20]

In time, the old reservation was returned to the Poncas. By then, however, conditions had improved in Indian Territory—mostly because of the glare of publicity that Tibbles and company had focused on the situation. Of the surviving Poncas, the majority decided to stay in Indian Territory and not return north. The Ponca tribe is divided to this day.

Thomas Tibbles and Bright Eyes continued to crusade for Indian rights for many years after the trial of Standing Bear, but Standing Bear himself soon returned home. He died in obscurity in 1908.

General Crook, meanwhile, was called to Arizona in 1882 to put down an Apache uprising. The general who had fought Crazy Horse in 1876 was thus pitted against another legendary warrior: Geronimo.

Crook nearly succeeded, and would have, but for a matter of honor. Not all the Apaches joined the rebellion, and Crook made certain promises to those who stayed out of it. When given orders requiring him to break those promises, Crook instead asked to be relieved from command. Another general would break faith with the Apaches. Crook would not.[21]

Years after Crook died, Tibbles wrote a new version of the events that led to Standing Bear's trial. Earlier, Tibbles had said that it was a fellow editor who had come to him late at night with news of the arrest; now he said that it had been none other than George Crook.[22]

Is that the truth? We may never know. The new version of the story appears in the same chapter of *Buckskin and Blanket Days* as Standing Bear's *revised* speech. In his later years, Tibbles was known to take some liberties with the facts. However, Crook and Tibbles had already collaborated on some pro-Indian rights articles by that time; they knew and understood each other.[23] And such a meeting, if it really took place, would naturally have been kept secret during Crook's lifetime, for the sake of his career.

Bancroft, Nebraska, May 26, 1903

At first, they just sat quietly, and that was enough. The house was as still and as silent as death, and two men—Thomas Tibbles and a young companion—sat together in the front room, keeping vigil through the long night.

At length, Tibbles spoke.

"I think you have never met her," he said. "Shall we go and see her now?" And he arose, taking his young friend by the hand, and led him into the adjoining bedroom.

Bright Eyes lay on the bed, covered with a sheet. A wet cloth was folded over her face. Removing the cloth, the old man said, "Isn't she beautiful?"

And he wept for her. They had been married nearly twenty-two years.

Despite his sorrow, Tibbles was glad for the company of his young friend, for he had almost had to spend that long night alone. He was not a popular man, not even with his late wife's family. He was sixty-three years old by then, and had made a career out of speaking his mind—a line of work that had made him neither wealthy nor well-liked. He was a political reformer, a radical, and a champion of underdogs. And so his sole companion that night was another oddball, an eccentric twenty-two-year-old poet named John Neihardt, who not long before—truth be told—had befriended Tibbles mainly because "when almost everybody seemed to 'have it in' for a man, I felt I must get acquainted with him."

And so they kept watch.

Finally, growing uncomfortable with the silence, Tibbles began to speak. As the hours passed, he reminisced about days gone by, reliving his many adventures, the trial of Standing Bear, and the long years of struggle on behalf of one cause or another. It was a "weird night of bittersweet remembering," Neihardt remembered years later:

> *Once when the night was getting old and he*
> [Tibbles] *had grown garrulous with weariness*

and the lapse of sorrow, he recalled an anecdote of General Crook. Having been invited to speak before the Indian Rights Society in Boston, the general had come all the way from the western plains to deliver one of the shortest and most effective speeches ever to fall from the lips of a man: "Ladies and Gentlemen," so, according to Tibbles, ran the speech, "I have been fighting Indians in the West for twenty-five years. During that time I have never known an Indian to break a treaty. I have never known a white man to keep one! I thank you."

Tibbles, overcome by the yarn, was seized by a spasm of explosive laughter. Part nasal nicker and high-pitched whinny, part raucous bray, the desecrating racket smote the mournful stillness of the house, to cease abruptly as he realized again what waited yonder.[24]

Thomas Tibbles lived another quarter-century after that long night. In 1904, he was nominated for vice-president by the Populist Party; in the following years he wrote his autobiography, remarried, and wrote editorials and features for the *Omaha World-Herald*—a job he held almost up to the time of his death in 1928, when he was eighty-seven years old.[25]

Chapter 15 notes

[1]*Dakota Territory:* The area referred to is now part of northeast Nebraska, just west of the town of Niobrara. *Indian Territory:* Known today as Oklahoma.

[2]Thomas Tibbles, *Standing Bear and the Ponca Chiefs,* Edited with an introduction by Kay Graber, Lincoln: University of Nebraska Press, 1995 (originally published in 1880), 18.

[3]Kay Graber, Introduction to *Standing Bear and the Ponca Chiefs,* xii.

[4]Tibbles, *Standing Bear,* 5-17; David J. Wishart, *An Unspeakable Sadness: The Dispossesion of the Nebraska Indians,* Lincoln: University of Nebraska Press, 1994, 200, 202-216.

[5]Tibbles, *Standing Bear,* 14, 15.

[6]Tibbles, *Standing Bear,* 2.

[7]Tibbles, *Standing Bear,* 25.

[8]James T. King, "'A Better Way': General George Crook and the Ponca Indians," *Nebraska History,* 50 (Fall 1969), 241.

[9]King, 239-256.

[10]Wishart, 292-298.

[11]Tibbles, *Standing Bear,* 33-35.

[12]May 2, 1879.

[13]To the modern reader, such a strategy sounds demeaning to the Poncas—and it was—but Webster and Poppleton had a solid legal reason for using it: Several years earlier, a Senate committee report concluded that the Fourteenth Amendment did *not* apply to Indians, except those who had dissolved tribal relations. In short, Standing Bear's lawyers were doing what they believed they had to do in order to win.

[14]Unless otherwise noted, quotations from the trial are taken from Tibbles, *Standing Bear,* 79-81.

[15]Tibbles, *Standing Bear,* 92.

[16]Thomas Tibbles: *Buckskin and Blanket Days: Memoirs of a Friend of the Indians,* Garden City, New York: Doubleday & Co., 1957, 200-202.

[17]Kay Graber, epilogue to *Standing Bear and the Ponca Chiefs,* 136-137.

[18]*Omaha Republican,* May 4, 1879. Regarding the authenticity of the speech: Tibbles' version of the speech did not appear in Tibbles' 1880 account of the trial (*Standing Bear and the Ponca Chiefs*), nor did it appear in the newspaper reports of the time; even the *Herald* printed a version of the speech almost identical to that printed in the *Republican.* I chose to include the *Republican's* version because the *Herald* merely summarized the last part of Standing Bear's speech.

[19]Tibbles, *Standing Bear,* 95.

[20]Kay Graber, epilogue to *Standing Bear,* 129-137.

[21]Robert M. Utley, *The Indian Frontier of the American West 1846-1890,* Albuquerque: University of New Mexico Press, 1984, 197-201.

[22]Tibbles, *Buckskin and Blanket Days,* 193.

[23]King, 241.

[24]John G. Neihardt, *Patterns and Coincidences,* Columbia: University of Missouri Press, 1978, 42-46.

[25]Graber, epilogue to *Standing Bear,* 136; "Publisher's Preface," *Buckskin and Blanket Days,* 7-9.

Chapter Sixteen

QUACKS

1880

To be told by a doctor that one has an incurable disease is one of the most dreaded things a person can experience. In the same way, to seek treatment for an ailment, and to have all known treatments fail one by one, is to experience a cycle of hope and disappointment that would test even the strongest psyche.

For Omaha's sick and suffering, January 1880 was a time of hope. A new year always brings new hope, but 1880 brought more than the usual share, for it brought Dr. R. J. La Fonzo, "the only and original Indian healer, from the Indian Medical Institute, of Chicago."

Within days of the great doctor's arrival, the streets were flooded with promotional literature, mostly copies of La Fonzo's *Medical Journal* (Vol. 3, No. 12), an illustrated eight-page booklet.

The doctor's credentials were impressive, to say the least. Among the booklet's illustrations were drawings with the following captions: "Dr. R. J. La Fonzo's visit to the Onondoga camp, where he made one of his greatest discoveries in medicine, the dyspepsia cure," and "The Osage Indians holding a pow wow, as thanks to the Great Spirit for the discovery of the herb 'Ar-gee-see-lota,' by Dr. La Fonzo, for the cure of consumption."

These were no small accomplishments. Though dyspepsia (i.e., indigestion) is not itself life-threatening, its successful treatment was no simple matter. The problem—not wholly understood at the time—is that chronic indigestion is not a disease in itself, but rather is a symptom of some underlying condition, such as a gallbladder inflammation or an ulcer. While this might seem to preclude the effectiveness of a one-size-fits-all cure, physical reality was no match for the genius of the great La Fonzo.

Nor was consumption (i.e., tuberculosis), which was both fatal and, at that time, incurable.

Though La Fonzo was not known to Omahans before his arrival, he was obviously an important man. The illustration on the *Medical Journal*'s first page showed a man with long, flowing hair, looking a little like the great Army scout Buffalo Bill. The following pages of the book told the doctor's story—a wild, romantic tale that read like a Beadle's Dime Novel. Clearly, this was just the sort of man in whom to entrust your physical well-being.

And there was more. Enclosed in each copy of the *Journal* was a little strip of blue paper, to be used by the reader as a diagnostic test. The reader was to dip the paper in his own urine, whereupon the paper would change color. As the *Bee* described the process, "The patient brings the paper to Dr. La Fonzo, who tells by the color to which it has been changed the disease with which the patient is afflicted, and treats it accordingly."

This was an important advance in diagnosis, simple and unambiguous. It was also, La Fonzo said in his *Journal*, his own invention, for which he had a patent pending. Other doctors who used it, he warned, would face legal action.

Of course the *Bee*—rude, cantankerous newspaper that it was—could not let this pass without comment. To the educated eye, the special test paper that Dr. La Fonzo had "invented" looked like nothing more than common litmus paper. More suspiciously, when tested, it behaved exactly like litmus, which turns blue when soaked in an alkaline solution and red when soaked in an acidic solution. The *Bee* pointed this out to its readers, suggesting that "the traveling Dr. La Fonzo ought to keep right on traveling."

Fortunately for the doctor, not everyone in Omaha read the *Bee*. As we have already seen, Ed Rosewater's paper tended to provoke strong opinions one way or the other. And so La Fonzo's medical practice thrived in Omaha for nearly a month.[1]

As in a Greek tragedy, in which a single character flaw leads inevitably to the hero's undoing, so it was with the great Indian doctor. His flaw—aside from a complete lack of moral integrity—was his inability to keep his mouth shut. He had a good thing going, and couldn't resist boasting about it to those who weren't his patients. Consider the following:

> *"I am no doctor," said La Fonzo; "I don't pretend to any one who knows, to be a doctor. I am a tinsmith by trade and worked in Chicago for a number of years. Becoming dissatisfied with my wages, I determined to strike for a richer stake. I accordingly decided to become a doctor, knowing how easily men can be imposed upon. I have never studied medicine an hour. I prescribe perfectly harmless remedies and allow their faith to work a cure. Why shouldn't it? People will be humbugged and I as well as the next man might as well be the humbugger."*

With those words, La Fonzo's Omaha practice came to a halt. He had talked to the wrong person, and his remarks appeared in the February 5 issue of the *Bee*. As if that wasn't enough, the *Bee*'s exposé also revealed something of the great doctor's attitude toward his new home:

> *He said that Omaha was the best place for d—n fools which he had ever struck, and boasted that if he was run out of it as he had been from others, he would leave with a handsome sum of money in his pockets.*

And so he did. As the next day's *Bee* reported, "With his usual candor he openly remarked that he 'guessed he'd better skip,' adding that there were plenty of other d—n fools in other parts of the country pining for his services." During his stay in Omaha, La Fonzo had been pocketing from $5 to $25 per case. His usual prescriptions had included such "Indian Herbs" as "Pond's Extract, turpentine, ascetic acid and lard."[2]

"Such scoundrels should be tarred and feathered," the *Bee* fumed.[3] Rosewater's paper had already exposed one quack a few weeks before La Fonzo's arrival; now it had three or four others in mind that it wanted to run out of town.

But somehow the *Bee*'s righteousness seems strangely inconsistent—that is, if one reads it directly from the microfilmed pages of the *Bee* itself. Take, for example, the evening edition of February 6, 1880, the same issue that trumpeted the departure of "The Bogus Doctor." In eight pages of newsprint, this issue ran advertisements for no fewer than twenty different patent medicines, almost all of which made health claims every bit as outrageous as those of "Doctor" La Fonzo.

There was the Excelsior Kidney Pad, which cured not only diabetes and Bright's Disease, but was also good for back pain, incontinence, and various female ailments.

There was Gray's Specific Medicine, for men, which cured impotence, "seminal weakness," and "all diseases that follow a sequence of Self-Abuse" [i.e., masturbation].

There was Hostetter's Stomach Bitters, a tonic whose widespread popularity was probably not hurt by the fact that it was nearly forty-five percent alcohol.[4]

There was Allen's Lung Balsam, a cure for coughs, colds, consumption, asthma, bronchitis, "and all other throat and lung conditions."

And there were various other medicines with wonderful names—Kidney Wort, Dr. Thomas Electric Oil, Dr. Wei De Meyer's Cure, The Genuine C. McLane's Liver Pills, Dr. Pierce's Golden Medical Discovery and Pleasant Purgative Pellets, etc.—which, taken all together, claimed to cure every ailment the *Bee*'s readers had ever imagined, and probably several more that they had not.

But we should not be too hard on the Omaha *Bee*. The other newspapers of the city—indeed, of the whole nation—were just as guilty. Newspapers were expanding rapidly in post-Civil War

America, growing both in size and in number. Fueling this growth was advertising revenue, the lifeblood of the newspaper. Patent medicines were sold increasingly by mail-order companies with nationwide distribution, and they bought lots of ad space. As a result, they also bought exemption from the type of editorial debunking that was sometimes inflicted upon small-time traveling quacks like R. J. La Fonzo.[5]

Medicine at this time was largely unregulated. It was perfectly legal to make false and misleading health claims for a product, to deceive the consumer as to its actual ingredients, or to market a product without bothering to do any research to establish either its effectiveness or its safety. Most of the so-called "patent" medicines (few were actually patented) were relatively harmless, if only for the reason that it's bad business to kill off customers who might otherwise buy more of your product. But many of the medicines contained high doses of alcohol or narcotics. Even products targeted at children sometimes contained drugs such as opium or cocaine.[6]

Doctors worked in a similarly unregulated environment. In Nebraska, not until 1881 did the law require practicing physicians to register with the county clerks and show some credentials. Before that time—and to a certain extent, even after it—credibility could be found in a variety of sources. For legitimate doctors, credibility with the public came from years of honest work and from associating with physicians' organizations such as the Omaha Medical Society.[7] For those with less exacting standards of professional conduct, a good marketing strategy was just what the doctor ordered.

R. J. La Fonzo is a good example of the latter approach. In his day, Indians were often despised as bloodthirsty savages, but they were also thought to possess valuable medicinal lore.[8] La Fonzo not only appropriated this mystique for his own purposes, but added to it a not-so-subtle impersonation of an American hero (Buffalo Bill), and—with the strips of litmus paper—a bit of scientific hocus-pocus. Claiming a patent was also a winner.

Though his shtick seems laughable now, in 1880 La Fonzo was pushing most of the right buttons. Had he found a way to include electricity or magnetism—both relatively new and mysterious then, and thought to have healing properties—he'd have pretty much had the whole of nineteenth century medical quackery covered in a single, shameless sales pitch.

It would have pleased me to conclude this chapter by noting that the quack doctors and their worthless medicines died out as the public became more sophisticated. It *would have*—if only it were true. Though a series of twentieth century laws required that drug labels be accurate (1906), that drugs be proven safe (1938) and effective (1962) before being marketed, [9] no law can change the eternal truth spoken by Dr. La Fonzo in 1880: People *will* be humbugged.

During the writing of this chapter, I interrupted my work for the necessary and sacred Nebraska ritual of watching a Husker football game. During a commercial break, a professional golfer hawked his "Energy Band," a gold-plated copper bracelet that featured two small magnets embedded in its inner surface. Wearing the thing was supposed to give you extra energy, and apparently, to improve your golf game. There was, of course, a patent pending on the magnets.[10]

Chapter 16 notes

[1]*Bee* (evening), January 9, 1880.

[2]*Bee* (evening), February 6, 1880.

[3]*Bee* (evening), February 5, 1880.

[4]David Armstrong and Elizabeth Metzger Armstrong, *The Great American Medicine Show: Being an Illustrated History of Hucksters, Healers, Health Evangelists, and Heroes from Plymouth Rock to the Present*, New York: Prentice-Hall, 1991, 167.

[5]Among the largest of the 19th century producers and distributors of patent medicines was the mail-order giant Sears, Roebuck, and Co. See Armstrong and Armstrong, 166.

[6]Armstrong and Armstrong 159-171, James Harvey Young, *American Health Quackery*, Princeton, NJ: Princeton University Press, 1992, 149.

[7]Harkins, "Public Health Nuisances," 483.

[8]Young, 54; Armstrong and Armstrong, 166-67.

[9]Young, 151; Armstrong and Armstrong, 170-171.

[10]So as not to offend anyone, I want to make it clear that I am not saying that the "Energy Band" is a worthless piece of humbuggery, or that it is a flagrant sham targeting ignorant credit card holders, or that the people who actually buy the thing deserve to lose their money for being such gullible idiots. I merely *suspect* that these things are so, and could be wrong. The reader can draw his or her own conclusions.

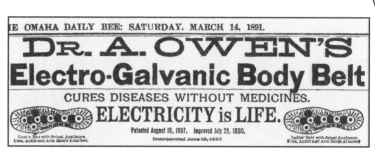

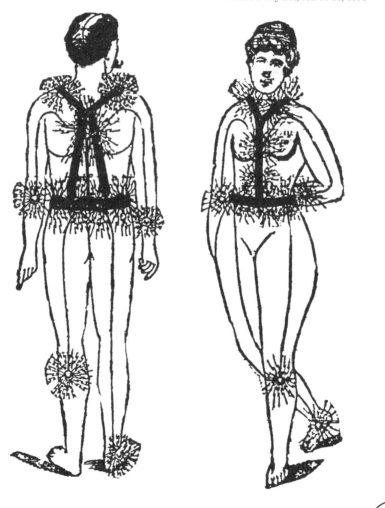

Omaha Daily Bee, March 14, 1891

Omaha Daily Herald, April 1, 1874

Omaha Daily Herald, May 16, 1883

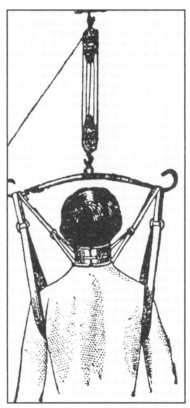

Omaha Daily Herald, Oct. 9, 1891

Chapter Seventeen

BUFFALO BILL

May 19, 1883

T he Indians were gaining. Screaming with savage fury, about fifty mounted warriors bore down on the helpless Monroe & Salisbury stagecoach. To a man, the braves were armed and painted for war. Their ambush had been sprung beautifully; they had caught the coach unawares, and with help nowhere in sight.

Atop the coach sat the driver—a hardened old mule-skin-ner—shouting and flailing away with the lash at his team of six mules. They were a fine team, running for all they were worth, and the dust trailed thick behind. But still the Indians gained. And the driver was only one man, and the four passengers below made only five in all. They were thus outnumbered ten to one, longer odds than Custer had faced at the Little Big Horn. Worse still, these passengers were dandies—city-dwellers—prominent men of the booming city of Omaha. In short, their situation was as hopeless as any which the West had seen.

They had been warned by the stage agent, warned quite sternly of the risk of ambush. And certainly they all knew the bloody history of the particular stagecoach in which they rode. It was known as the "Deadwood" coach, having been attacked some years earlier by road agents near Deadwood in the Black Hills.[1] But neither passengers nor driver had paid any heed to

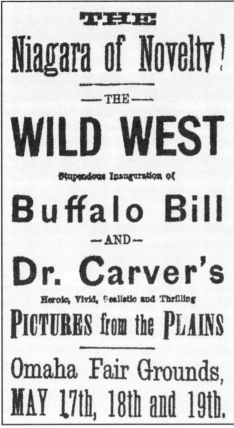

THE

Niagara of Novelty!

— THE —

WILD WEST

Stupendous Inauguration of

Buffalo Bill

— AND —

Dr. Carver's

Heroic, Vivid, Realistic and Thrilling

PICTURES from the PLAINS

Omaha Fair Grounds,

MAY 17th, 18th and 19th.

Omaha Daily Herald, May 16, 1883

the warnings.

The Indians began firing as they drew near to the stagecoach. Reaching out the windows, the passengers returned fire with their revolvers—with no apparent effect. The scene was dizzying: the speed of the chase, the thunder of hooves, the flying dust, the shouts and war cries and clatter of gunfire.

But soon the end was in sight. Relentlessly, the Indians began to close around the coach, the prey within their grasp. And just at that moment, when all seemed lost, something remarkable happened.

Just as in a bad Western, where the cavalry rides in to save the day, so appeared on this day a party of scouts, buckskinclad and beautifully mounted. Their shirts and trousers were trimmed with gaudy fringe, their hats were broad-brimmed and their rifles were at the ready. Their leaders, riding out in front, were two men with long, flowing hair, one man wearing a mustache, the other with a mustache and goatee. They looked like seventeenth century cavaliers come back to life in the American West. And though riding hard and shooting from horseback, when they fired, men fell.

Strange as it may seem, the formerly ill-fated "Deadwood" coach had the good fortune that day to be rescued by a remarkable group of men. To a man, these scouts were highly-skilled cowboys and frontiersmen—Nebraskans, mostly—and of the two Nebraskans at their head, one was Dr. W. F. Carver, a renowned marksman and trick shooter. The other was a world-famous Army scout known as "Buffalo Bill" Cody.

Quickly, the scouts and Indians clashed, the Indians soon being driven off in confusion. Those who didn't get away fast enough were shot off their horses by the scouts, and were scalped where they fell.

And the dusty stagecoach came to a halt, safe at last.

And here the story takes another strange twist, for even before the noise of gunfire was stilled, the air was filled with another sound, one which may disappoint you if you've been caught up in all the excitement: it was the sound of 8,000 voices cheering. Back in the grandstand, beside the racetrack on which the stagecoach had been traveling, the audience stood on their seats, clapped, hollered, and demanded a repeat performance. They had never seen anything like it before, and they loved it.[2]

Such was one scene of an outdoor extravaganza which came to be known as Buffalo Bill's Wild West. During the next thirty years—throughout the United States and Europe, before countless men, women, and children, before common folk and heads of state—thousands of performances were to follow. This was the first.

The long-awaited performance had been hyped in Omaha's newspapers with Barnum-esque bombast. After being postponed for two days because of rain, a front-page ad appeared in the Omaha *Bee* on the evening of May 18, proclaiming that:

THE SUNSHINE
OF
SUCCESS!
At last illuminates the Great Garden
of Merit, where the Wild Flowers
of Western Talent are destined to
Bloom in rare and extraordinary profusion.
EVERYTHING INDICATES THAT THE EVE
OF
AN EVENT
Which will mark an epoch in the History of the

Amusement Universe, has at length arrived, and
that Cody & Carver's
"WILD WEST"
WILL BE POSITIVELY INAUGURATED
Saturday, May 19th, as Advertised

This wonderfully overblown prose contains yet another sur-
prise: the first Wild West show, in which the Wild Flowers of
Western Talent bloomed at the Omaha Fair Grounds[3], really
did mark an epoch in the History of the Amusement Universe.
In its day, Buffalo Bill's Wild West became something of an
American institution. Well into the twentieth century, Buffalo
Bill *was* the West to many Americans. His persona and his show
helped create the mythology by which the West was understood.
In other words, performances such as the Deadwood stagecoach
rescue, which seems to us like a stereotypical scene from an old
Western movie, seems so familiar precisely because it was the
predecessor of the Western movie. In a metaphorical sense,
John Wayne was Buffalo Bill's grandson.

Unlike the movie stars of the next century, however, Bill
Cody had really lived the Old West he sought to portray. Born in
Iowa in the year of its statehood, 1846, Cody moved with his
family to Kansas Territory, where he grew up amidst the bitter
"Bleeding Kansas" struggle between Northern and Southern
settlers. In 1855, Cody's father, Isaac, was stabbed near Fort
Leavenworth while giving an anti-slavery speech.

When Isaac Cody died of illness two years later, eleven-year-
old Billy went to work to help support the family. Working for a
team of "bull-whackers" on a wagon train, he met James B.
Hickok, later famous as "Wild Bill." Ten years older than Cody,
the future gunfighter took a liking to the boy; they were friends
for the rest of Hickok's short and violent life.

At age fourteen, Cody began riding for the Pony Express,
once making a round trip of 322 miles in less than a day.
Changing horses every hour, Cody finished his ride in twenty-
one hours, forty minutes.

During the Civil War, Cody enlisted with the Seventh
Kansas Cavalry. As an eighteen-year-old private, he fought
with General A. J. Smith's troops when they defeated the leg-

Omaha 1889

endary Confederate cavalryman Nathan Bedford Forrest at the
Battle of Tupelo.

After the war, Cody and a partner founded the town of Rome,
Kansas. When the town failed, Cody was financially ruined—
and not for the first or the last time. Later, hired to supply the
Kansas Pacific Railroad with buffalo meat, Cody killed more
than 4,000 bison; in addition to his pay, the twenty-two-year-old
earned himself a new nickname: Buffalo Bill.

As a scout for the U. S. Army during the Indian wars, Cody
earned his commanders' respect for his willingness to carry out
dangerous missions for which no one else would volunteer. He
fought in numerous engagements, and in 1872 was awarded the
Medal of Honor.

Cody's fame spread. He served as guide for foreign royalty
who came to the plains to hunt, receiving glowing press coverage in European newspapers. He traveled East and created a
sensation with his genteel manners and dashing appearance.
And he began to realize that his larger-than-life image could
earn him the kind of income of which Army scouts could only
dream.

He started in the theater, touring with his own stage company, the Buffalo Bill Combination. He toured in the winter, scouted for the Army in the summer. His shows featured incomprehensible plots, corny dialogue, terrible acting, and non-stop action, fights, horses, and shooting. Audiences loved it.

The theater earned Buffalo Bill a handsome income, but eventually he found the stage too confining. As he explained years later, "the theater was too small to give any real impression of what Western life was like. Only in an arena where horses could be ridden at full gallop, where lassos could be thrown, and pistols and guns fired without frightening the audience half to death, could such a thing be attempted."[4]

When Cody's fellow North Platte citizens put him in charge of their Fourth of July celebration in 1882, he had the chance to try out his ideas on a large scale. The resulting "Old Glory Blow-Out" showed Cody that a large outdoor show could work. Joining up with fellow North Platte resident Dr. Carver, Cody began assembling his Wild West company.

So Buffalo Bill made a big gamble, sinking all his money and energy into an elaborate and enormously expensive show. Aside from the stagecoach ambush, the show featured races, a Pony Express demonstration, fancy shooting, lassoing, and a tiny herd of buffalo—which by 1883 had been hunted nearly to extinction.[5]

The verdict of the Omaha press was that Cody had struck gold. The Omaha *Herald* ran its story under the headline:

CODY'S CYCLONE.
The "Wild West" Sweeps All Victoriously Before It.[6]

The *Bee* also praised the show, but more importantly saw in it an opportunity to suggest a new line of work for the *Herald's* editor, Dr. George L. Miller. In a story which Rosewater may have tinkered with, the subject of P. T. Barnum's famous circus comes up during a barroom conversation:

> *"Where is Barnum now with his greatest show on earth" laughed Bill Cody, Sunday afternoon after asking the crowd up to drink for the fiftieth time at a popular bar. "I'll come back to Nebraska*

next fall with my celebrated Deadwood stage coach chuck full of dollars. I tell you the "Wild West" is bound to take east. It is a genuine Niagara of novelties all lariated from Nebraska and complete in every particular." "Not quite complete," chipped in the Hon. Pat O. Hawes, who had been examining the ceiling through the bottom of a tumbler. "Not quite complete. There are several western curiosities which you might add with profit. Dr. George L. Miller in [a] great ground and lofty tumbling act would take like wildfire. Nothing like it has ever been seen in the eastern editorial circles . . . ."[7]

After Omaha, the Wild West traveled to Council Bluffs, then to Springfield, Illinois, then Chicago, and on east. Though popular, the show was poorly managed and lost money at first. Dr. Carver, drunk and surly much of the time, became increasingly jealous of Cody's enormous popularity. Buffalo Bill, a heavy drinker himself, spent two weeks in an Indianapolis hospital after trying to ride an especially mean buffalo during a show. A friend of Cody's later recalled that the first time he saw Buffalo Bill completely sober that summer was when the showman rejoined the tour after his hospital stay.

That turbulent first season, which for Cody was also marred by marital strife and the death of his eleven-year-old daughter, ended back in Omaha for a final show. Cody and Carver then divided their assets by coin-toss and parted ways, each glad to be rid of the other. But though Carver was to tour for years with his own Wild West show, the future belonged to Buffalo Bill.

Chapter 17 notes

[1]The Deadwood coach: William F. Cody, *An Autobiography of Buffalo Bill*, New York: Rinehart & Co., 1920.

[2]*Bee* (morning), May 21, 1883; *Herald*, May 20, 1883.

[3]Fair Grounds: Also known as the Driving Park. Located just northwest of 16th and Sprague.

[4]Cody, *Autobiography*, 314.

[5]Cody bio: Don Russell, *The Lives and Legends of Buffalo Bill*, Norman, OK: University of Oklahoma Press, 1960, 13-35, 290-91; Eric V. Sorg, *Buffalo Bill: Myth & Reality*, Santa Fe, NM: Ancient City Press, 1998, 6-17.

[6]*Herald*, May 20, 1883.

[7]*Bee* (morning), May 21, 1883.

Chapter Eighteen

CITY OF HARLOTS

1870s-1910s

W hen Josie Washburn shot herself on July 17, 1879, the newspapers reported it as an accident. And it may have been. According to the *Herald*, she was "wounded by the accidental discharge of a revolver which she was handling." She survived, but carried the bullet in her shoulder for the rest of her life.[1]

In her writings of her later years, Washburn never mentioned the incident—and generally said little about herself as an individual. When she wrote about women like herself, she usually spoke of them as a group, a social class.

"Our suicides are many," she wrote, and gave the idea special emphasis, coming back to it again and again. But as to her own intimacy with that peculiar temptation—if she had any—she said nothing.[2]

Josie Washburn was a prostitute. As such, the story of her life is, as historian Sharon Wood put it, "a narrative of gaps, silences, and mysteries." Piecing together various versions of her story, one concludes that she was:

> *born probably around 1853, in Rhode Island, or Maine, or Wisconsin, to parents who were natives of Scotland, or Maine, or Norway. Or she may*

have been born somewhere else, to parents of yet
another ancestry. Her name then was not Josie,
but may have been Helena. Like many prostitutes,
Washburn used at least one pseudonym in her
work and created various false histories to go with
it. The stories were part of the fantasy created for
men, as well as a means of maintaining self-
respect.[3]

At age seventeen, Josie—or Helena, or a girl of some other name—came to Omaha.

"After a day or so I found myself in the establishment of Anna Wilson on lower Douglas Street—I have no space to go into the details—nor have I a desire . . ." Shedding her old identity, she entered into a life that she would later refer to as the *underworld.*[4]

A few details of that life can be stated with some confidence. Washburn worked in Anna Wilson's brothel for eight years, appearing almost monthly before the police court on prostitution charges. Then, in July 1879—the month she shot herself—the arrests stopped. Years later, Washburn wrote that she got married that summer (though no public record of this has been found). For the next fifteen years, her whereabouts are unknown. She entered into the marriage full of hopes for a "pure angelic life," but her "profligate" and "degenerate" husband eventually abandoned her.

Single again in the midst of the economic depression of the 1890s, Washburn returned to prostitution, this time as the madam of her own brothel in Lincoln. In 1900, she sued a man named Fred Nagel for breach of promise and for repayment of loans. The promise had been marriage; the loans totaled almost $4,000 dollars. Simply put, Nagel had accepted the money, then married someone else. The lawsuit was unsuccessful.

In 1906, Washburn was involved in another court case, this time involving Lincoln's chief of police and city detective. Along with six other brothelkeepers, Washburn testified that the two officials had been blackmailing them. The women testified, but the men were acquitted. The word of a prostitute carried little weight.

A year later, Washburn retired from the business and moved back to Omaha. In 1909, she wrote and published a book called *The Underworld Sewer.*[5]

This is where our story moves from summary to substance. In her book, Washburn gives us a rare inside look at the life of a prostitute. It is not a glamorous portrait. After all these years, this angry, articulate little volume still packs a wallop.

"A girl or woman who comes to the underworld institution must undergo a long siege of experience before she is able to understand the meaning of the underworld," Washburn writes.[6] And she gives us the following description of a single night; the scene is "the week of the state fair, or a big political doings, or a fraternity meeting, or a convention night; this is our harvest time":

> *Crowd after crowd come to the different doors and yell for admission.*
>
> *They are drunk, we fear them; WE NEVER GET OVER THIS FEAR, although we have seen the same performances daily year after year.*
>
> *A drunken bunch has arrived, they are young and handsome fellows, they use vile language . . . They are society dudes and imagining they are making a hit with our girls, by exhibiting their toughness, and failing to find an appreciative audience, they pinch and hurt the girls just to hear them scream, and curse and call them names . . .*
>
> *The next visitors are hilarious in the extreme; they push, leer, crowd against each other in the hallway and march to the tune of a vile song; they demand beer, which we furnish; they sing more songs of smut, and order more beer at a dollar a bottle . . .*
>
> *They are beginning to tell jokes everywhere. The jokes we have heard before, but we laugh; this is one of the parts we are required to learn to act when we first enter the underworld.*
>
> *They drink more beer and tell more stories with*

whiskers upon them. They ask for a dancer; a girl is found who can supply their demand, and whether it be a jig or a rag, or a hoochee-koochee, it amuses them extremely . . .

The house is now filling up with crowds who are very tired and awfully drunk. They all call for beer at the same time, which we serve as fast as possible; any lagging brings a volley of oaths. Their songs, their stories and their beer buying does not vary from the former callers, but these crowds are drunk, ugly, and abusive.

All of our judgment which we have stored up from years of experience is called into action to keep rows down, which means a strain upon our nerves and activity in the severest sense . . .

It is now 4 o'clock a.m., and time to close. All the rooms upstairs have been rented.[7]

The effects of this life upon a young woman were predictable. "After a year of this life," Washburn writes, "she turns into one of three channels, either becomes a tough, hardened creature who is always ready to take a part in every kind of depravity, or is stupefied with dope, lovers, and more dope. Or else she is awakened to the horrors of her plight and makes every plan to extricate herself therefrom."[8]

A brothel was not the only type of establishment where prostitutes were available. Another type of setup was a row of "cribs," little one- or two-room shacks. In Omaha's vast vice district, one of the most notorious areas was a place known simply as "the Cribs." Sprawling through the alleys of Capitol Avenue between Ninth and Tenth Streets, this area featured vice at its most audacious.[9] Washburn describes it as follows:

Each crib consists of two small rooms, about six feet high; a door and a window forms the whole front. Each crib has a projecting corner, and a casual glance down the line gives it a scalloped appearance, which is meant to be artistic.

*These alleys are paved, regardless of expense,
and have heavy iron gates at each end. One of
these alleys is covered by a fancy roof, the ceiling
has a showy red design, embellished with many
electric lights.*

*Some of the girls who exist in these alleys are
those who have seen years of suffering, and are
now addicted to dope and liquor. But the majority
are the very young girls who are carried away by
the excitement. There is the girl-chum of her own
age, there is the din, clatter, and hum of many
voices, the bright light, men constantly passing,
and at times the alley becomes a surging mass of
humanity, all of which has a hypnotic effect upon
a young girl.*

*. . . These girls who occupy the crib are always
under the influence of a lover, who fleeces them of
all money above their bare living expenses. Some
of these girls with their pretty faces seem so young
and frail as to be mere children. Their condition is
pathetic in the extreme, as they do not even realize
that they are in the worst of slavery.*[10]

Later, Washburn quotes from a 1907 grand jury report that
includes the following:

*The worst feature of the district is what is
known as the crib system. At night these cribs are
brilliantly lighted, the shades are never drawn,
and through the glass front or large windows
therein, that which transpires on the inside may
be observed from the street. High school boys and
boys of tender age are allowed to visit the district
and here take their first step in vice.*[11]

The "district" referred to was the notorious "Burnt District,"
which extended from Douglas Street six blocks north to Cass,
and from the river west to Sixteenth. During the late nineteenth and early twentieth centuries, the Burnt District was

The Underworld Sewer
"Our suicides are many."

"where sin held full sway and Satan reigned supreme."

Several of the Burnt District properties, including the Cribs, were owned by one man, M. F. Martin, who made a fortune from the saloons and restaurants servicing the crowds—and from the one to five dollars in *daily* rent he charged the 200-or-so crib women.[12] Josie Washburn despised him, referring to him in her book as the "man-landlady" or "the monster." Crib women who could not pay their rent in advance had their belongings thrown out on the street; Martin lived comfortably in a fine house in a respectable neighborhood.

A few points bear emphasis. First, a large-scale sexual carnival such as the Cribs—with its electric lights and voyeuristic windows—could hardly operate in secret. That such a place existed for some twenty years before being shut down is hardly a testimony to the moral will of Victorian-era Omaha.

Second, when she refers to "very young girls," Washburn is not exaggerating. She means teenagers. The prime age for prostitution was between fifteen and thirty, though prostitutes as young as eleven were known in the West.[13]

The girls come to the underworld, Washburn writes, by "two broad ways, men's double-dealing, deception and lust; and by deprivation, poverty and abuse."[14] The "deception and lust" story is a familiar one: a man and a young woman become romantically involved; he promises marriage; she gives in to his desire—then comes the scandal, the broken relationship, the disgrace of the woman. *He* has been sowing his wild oats; *she* is a slut. *He* can always move on to another place; *she* has no such power to earn a decent living, especially without proper references. Washburn describes the plight of servant girls as follows:

> *The girl who labors for others is often required to sleep in cold corners in winter, and hot garrets in summer, not always free from vermin.*
> *They have no place to receive their company except in the kitchen or upon the street.*
> *These girls who do your washing, cleaning, and cooking, who are earning a respectable living by the "sweat of their brow" are treated as slaves.*
> *These good girls are made to feel that the work they do disqualifies them from being respected, or noticed by friends and visitors of the family.*[15]

For single mothers with children, the "starvation wages" available to women made survival even more difficult.[16] To the mothers who turn to prostitution to keep their children out of an orphanage, Washburn shows her highest sympathy and praise:

> *It is said that "Greater love hath no man than this, that a man lay down his life for his friends."*[17] *But it is not the hardest act to DIE for those we love, BUT TO LIVE IN DISGRACE, SELL BODY AND SOUL, and to devote a life to a condition where men expect us to take a part in all kinds of degradation for their entertainment, IN ORDER TO SUPPORT OUR CHILDREN, is a far GREATER SACRIFICE THAN DEATH.*
> *Such a woman is always an angel ALTHOUGH she is in the midst of vice . . . .*[18]

In Omaha, the kingdom of vice was vast, the Cribs being only one part of it. Many brothels existed, catering to varying classes of men. And from time to time the women would be arrested, the madams fined, and occasional letters would be written to the newspapers, occasional citizens' committees would form and would hold meetings in which everyone would shake his head and lament the continued presence in the city of the "social evil."

And nothing would come of it. A prostitute might be arrested, but she was not kept out of the brothel or off the street for long. She was fined, then sent back to work. And so the money kept rolling in, filling city coffers and the pockets of policemen, and of judges, and of city officials—and making rich men of those who owned property in the vice district, where exorbitant rents could be charged. Yes, prostitutes were arrested, but never their customers, and never men like the "man-landlady," M. F. Martin.[19]

"Good people," Washburn addresses her readers at one point—though by then it is too late to call them *good*, too obvious that she does not believe it—"I continue this history in order to prove THAT YOU REALLY WANT THE SOCIAL EVIL TO CONTINUE."[20]

On this point (among many others) we don't need to take Josie Washburn's word for it, don't need to wonder if this isn't all just a passionate work of rationalization flowing from a guilty conscience. That may very well be part of it, but it isn't all. A series of *Bee* articles from 1876-77, summarized below, provides ample evidence of what Omaha really wanted:

November 29, 1876. A citizens' committee petitions the City Council to do something about the "disreputable houses" near the Dodge Street School at Eleventh and Dodge. The petition was referred "for investigation" to the council's delegation from that part of the city. A second, similar petition, from a different group of citizens, was referred to the city marshal, "with instructions to do his duty."[21]

December 6, 1876. The delegation reports back on last week's petition, saying that "the matter had been placed in the hands of the city marshal." The marshal reports that he had "caused" all the brothels near the school "to be vacated."

February 21, 1877. The City Council adopts a resolution instructing the city marshal to enforce the law by closing the brothels "from Tenth Street to Twelfth Street West, and from Douglas Street South to Capitol Avenue North"—in other words, the area that the marshal claimed to have cleaned up back in December. In its resolution, the council did not address the brothels outside those limits, though they were also illegal.

April 18, 1877. The City Council adopts a resolution to ask the Committee on Police to think of ways to remove the brothels from the vicinity of the school and "to devise some plan by which the social evil, so called, can be better *controlled and districted* than heretofore." (Emphasis mine.)

May 2, 1877. Another citizens' petition protests the brothels near the school.

May 9, 1877. The Council adopts a resolution "calling the Marshal's attention to ordinances in regard to houses of ill-fame."

And then—after nearly half a year of useless petitions and resolutions—no further mention is made of the matter. No reports of housefuls of prostitutes moving to new addresses; no reports of further protests. Nothing. It appears that the dreamy idealists who wanted to keep the sex trade at least two blocks away from a schoolhouse finally recognized that—in Omaha, at least—they were asking too much.

Of course, not all Omaha schoolchildren had to walk past 'houses of ill-fame' on their way to school. Vice was not tolerated in the more respectable (i.e., wealthier) neighborhoods. This was part of an unwritten code that segregated the city into zones of propriety and zones of vice. The existence of prostitution was taken for granted by many people as a necessary evil; it was thought to help protect "good" women from sexual assault. Hence, as Josie Washburn writes, the underworld served as a "sewer, through which to DRAIN ALL MORAL IMPURITIES FROM THE CHRISTIAN WORLD."[22] It went without saying that "bad" women needed no protection from sexual assault or harassment; for women who had no honor to preserve, *all* sex was consensual. No one was ever convicted of raping a prostitute.[23]

Thus there were two worlds, and for a woman to cross from

one to the other was always a one-way journey, and always from respectability to disgrace.

Men, on the other hand, were allowed by the code to move freely between the two worlds—and move they did. In the 1880 census, Omaha reported seventeen houses of "questionable character." By 1890, the number had risen to forty-three. By 1910, according to one historian, it had topped 100.[24]

Though it is a little late for our nineteenth century purposes, a 1918 health commissioner's report contains some fascinating assertions: the commissioner said that at least 1,600 women were working in Omaha's "vice trade."[25] The method of estimate was crude, but not entirely without merit: a U.S. Health Survey investigation of Sioux City, Iowa, had found about 800 prostitutes there. Omaha's health commissioner concluded that Omaha had at least as many in proportion. Furthermore, based on other U.S. Health Survey data, the Omaha commissioner estimated that of the men who had lived in Omaha for ten years or more, fifty percent "have, or have had, social [i.e., sexually transmitted] diseases."

Regarding women and social diseases, the commissioner prudently said nothing (and thus probably saved himself from being run out of town). Nevertheless, he and everyone else believed that almost all prostitutes carried disease.

The report was greeted with something less that warmhearted enthusiasm. Omaha Mayor Ed Smith publicly condemned the fifty percent estimate as "a libel upon the men of the city." Perhaps he was being too harsh. There was, after all, a bright side: Omaha men compared favorably to those of Chicago, for whom the government estimate of present and past infection was *eighty percent.*

These estimates may have involved more guesswork than actual data, but one figure is beyond dispute: of the men inducted into the U. S. Army during the previous year (World War I had just ended), ten percent had proved to be infected with a sexually transmitted disease at the time of their induction. Whether or not this translates into a fifty percent risk of infection over time is left for the reader to judge. [26]

Incidentally, Mayor Smith was notably selective in his

charges of libel. He did not dispute the estimate of 1,600 Omaha prostitutes.

Perhaps the most striking thing about the 1918 health commissioner's report—other than the numbers themselves—is the obvious ignorance with which city officials greeted the report. Though the estimates were crude, they represented more information on the subject than the city had previously possessed. Even the police commissioner admitted that he did not know how many prostitutes resided in Omaha. Though the "vice trade" had existed openly for years, the women themselves had always been invisible as human beings. Other than arrest records, they mostly lived and died in anonymity—and nobody even knew how many of them there were.

Only one of the underworld women managed to carve her name prominently into Omaha history, and it was not Josie Washburn. Until *The Underworld Sewer* was re-issued in 1997, both the book and its author had been forgotten. Instead, it was Washburn's former employer, the remarkable Anna Wilson, who achieved legendary status. It is probably no accident that of all Omaha's underworld women, the one remembered is the one whose wealth and glamour lived up to the mythology surrounding the trade, and whose life stood in stark contrast to the ugly reality of Washburn's "sewer." This, in brief, is Anna Wilson's story:

Like "Josie Washburn," "Anna Wilson" may be a pseudonym. She was born in Georgia in 1835, a Baptist preacher's daughter, and was raised by her uncle after her parents died. A beautiful, intelligent woman, Wilson was also said to be infatuated with military officers. She got one, a captain. But then something drastic happened—just what that was is unclear. Suddenly in 1867, the thirty-two-year-old Wilson left her old life and came to Omaha, where she opened a brothel.

This is all quite sketchy, but it's more than anyone in Omaha knew about her at the time. They only knew that Wilson was said to have come to Omaha from New Orleans. To her dying day, she claimed to have no living relatives.

What she had, for thirteen years, was a companion named

The Underworld Sewer

"*Let her in.*"

Dan Allen. He was a gambler by trade, and he and Anna were the Omaha underworld's most famous couple.

Unlike Canada Bill and his "cappers," Allen was known as an honest man. In his popular saloon and gambling house, the games were not fixed (at least, not beyond the usual house advantage), and the second-story gambling room was connected by a dumb waiter to a pawn shop below. This was a great convenience for the players, and they appreciated Allen's thoughtfulness. A player who lost all his money did not even need to leave the table; he could send down a watch or other valuables on the dumb waiter, and the pawnbroker would send up money. If the player then started winning, he could redeem his property—after, of course, paying considerable interest to the pawnbroker. In the gambling world, this was considered "a square deal," and it won Dan Allen the respect of Omaha's sporting men.

He and Anna Wilson were well-matched, then, for she also had a reputation for integrity, and it was said that she would not accept a new girl into her employment unless said girl was already "ruined." It was also said that Wilson encouraged her women to marry if they could and get out of prostitution. Both she and Dan Allen were known for helping the needy.

Even so, they lived extravagantly. In 1875, Wilson attended a masquerade ball hosted by a man named Harry Clayton, a saloon owner. Lavishly dressed and adorned with diamonds, Wilson became drunk on champagne and was taken home in a hack.[27] Next morning, she discovered that the diamonds she had been wearing were gone. *Ten thousand dollars' worth of diamonds.*

The evidence pointed to Harry Clayton as the culprit, and Dan Allen wasted no time in recovering his sweetheart's property. After Clayton and several of his men had been arrested, Allen sent word that he had enough evidence to send them all to prison unless the diamonds were returned. Clayton told Allen where to find the diamonds—but was sent to prison anyway.

In time, Allen's health declined, and he died in 1884. Anna Wilson had him buried at Prospect Hill Cemetery and ordered an elaborate monument built over his grave. For years afterward, she visited the cemetery almost daily, and spent a fortune on fresh flowers for the grave.

Anna Wilson closed her brothel in the 1890s. From then on, she lived quietly, investing in real estate and growing increasingly wealthy. She gave generously to charity, and wrote a detailed will in which she distributed her fortune to various charitable causes. [28]

She even gave away the house that had been her brothel. In 1911, Wilson, now seventy-six and in declining health, announced that she would give the posh, three-story, red brick Victorian house at Ninth and Douglas—the one with the stone porch columns of carved nude women—to the city of Omaha, to be used as a hospital.

Omaha needed a new hospital building, and Wilson's twenty-five-room house was worth $100,000. Even so, the city council turned it down until Wilson suggested that, until her death, the city pay her $125 a month in rent. Satisfied that it was better to rent a bawdy-house than to get it free, the council agreed. The naughty stone columns were replaced with plain wooden ones, and the house served as a hospital for many years. Eventually it housed a venereal disease clinic. [29]

When Anna Wilson died later that year, the papers printed glowing obituaries, citing the half-million dollar fortune she had left to charity, and saying little or nothing about how it had been acquired.

Through her philanthropy, Anna Wilson accomplished something that no woman from Omaha's underworld had ever done. She achieved a measure of dignity.

She could never be truly respectable, of course—not even after she retired—because there was no redemption for a fallen woman, no saving grace. "Will a woman from the underworld be allowed to reform?" Josie Washburn asks:

> *The Christian world is delighted to have a MAN who has been a drunkard, and burdened with all of the sins which go with that condition, reform. He is encouraged, invited into business circles, into the home, into the church, upon the platform, and into public life. He is not obliged to hide behind false colors.*[30]

But the prostitute who wishes to reform is shown no such grace. Either she accepts the brand of "RESCUED"—and the snubs, the mistrust, and the condescension attached to the label—or she hides her past, creates yet another false identity, and prays that she is never found out. In other words:

> *The methods adopted to reform fallen women are not only worthless but heartless. When the church societies undertake to REFORM THE WOMEN IT IS IN THAT LOFTY SANCTIMONIOUS MANNER WHICH IS SIMPLY INTOLERABLE to any woman except one ready to die . .*
> .
>
> *The following is an example of a girl that was rescued by the rescuers. They found a home for her in a family as a domestic. She slaved all day, and at night she had the baby to care for. Without any relaxation this girl toiled on. Each day she was*

reminded by her mistress how fortunate she was in having a home with respectable people who loved her. She bore this burden as long as she could—but—you can guess what became of her.

What became of her is that she returned to prostitution. "Is such redemption any redemption at all?" Washburn asks.[31]

For of course *redemption* was the very thing they were all seeking—Josie Washburn, Anna Wilson, and all the countless, nameless women of the underworld—redemption, an experience of that elusive, amazing *grace* that the "Christian world" claimed to offer.

Considering her experiences, perhaps the most remarkable thing about Josie Washburn was her own Christianity. She may have bashed the "Christian world," but she did so by preaching to it, by calling it to repentance, by charging it to exhibit the grace which she knew to exist at the heart of the Christian faith.

Of the four illustrations Washburn commissioned for her book, the last is the most striking. A woman—wearing a sleeveless dress, her bare arms advertising her profession—stands at the door of heaven. The door is closed to her. The woman is crying, face in her hands, too ashamed to look at the angel Gabriel, who peers out at her from a window. Behind Gabriel stands Jesus, who says to the angel,

"LET HER IN."[32]

Chapter 18 notes

[1] *Herald*, July 18, 1879.

[2] Josie Washburn, *The Underworld Sewer: A Prostitute Reflects on Life in the Trade, 1871-1909.* Introduction to the Bison Books Edition by Sharon E. Wood, Lincoln: University of Nebraska Press, 1997. Originally published: Omaha, Washburn Publishing Co, 1909, 263.

[3] Sharon E. Wood, Introduction to *The Underworld Sewer*, vi.

[4] Washburn, quoted in Wood's introduction, vii.

[5] Wood, vi-xii.

[6] Washburn, 327.

[7] Washburn, 188-96.

[8] Washburn, 327-328.

[9]Federal Writer's Project, *Omaha: A Guide to the City and Its Environs*, 108.

[10]Washburn, 45-46.

[11]Quoted in Washburn, 71.

[12]Federal Writer's Project, 107-108. Regarding the rent: by way of comparison, in those days a laboring man might earn only a dollar a day.

[13]Anne M. Butler, *Daughters of Joy, Sisters of Misery: Prostitutes in the American West, 1865-90,* Urbana: University of Illinois Press, 1985, 15-16.

[14]Washburn, 107-108.

[15]Washburn, 276-277.

[16]Washburn, 153.

[17]She is quoting the Bible: John 15:13.

[18]Washburn, 140.

[19]During the 1907 crackdown, Martin was fined $100 for using property for immoral purposes. This token fine appears to be the extent of his punishment. See Federal Writer's Project, 108.

[20]Washburn, 76.

[21]City Marshal: William P. Snowden. With his wife Rachel, he set up housekeeping in Omaha on July 11, 1854, just one week after the Independence Day picnic described in Chapter 1. They were Omaha's first settlers.

[22]Washburn, 239.

[23]Butler, 111. Even prosecutions in these cases were almost unheard of.

[24]Michael J. Harkins, "Public Health Nuisances in Omaha, 1870-1900," *Nebraska History,* Vol. 56:4, Winter 1975, 492.

[25]Omaha's population that year was estimated at 235,000—or about double what it had been twenty years earlier. (See *City Directory of Greater Omaha 1918,* 23.)

[26]*Omaha Evening World-Herald,* Dec. 31, 1918, 1.

[27]Hack: A horse-drawn taxi.

[28]Sorenson, *The Story of Omaha*, 472-474; Fred Thomas, "Benevolent Madam Rests at Prospect Hill," *Omaha Morning World-Herald,* Jul. 27, 1998; Don Beckman, "Frontierwoman Was Saint and Sinner," *The Metro*, June 4, 1975, 15.

[29]*Bee* (morning), August 2, 1911; Federal Writer's Project, 98. The house is gone now. The site is now occupied by the on-ramp from Douglas Street to the I-480 bridge.

[30]Washburn, 287. No redemption: 316.

[31]Washburn, 291, 292, 294.

[32]Washburn, between 315 and 316.

Chapter Ninteen

The Giggling Horror of It All

1880s

One night, a man awoke from a sound sleep to discover that he was dead. Through the sheet that covered him, he could see the light of many candles. His head buzzed with alcohol and with the ear-splitting report of a gunshot.

Perhaps that was the shot which had killed him. Sitting up and drawing back the sheet, he looked all around, struggling to comprehend his destiny. Alone in a somber room, he lay on a little cot, surrounded by glowing candles. By the candlelight he could make out the stacks of coffins against the walls. Perhaps in the eerie half-light he could even distinguish the bad from the good, the cheap pine boxes from the polished black caskets with plush, pillowed interiors; perhaps he even noticed how the candlelight glinted off the plate-glass windows on the front of the finer models.

His coffin would be one of the fine ones. He was a prominent businessman; he would go in style. The papers would print admiring obituaries, and wealthy and respected men would stand hats-in-hand at the graveside. No one would mention the drinking. Death was too polite an occasion for that. But everyone knew, and later they would talk about it. They would assume that drink had had something to do with it, with whatever it was *(Was it the gunshot?)* which had brought him here to this place of death, this place of inescapable and horrifying *death*.

He began praying aloud, though he must have known it was too late for that. It was all over. He was dead.[1]

"Omaha, Nebraska, was but a halting-place on the road to Chicago," wrote Rudyard Kipling of his 1889 visit, "But it revealed to me horrors that I would not have willingly missed." The twenty-four-year-old Englishman was making his way back home from the Far East, where he had just spent seven years in India. The future author of *The Jungle Book* was a cosmopolitan young man, knowing the customs and beliefs of many exotic peoples; he knew, for instance, how corpses were burned in India. But that didn't prepare him to meet Gring the undertaker in Omaha.

". . . I wish I could live a few generations just to see how my people keep," Gring said with enthusiasm. "But I'm sure it's all right. Nothing can touch 'em after *I've* embalmed 'em."

Kipling had been sauntering down Farnam Street when he came upon "a shop the like of which I had never seen before: its windows were filled with dress-coats for men, and dresses for women. But the studs of the shirts were made of stamped cloth upon the shirt front, and there were no trousers to those coats— nothing but a sweep of cheap black cloth falling like an abbe's frock." This was Gring's shop. The clothes on display were for burial. Gring explained,

"As you see here, our caskets have a plate-glass window in front . . . and you don't see anything below the level of the man's waistcoat. Consequently . . . " Gring then "unrolled the terrible cheap black cloth that falls down over the stark feet, and I jumped back."

Kipling was appalled. "Can you imagine anything more awful," he wrote, "Than to take your last rest as much of a dead fraud as ever you were a living lie—to go into the darkness one half of you shaved, trimmed, and dressed for an evening party, while the other half—the half your friends cannot see—is enwrapped in a flapping black sheet?"

"I tried hard to make Mr. Gring comprehend dimly the awful

JACOB CISH,
261 Farnham St., Bet. 14th & 15th

UNDERTAKER

heathendom that he was responsible for—the grotesquerie—
the giggling horror of it all. But he couldn't see it."[2]

People of the Victorian era had a strange relationship with
death. Death was enshrined in the culture to a degree which
seems maudlin and depressing to us—in gushing obituaries and
grand funeral orations, in black mourning clothes, in gaudy
monuments, even in popular art and music. *We have roamed
and loved 'mid the bowers*, wrote Stephen Foster in a popular
song of the 1850s:

> *When thy downy cheeks were in their bloom;*
> *Now I stand alone 'mid the flowers,*
> *While they mingle their perfumes o'er thy tomb.*[3]

In the days before modern medicine and sanitation, death
was always lurking nearby, even for the young and healthy. It
wasn't that death was more common then—they all died sooner or later, just as we do—but in those days, death was more
likely to come for you sooner than later, and without warning.
Especially in a wicked town like Omaha, where a man just
might hear a gunshot and wake up dead.

Farnam Street, in front of the *Bee* Building, circa 1890.

Not that everyone went about with sad faces. Some even made a mockery of death. Take the Coffin Club, for instance. This social club—newspaper men, mostly—had as its headquarters the undertaking parlors of Drexel & Maul, near Fourteenth and Farnam. The presence in their meeting room of caskets, burial clothes, and frequently, corpses, did not interfere with club business. The room was even equipped with a cot, in case someone wanted to take a nap less permanent than the sleep of the dearly departed nearby.

One night a stranger came in while the club was meeting. He had no place to sleep for the night and apparently felt that an undertaking parlor would be quiet enough. The club members, which included Drexel and Maul themselves, had no objections. They offered the cot—which was not being used, though it sat just ten feet from a casket which was.

As soon as the meeting ended, the stranger was alone on his cot in the darkness, happy to be in for the night, and apparently untroubled by the nearby corpse. He fell asleep.

Thump. The stranger awoke, thinking he had heard something. He looked around, but was blind in the darkness. He listened, and thought he heard something that sounded like . . . like somebody breathing—snoring, even—and the sound was coming from nearby, in the direction of the coffin.

Thump. He was wide awake now. He was not dreaming, not imagining anything. The rasping, snoring sound of breaths being drawn in and exhaled, drawn in and exhaled, had grown stronger, even as a terrible thought had grown stronger in the stranger's mind, grown till he could no longer deny it: *The dead man was trying to get out of the casket!*

Thump.

At once the stranger leapt to his feet and ran for the door. In the next moment his feet were knocked from under him and he crashed to the floor face-first. He had tripped over a coffin—yet he was sure there had been no coffin in that spot when he had gone to bed! Again he leapt up and made for the door, but again he tripped and fell flat—over a second coffin!

In fact, several coffins lay between the cot and the door, none of which had been there earlier. He tripped over each of them. Finally reaching the door in a blinding frenzy of panic, the stranger found it locked. Rearing back and crashing into the door, he broke it down and ran into the street.

No explanations could have induced the terrified man to return to his lodging. One might have explained that the dead man was still dead, still silent, and still in his coffin. One might have added that the snoring was produced by a dog, a butcher's dog, in fact—"a large fat animal"—a dog which not only snored, but which thumped his tail on the floor while he slept. And one might have explained that the dog was led into the room by a member of the Coffin Club, the same group who so thoughtfully arranged the coffins between the cot and the door. But it probably wouldn't have done much good.

Of course, no one could offer any such explanation to the stranger, since, as club member Ed Morearty wrote in his memoirs, he "never was seen nor heard of since, and for aught I know he is going yet."

Which brings us back to our dead, drunken businessman, lately awakened to his state of demise. Gradually, he began to recognize his surroundings. He realized that he lay on his usual cot at the undertaking parlor of Drexel & Maul, the place where he commonly went to sleep off a drunk. Confused, he got up and walked out the back door, never to enter the parlor again.

It had been Drexel's idea. (Who says that undertakers don't have a sense of humor?) The club had grown tired of this man staggering in "every time he got beastly drunk," so Drexel arranged the sheet and the candles, while another club member hid in a pile of coffins and "fired off a gun that sounded like a cannon."

In 1917, Ed Morearty wrote of the businessman, "I see that man every day, and he has never drank a drop from that day to this, yet he is still in ignorance as to who caused it, and will be so unless he reads this story."

Chapter 19 notes

[1]Ed F. Morearty, *Omaha Memories: Recollections of Events, Men and Affairs in Omaha, Nebraska, from 1879 to 1917*, Omaha: Swartz Printing Co., 1917, 25-26.

[2]Rudyard Kipling, "Omaha Between Trains," in *Roundup: A Nebraska Reader,* Virginia Faulkner (ed.), Lincoln: University of Nebraska Press, 1957, 168-169 (originally published in Rudyard Kipling, *From Sea to Sea: Letters of Travel,* New York: Doubleday & McClure, 1899).

[3]Stephen Foster, "Gentle Annie," *Songs By Stephen Foster,* compact disc, performed by Jan DeGaetani, Leslie Guinn, and Gilber Kalish, Elektra/Asylum/Nonesuch Records, 1972, 1976, 1987 (song composed in 1856).

Extra! Extra!

Council Bluffs is drunk again. If you don't believe it, read the following from the Council Bluffs Nonpareil: "And who shall say that within the next quarter of a centennial Council Bluffs will not be the city wherein the capital of the United States will be established? Stranger things have come to pass since the landing of the Pilgrims."
—Omaha *Daily Bee*, March 4, 1876

* * *

Custer's Command Cleaned Out.

___

The Indians Almost Annihilate the U.S. Forces—Three Hundred Soldiers Killed.

___

Gen. Custer, His Two Brothers, Nephew and Brother-in-Law Killed.
—Omaha *Daily Bee*, July 6, 1876

* * *

RED DEVILS.

___

Custer's Death Confirmed.

___

Latest Dispatches from General Terry.

___

How the Terrible News Was Received.
—Omaha *Daily Bee*, July 7, 1876

* * *

JOHN CHINAMAN HE LIKEE MELICAN WOMAN.

Marriage of Warry C. Charles, a
Chinese Laundryman, to Mary
E. Whiting, an American Miss.
—Omaha *Daily Bee*, March 15, 1876
(Charles, age 21, operated a laundry business on Harney Street)

* * *

THE MONGOLIAN HORDE.

Swarms of Opium-Soaked Heathens Constantly Flocking To Our Shores.

And Superseding the Natives in All Kinds of Remunerative Labor.
—Omaha *Daily Bee*, February 15, 1879

* * *

Hon. A. J. Poppleton lectured last evening at the Masonic Hall . . . He spoke of the press as a moulder of public opinion, and how it was controlled and throttled by corporations, such as the telegraph companies, who give the press its power . . .

Of Congress, he said ninety-nine per cent are about as competent to perform their duties as a cabin boy to take the helm of a ship . . . Of the lobbies, he said they were agents of corporate capital, composed of picked men, trained and particularly qualified, and there was but one test, and that was success. The "third house" is the true legislature of the country, and nine-tenths of the legislature was inspired by them.
—Omaha *Daily Bee*, April 23, 1879

* * *

SHAW SLUGGED

How an Irate Woman Vented Her Wrath.

A Beer Glass Hurled With Nearly Fatal Aim.
—Omaha *Daily Bee*, May 15, 1883

* * *

Do you feel broken down? Try Wheat Bitters and jump for joy. They will restore you.
—Omaha *Daily Herald*, May 17, 1883

* * *

"Worth her weight in gold" is not the most complimentary thing that can be said about a woman, as she would have to weigh 300 pounds to bring her value up to $100,000.
—Omaha *Daily Herald*, May 20, 1883

* * *

Mart Kennedy has a wolf in his collar trapped about a week ago near Florence. He proposes to turn it loose in the country some day next week and inaugurate a grand wolf hunt.
—Omaha *Daily Bee*, March 4, 1880

* * *

At the fall election of that year [1882] *the people were called upon to vote on the constitutional amendment . . . which contemplated giving and granting to women the right to vote. . . Edward Rosewater accepted the challenge of Susan B. Anthony, the joint debate taking place in Boyd's Opera House in September of that year, and was enjoyed by the crowded house that attended, each side being applauded as their respective clinching arguments were made. Mr. Rosewater, however, judging from the applause, merited the decision. . . A few days thereafter, Gilbert M. Hitchcock, now editor of the World-Herald and United States senator from this state, accepted the challenge of Phoebe Cousins . . . During the debate he became so enthused in his subject that he invoked the wrath of his opponent to such an extent that she arose from her seat to attract his attention, and pointing her long bony forefinger at him menacingly, exclaimed: "Mr. Hitchcock, you are a disgrace to the mother who bore you!" He was applauded to the echo and won the debate on its merits.*

—Ed Morearty, *Omaha Memories* (1918)

* * *

Notwithstanding the high flown declarations in our declaration of independence our government was founded on the bones and blood of slavery and on the disenfranchisement of half its population.

—Susan B. Anthony, from her debate with Edward Rosewater, quoted in the *Bee*, October 14, 1882.

* * *

In my estimation the highest aim that a woman in this country may have, more than she could achieve by the enfranchisement of her sex—to be the mother of a manly man like James A. Garfield.

—Edward Rosewater, praising the mother of the late president during his debate with Susan B. Anthony.

* * *

FOUR MORE GOOD INDIANS.

They Are Made by the Rope Route at Missoula, Mont.

FOR ATROCIOUS CRIMES COMMITTED.

—Omaha *Daily Bee*, December 19, 1890

* * *

A large number of squatters' houses along the bank were completely surrounded, the water in many instances reaching the houses and flooding them. Just north of the bridge a row of a dozen of houses were completely cut off by a stream of the flood that ran between them and the railroad tracks. In some of these houses strange scenes were presented. In all of them the furniture was packed ready for removal at a moment's notice, while strong wooden rafts were tied at the door to be used in case of a dangerous increase of the flood. In one house the family, about a dozen in number, were seated at the dinner table in a room—the only one in the house—in which the water was at least a foot deep, and unchained articles of furniture floating around them. The house in question was anchored to the railroad tracks by the means of strong rope cables and the family sat at their noonday meal as apparently unconcerned as though they were occupying a mansion upon the highest point of the city. A consumptive looking barn and chicken house that belonged to the family named occupied a higher position and was free from flood, its occupants, a cow and several dozen chickens, faring more comfortably than their owners.

—Omaha *Daily Bee*, March 28, 1887

Chapter Twenty

THE LYNCHING OF GEORGE SMITH

1891

"Men who stand high in the esteem of the public for christian character, for moral and physical courage, for devotion to the principles of equal and exact justice for all, and for great sagacity, stand as cowards who fear to open their mouths before this great outrage. They do not see that by their tacit encouragement, their silent acquiescence, the black shadow of lawlessness is spreading its wings over the whole country."
—Ida B. Wells, 1892.[1]

Part I: "He is Too Vile To Live"

Wednesday, October 7, 1891, about 4:20 pm.

Five-year-old Lizzie Yeates came running into the house, crying. Her clothing was in disarray and straws of hay stuck from her hair. Asked what was the matter, she replied that "that man" had hurt her. Though she could not have comprehended the meaning of it, Lizzie showed her mother and grandmother what had been done to her.

She had been raped.

Immediately, the two women ran outside to look for the

assailant, but saw no one. Lizzie's grandmother, however, believed she had seen the man about twenty minutes earlier.

Lizzie had been playing in the yard at the time. Through a window, Grandmother Yeates had noticed a young man in the back yard, and went out to see what he wanted. He explained that he was looking for garbage to remove. There wasn't any, Grandmother Yeates replied, and the man departed by way of the alley. She thought nothing more about it.

Now, less than half an hour later, she found herself unable to form a clear mental picture of the man. The encounter had been so brief, so ordinary, so innocent. Now, in a few minutes' time, it had become a precious link between a vicious crime and swift justice.

Of a few things she was sure: he was a young man, of medium size, and neatly dressed in a blue checkered suit and a derby hat. None of this was particularly noteworthy. But there was one other thing, and this would influence all the events which followed:

He was black.[2]

"The year 1891 was not one of great achievement for Omaha," recalled Ed Morearty, whose Coffin Club exploits we read about in a previous chapter. "The general stagnation of business throughout the country was beginning to be felt here as elsewhere. This, added to the drought which prevailed for some time in the middle west, causing the loss of crops, much depreciation in land values and general unrest among the people."[3]

After the heady boom years of the 1880s, hard times were coming to Omaha. The city's population—more than 120,000 by 1890—would shrink 30,000 by mid-decade, as people moved away in the hope of escaping unemployment and poverty. In 1891 the depression was just getting under way, but the usual companions of hard times—political and social unrest—were already becoming apparent.[4]

Part of the unrest expressed itself as suspicion toward people seen as racial or cultural outsiders. In 1889, Rudyard Kipling had found Omaha to be "populated entirely by Germans, Poles, Slavs, Hungarians, Croats, Magyars, and all the scum of the Eastern European States . . ."⁵ He was exaggerating for effect, of course—and displaying his prejudices—but Omaha's ethnic and cultural diversity was undeniable, and as hard times set in, was seen as less and less tolerable. The American Protective Association became influential in Omaha that year. Proclaiming itself dedicated to "Patriotism and Religion," the APA was in fact anti-immigrant, anti-Catholic, and anti-anything-not-white-Anglo-Saxon-Protestant. In such hateful times, it is not surprising that Omaha's black population should also come under greater suspicion.⁶

Thursday morning, October 8.

On page four of the *World-Herald*, a headline proclaimed:
HE IS TOO VILE TO LIVE

Every Reason for the Lynching
of a Lustful Young Negro.

A Little Girl Outraged in the Heart of
the City—Room for a Lynching Committee.

Included in the article was a summary of Lizzie's brief but harrowing account of the crime:

> *When they [the mother and grandmother] returned to the house the child told them that the negro had picked her up, carried her across the alley into Mr. McClanahan's barn, thrown her on the hay, torn her underclothing off and then accomplished his vile purpose with her person. She could make no outcry, for as soon as the lustful brute took hold of her he grabbed her by the throat and choked her. The violence of his grasp was still attested by the finger marks on her neck.*
>
> *Dr. Ross was called and found that the child had been terribly lacerated. He states that she is not, however, seriously injured.*

A police search was in progress, the article said, and though the grandmother "could give no very accurate description of the fellow," the brief description she gave was reported. Omahans had reason to believe that a dangerous black fiend was prowling the city, house to house, in search of victims. Until he was caught, Omaha's wives and daughters would not be safe. Such a threat, in the *World-Herald*'s view, required swift and brutal justice of a kind which could not be entrusted to the judicial system.[7]

To understand the *World-Herald*'s views on crimes "of a certain nameless nature," consider the following excerpt, taken from an editorial published the following spring. The subject is Southern lynchings:

> *The law can never adequately punish these crimes. Neither can it give to the injured any reprisal. Seated in the deepest instincts of the human heart is the desire to avenge personally and with deadly effect such crimes as those which are every few days perpetrated and most often by the negroes. Why they are so frequently guilty of such heinous outrages the physician can perhaps tell better than the moralist. But it is the first outrage which is the cause of the second [i.e., lynching], and it might be well to level the guns against the cause as well as against the effect.*
>
> *It is not in the nature of Americans to be law breakers except when they are confronted with terrible situations. When it comes to a question of defending his home, no man pauses to reflect much about code and statute. That is the whole of the matter.*[8]

By the 1890s, the idea that black men were somehow naturally prone to raping white women had become firmly entrenched in the minds of white Americans. It is clear now that the myth of the heightened sexuality of the black male persisted mainly because it served a purpose in society, especially in the South, where the myth originated. That purpose was to provide a powerful justification for the lynching of thousands of black men, which in turn served the purpose of keeping blacks

Douglas County Courthouse, circa 1890.

in a subservient position close to that in which slavery had formerly held them.

For these reasons, the myth was immune to argument and common sense. The great orator and abolitionist Frederick Douglass pointed out that during the Civil War, many white Southern women were left at home with their slaves, but during four years of war, rape by black men was unheard of.[9] Editor and pamphleteer Ida Wells, who began her bold and eloquent war of words against lynching in 1892, at age twenty-three, showed that in most lynchings, the victim was not even accused of rape, but was hanged on some other pretense. Furthermore, Wells enraged her adversaries by proving that many of the so-called rapes were actually cases of inter-racial romance, between consenting adults, which—once discovered—led to the violent death of the negro at the hands of an angry mob.[10]

But the reality of the 1890s was that most people were far more familiar with the racial views of papers like the *World-Herald* than they were with Frederick Douglass or Ida Wells. And in the Lizzie Yeates case, not only did a rape unquestionably occur, but also—if the little girl's story has been reported accurately, and "that man" was indeed the black man who had been seen earlier in the yard—the race of the perpetrator seemed to confirm the stereotype which the people already accepted.

Thursday, noon.

The arrest occurred at Twentieth and Lake, less than half a mile from the Yeates home. Cornered in a hay loft, George Smith, negro, was taken into custody by two Omaha police detectives. Details are sketchy. Apparently Smith gave an alias to the police, calling himself "Joe Coe." As the *Bee* reported that evening, the man who had been hiding "proved to be George Smith," who, incidentally, "had been taken to Council Bluffs a few weeks ago to answer for a similar crime but managed to get clear."

How did it happen? Did the police track this man and then learn that he was George Smith, or were they looking specifically for Smith in the first place? The distinction, as we will see later, may be an important one.

At any rate, the *Bee* was pleased with the arrest, noting that, though he was wearing a different suit of clothes, he:

> *was identified by the little girl and by a woman who had seen him in the vicinity of the house. It is understood that he pawned the clothes last night that he wore yesterday; and the police are now looking for them as a link in the chain of evidence against him.*

For all his disdain for the competition, on this day Edward Rosewater's *Bee* was in full agreement with the *World-Herald*. The *Bee*'s story ran under the headline, HEMP NEEDED.[11]

Friday morning, October 9.

So quickly did the arrest occur that a *World-Herald* squib was already partly obsolete before the morning edition hit the streets: "If the black rascal who committed the foul crime on little 5-year-old Lizzie Yeates can be caught in time, the Neal gallows might properly do double duty."[12]

Ed Neal was a white man, a convicted murderer, whose hanging was scheduled for Friday noon. A gallows had been built next to the county jail, hidden from the public's view by sixteen-foot-high walls. Though only about 250 people were fortunate enough to have been given tickets to the hanging, the whole city was filled with suppressed excitement.

The case—in which Neal was charged with the murder of an elderly farm couple—had been frustratingly slow. After a trial which lasted more than a week, nearly a year and a half passed while Neal's attorney appealed the verdict all the way to the Supreme Court. Finally, Neal's last card was played out, and justice was only hours away.[13]

How long would Lizzie Yeates have to wait for justice?

George Smith was being held in the city jail at Fourteenth and Davenport, awaiting his preliminary hearing, his bail fixed at $2,000. Hearing or no hearing, the *Bee* had already pronounced him guilty, identifying him in a headline as "George Smith, Who Assaulted Little Lizzie Yates [*sic*]."[14]

Smith was a waiter by trade. He was married, had a three-year-old son, and lived in a frame shanty in the alley between Eleventh and Twelfth streets near Izard. From here, if you were to head northwest across the railroad tracks, the Yeates home was just half a mile away.

Besides his wife and child, Smith's family consisted of his mother, who worked as a laundress and lived near Fourteenth and Howard in a dwelling similar to George's; his father, who lived in St. Joseph, Missouri; his sister, Kate, who "recently ran away with a soldier"; and his brother, John, who like George was a waiter. None of this, however, was reported at the time.[15]

Friday, about 11:30 a.m.

Since 8 a.m., a crowd had been gathering around the county jail. Faces looked out from every window of the nearby buildings. The roofs were crowded, while on the street popcorn merchants and fruit peddlers kept up a steady trade. Young men, old men, women pushing baby carriages, white and black, all waited in anticipation. Ed Neal was just thirty minutes from eternity.

To some, the morbid crowd was embarrassing. The *Bee* would lament later that the scene "did not furnish an edifying commentary upon human nature . . ."

Over at the *World-Herald*, something stronger was being set in type. For all its bloodthirsty bombast of late—out-Rosewatering Rosewater—someone there abhorred the whole proceeding and gave us this description, entitled "A Legalized Murder":

> . . . *Around the grim little brick structure on Harney street a number of men and boys have clustered for the last forty-eight hours. They were there to be entertained. They wished mainly to hear the hammer that pounded the nails into the scaffold; to catch the sound of the young murderer's voice, to hear the footfall of the death watch. The morbid folk who are not ashamed to confess their vulture-like appetites, have been feasting their souls to gluttony on the hideous fact of Neal's fate.*

There was talk among the crowd, talk of Neal, talk of George Smith, talk of Lizzie Yeates. And around this time the story began to spread that the little girl had died from her injuries. Inside the sixteen-foot walls, violent indignation spread from person to person like a virus, swelling into an epidemic of vengefulness. "Feeling ran so high," the *Bee* reported that evening, "that had there been a leader, a rush would have been made for the cell of the colored brute and the latter would have followed Neal upon the scaffold."

But soon the crowd's attention was diverted by the long-awaited appearance of Ed Neal.[16]

Friday afternoon.

"JUSTICE AT LAST," proclaimed the *Bee*'s evening headline. Neal had died on schedule, and the *Bee* had all the details.

Included in the report was the following sentence: "About this time the news was received in the crowd that the little girl who had been criminally assaulted by the negro, George Smith, had died." As quoted earlier, the paper went on to explain the crowd's reaction to this "news."[17]

By failing to investigate this rumor before printing it and calling it *news*, the *Bee* effectively confirmed the story. The results of this act of sloppy journalism were— or should have been—predictable.

Governor James Boyd

"Heafey and Heafey Undertakers and Embalmers" read the sign on Fourteenth Street just north of Farnam. There, Ed Neal's body was on display for anyone who cared to stop by. That afternoon, 23,425 people did.[18]

Friday, 4 p.m.

George Smith stood before Lizzie Yeates, but she would not look at him. There in the Yeates's parlor, the police were hoping for someone to positively identify Smith. (Police line-ups were still in the future.) Unfortunately, Lizzie refused to look at any of the strangers just then, so she was of no help.

What the papers had already reported—that Lizzie and her grandmother had already identified Smith—was not true. Whether either of them had seen George Smith before was precisely the question at hand.

What the grandmother told the police comes to us through a *Bee* reporter who visited the family later that day:

> . . . *Mrs. Yates* [sic] *was quite certain that he was the negro who had been prowling around the place and represented himself as a garbage man. She said she would not be willing to swear posi-*

> *tively as to his identity, but she firmly believed*
> *that he was the brute who had assaulted her*
> *child.*

She was sure; she was not sure; she was sure. Grandmother Yeates's hedging response—as though she really *wanted* to believe, but was not quite convinced that this was the man—came too late to make the evening papers. It would not appear until Saturday morning.

So the police loaded Smith back into the patrol wagon and took him away. Lizzie's father stood watching. "It is difficult to identify the parties in some instances," he told the *Bee* reporter, "And perhaps there would be in this, although I am satisfied in my own mind. Self control is not always easy, and it was hard for me to let that damned scoundrel get out of the yard alive."[19]

About 5 p.m.

With the evening papers out, the talk of a lynching became more serious. Small groups of men gathered on street corners, talking about what to do, waiting for something to happen.

Meanwhile, Smith was quietly transferred from city to county custody. Mayor Richard Cushing, worried about mob action, had ordered Smith taken to the county jail, which was larger and more secure than the city facility. It was here, incidentally, that Neal had been held and had that morning been hanged. Smith may have been taken there directly from Yeates's house; at any rate, the transfer went smoothly and without attracting attention.[20]

Across the river, the Council Bluffs *Globe* reported "THREATS OF LYNCHING," with the subheading, "A Negro Rapist Liable to Be Mobbed." Like the Omaha *Bee*, the *Globe* reported that Lizzie Yeates was dead. As the word spread, groups of Council Bluffs men began crossing over into Omaha.

The *Globe* also identified Smith as "the same negro who some time ago assaulted little Dottie Gunn on Cut-Off."[21] This charge, alluded to earlier by the Omaha papers, seemed especially damaging to Smith's case. Smith appeared to have escaped a similar criminal charge just weeks earlier due to a bizarre legal loophole caused by a loop in the Missouri River.

It all started with high water back in July 1877. During that month, the Missouri River complicated the Nebraska-Iowa state line by cutting a new channel for itself. A four-mile loop was cut off from the winding river when high water wore a new channel through the neck of the loop. Suddenly 1,600 acres of Iowa land lay west of the Missouri River. Was this land now part of Nebraska, or still part of Iowa? Eventually, the U.S. Supreme Court ruled in Iowa's favor (today Cut-Off is incorporated as the town of Carter Lake, Iowa), but in 1891 the issue was still unresolved.[22]

In September, 1891, George Smith faced a grand jury in Council Bluffs, accused of assaulting a minor, Dottie Gunn, on Cut-Off Island. The grand jury, however, chose not to indict Smith. As reported later, the grand jury held that the crime, if committed at all, had happened in Nebraska, not Iowa. Smith was released. By October 9, the Cut-Off case was being cited as an instance when George Smith "managed to get off" and escape justice. It was precisely the sort of thing that might lead a person not to trust the legal system to deal adequately with dangerous criminals.[23]

Nationally, a precedent had already been set. In addition to the countless news items relating one lynching or another (mostly in the South), a famous mass lynching had taken place in New Orleans in March of that year. In this case, the occasion was the gangland-style murder of the chief of police, who had recently begun an investigation of the New Orleans Mafia. After a trial acquitted several of the accused, a mob stormed the jail and seized eleven of the men—Italians all—and killed them. Two were hanged; the rest were shot to death.

Though the incident led to a temporary severing of diplomatic relations between Italy and the United States, Omaha newspapers praised the lynching of the "Sicilian assassins." The *World-Herald*'s report emphasized the failure of the court, the orderliness of the mob, and the high social standing of many of the participants. The *Bee* added that "Judge Lynch is not always above reproach, but law-abiding citizens must feel that he did his duty in New Orleans on Saturday."[24]

Friday, 8:30 p.m.

A crowd had gathered around the city jail. They were orderly enough, and in true democratic fashion, chose a committee of representatives. The committee then went inside and asked about Smith. He wasn't there, a jailor told them, he'd been taken to the county jail just a few hours earlier.

Only about a hundred people had been hanging around the county jail—mainly, it was supposed, due to lingering curiosity about Ed Neal. Suddenly, the crowd began swelling rapidly, probably just as soon as the city jail crowd walked the eight blocks to Seventeenth and Harney. Word spread rapidly.

Sitting on the curbstone of Seventeenth Street was a row of black women. One observer noted that they "seemed to know what was coming."[25]

Part II: Steel on Steel

Sheriff John Boyd was already in bed. It had been a long day. Because Ed Neal had been a county prisoner, it had been Boyd's responsibility to arrange the hanging and see that the carnival in the surrounding blocks didn't get out of hand. It had all gone smoothly; now Boyd was ready to get some much-needed sleep. Then the phone rang.[26]

We don't know who called him or what he was told. The most likely version is that Boyd, knowing nothing of the transfer of Smith to county custody, was simply told that there was some sort of trouble at the jail and that he had better get down there. The jail's phone line was probably already cut. When Boyd arrived at the jail around 9 p.m., he found a thousand people gathered outside. The doors were locked. As soon as he was let in, the sheriff immediately demanded to know what was going on.

Hearing that Smith was now his responsibility, Boyd immediately recognized that the situation could get ugly. He ordered Smith taken from his cell and moved into the cage, the solitary confinement cell, the most secure spot in the whole building. Conveniently, the cage was empty, having just been vacated that morning. Its previous occupant was Ed Neal.

As the jailors led Smith to his new cell, the sheriff assured him that he would protect him to the best of his ability. But,

Boyd quickly added, if it weren't for duty, he'd be tempted to furnish the rope with which to stretch him.

Outside, people were streaming in from all parts of the city. Word was out: the thing was underway. And the police did nothing to interfere.

According to later reports, the authorities did not immediately recognize the nature of the gathering. Thinking that people were curious to visit the site of Neal's hanging, they did not realize that another hanging was what the people had in mind. This, at least, is the interpretation most favorable to Police Chief Webb Seavey, who was notably absent at the time. The police department had apparently made no plans for crowd control.

As the people continued to gather, they talked among themselves, talking openly of lynching, making no secret of their purpose. Suddenly, someone shouted,

"Hang him!"

And the crowd responded. As one observer described it, "There was a silence for a second and then the very heavens were rent with an angry shout from hundreds of throats. 'Lynch him! Lynch him!,' they yelled, and the roar died away like distant thunder, only to rise again in an angry volume as the crowd was augmented."

Lynch him! Lynch him!

The crowd was growing impatient. Inside the jail, a single light shone from the window of the jailor's office.

Bring out that damned nigger!

Some men began to talk of breaking down the door, but no action was taken. A few police mingled with the crowd, but did nothing. By now, the people were too numerous to be easily controlled by a few bluecoats.

"Let me get there!" shouted a gray-haired man as he pushed his way through the crowd toward the door. It was "Uncle Jimmy" Cannon, an old army scout. Uncle Jimmy was from

North Platte, Buffalo Bill's town, but he was well-known in Omaha. Mounting the steps, he shouted, "Fellow citizens, follow me!"

Nothing happened. As a reporter later explained, "Nobody followed because he did not lead anywhere."

With Smith in the cage and the jail prepared for defense, Sheriff Boyd came outside to try to diffuse the situation. Not liking the strength of the cards he was holding, he tried to bluff. Standing on the steps of the east door, he addressed the people,

"Boys, I know the sentiment of your crowd, and accordingly I removed Smith from the jail. I told him when I took him away that if it was not my duty to protect him I would furnish the rope to hang him."

What the sheriff said next was lost in the shouting of the crowd. Regaining their attention, he continued, casually:

"I'd been at home trying to rest. I was telephoned that you were here, and I came over. I was aware of this this afternoon. He was in an upper cage and I took him—"

The crowd interrupted again, dissatisfied with what the sheriff was saying. When next heard he was again trying to empathize with the crowd, to show them he was one of them, so as to win them over:

"If he were here and I were not the sheriff, I'd be the first to make a noose."

The crowd howled with impatience. None of them was the county sheriff; let them make the noose. How could the sheriff object to that?

"You can't make us believe he isn't here!" someone shouted. A cry went up,

"Bring a battering ram! Get that rope ready!"

This was not going as the sheriff had hoped. The crowd was growing before his eyes in both size and aggression. Groups of fifty to 150 men kept arriving and adding their voices to the mob. The situation escalated further when the crowd appointed a five-man committee. The committee demanded to be allowed to look for Smith inside the jail, but Boyd refused to let them in.

And suddenly, the sheriff wasn't there anymore. Some said they saw him leave of his own accord; others said they saw him

Durham Western Heritage Museum
South side of the courthouse and jail. Smith was dragged down
the driveway to the street. The *Bee* Building is on the right.

being shoved out into the crowd, where he was told he wasn't
wanted anymore. Either way he was gone. He did not return.

Another man named Boyd worked his way to the front. It
was the sheriff's brother, James, a former Omaha mayor who
lately had been elected governor of Nebraska. Just months into
his term, he was already an ex-governor. The Nebraska
Supreme Court had ruled the Irish-born politician ineligible for
office, declaring that he had never become a U.S. citizen. Later,
the U.S. Supreme Court would overrule this decision and rein-
state Boyd, but for the time being the ex- and future governor
was in Omaha attending to private business. His new show-
place, Boyd's Theatre—just across the street from the courthouse and jail—had just opened to the public a few days earlier.[27] Hearing of the trouble (the theatre had emptied during an
intermission), Governor Boyd had come to lend his prestige to
the cause of law and order.

He was greeted with howling and cat calls. Waving his hand,
he shouted,

"Gentlemen, you all pretend to be good citizens, don't you?"

"Yes," they shouted.

"Then let the law take its course."

The crowd's reply was neither pleasant nor respectful.

"For the honor of Omaha, men, desist!" the governor pleaded. "Your actions are a disgrace to the city and will bring shame to every man in it. I implore you to cease and let the law take its course. Be men and disperse."

"Give us the nigger!" came the reply. "We'll tear him limb from limb!"

Whatever else James Boyd said was lost in the noise. Though he continued to hold his position at the jail's east door, the crowd was no longer listening.

Ed Morearty had come up in the world since his Coffin Club days. Now a city councilman, he noticed the crowds as he left a meeting about a quarter mile from the jail. Wave after wave of excited people rushed past him on the street, and Morearty followed, wondering what was going on.

He arrived while Governor Boyd was addressing the crowd. It was not going well. Soon, a local judge tried to calm the crowd, but was equally unsuccessful. Someone spotted Morearty, encouraged him to give a speech, and got him up on a window ledge a little above ground level. Even those who couldn't hear him could see him. He was a tall man, wearing a gray overcoat and probably a derby hat, too. For added style, the thirty-one-year-old councilman carried a cane.

Morearty had just begun to address the crowd "along the same lines as the previous speakers" when disaster struck. Holding the cane as he spoke, he was pushed off balance by the jostling of the crowd. The cane struck the window, shattering it.

The result was immediate. With the loud breaking of glass, the first act of physical aggression had been committed—or so the crowd thought. With this psychological barrier down, the crowd surged forward. The attack was on. Morearty recalled, "In the mad rush of the infuriated mob I was thrown to the ground and barely escaped with my life."[28]

That, at least, is Morearty's version. As a city councilman unfriendly to some of Edward Rosewater's opinions, Morearty had the misfortune of being frequently vilified in the *Bee*, which reported:

> *Councilman Morearty grabbed hold of the bars over the window of the jailer's office and urged the mob on. Morearty started the ball rolling by thrusting his cane through the bars and breaking the windows. This act was met by applause and the councilman continued until every pane of glass in the two windows was shattered.*

Governor Boyd was still standing in front of the east door when the battering ram arrived. It was an eighteen-foot oak beam, carried by a group of men who charged toward the door like medieval soldiers storming a castle gate. At last, the powerless ex-governor stepped aside. In a moment, the collision of ram and door echoed off the surrounding buildings. The door held, but the men kept up the assault, ramming again and again. The crowd cheered each blow.

Notable by its absence was any coherent presence of law enforcement. A few police were mingling with the crowd, moving about, but neither supporting nor trying to prevent the assault on the jail. They were too few and had no leadership to make any difference. Where was Webb Seavey, the chief of police? And where did Sheriff Boyd disappear to?

It wasn't that Sheriff Boyd didn't want to come back. After he left (or was pushed away from) the east door, he tried circling around to the north door. But he found that he was expected.

Nine men surrounded him, their faces masked with handkerchiefs. Reaching for his revolver, Sheriff Boyd was in the act of drawing it from his pocket when his arms were pinned behind him. He was disarmed, picked up, and carried away.

"My God, boys, you have got me into a wretched fix," he told his captors, or at least reported himself as telling them. "You have put me in a compromising situation."

Sheriff Boyd spent the rest of the evening five blocks away, under guard behind the high school. Though he pleaded to be released, his captors refused. They were well organized, he said later, and had couriers to keep them informed of the progress of events.

Back at the jail, the battering ram crew continued their assault on the door. But try as they might, the door would not give. The crowd grew impatient. Even worse was the news from yet another man who pushed his way to the front:

"There's another door inside after you break in that," he shouted.

But they kept on.

Meanwhile, another group of men circled around the building and got the south door open. Their method? They knocked.

They were led by a "big burly red faced man." He pounded on the door, and it opened. It was that easy.

Then came the hard part: in the doorway stood Captain Cormack of the police department.

"What do you want?" Cormack asked angrily.

"We want in!" they yelled.

Immediately, Cormack's revolver was pointed in the big man's face.

"Get out of here," Cormack said. "If you make another move to get in this door I will kill you." The police captain had a reputation as "a man of nerve and a dead shot." The crowd responded accordingly. They backed down.

Back at the east door, a second gang of men brought another heavy timber, but the door got the better of them too. This was getting nowhere.

Then "Uncle Jimmy" Cannon, the old scout, spoke up again. Pointing at the jailor's office window with his cane, he said,

"Here is where you want to exert your force."

Of course. The window was barred, but not nearly as formidable as the heavy door. After a good deal of pounding, the upper window guard was bent, twisted, and finally forced out. The way inside was open.

"Go in there!" the crowd shouted. No one went. Not sure what to do, the men near the window began pounding on the lower window guard. Soon it too was out of the way, but again no one seemed eager to face the armed jailors and police inside.

Once again, Uncle Jimmy stepped forward. With the crowd cheering him, he climbed in the window.

Like the men who had faced Captain Cormack at the south door, Uncle Jimmy found himself staring down the barrel of a Colt's revolver—several revolvers, in fact. Jailor Lynch (the name is real) warned the old scout to stand back.

"Never mind him," said another man. "He won't shoot a gray head."

Warned again, however, Jimmy Cannon backed down, climbing out the window to the hisses of the crowd. Undaunted, the other men shoved a twenty-foot plank into the office; the jail's defenders were "prodded in the ribs" until they retreated to the corridor.

Were the heavily-armed defenders really forced out of the office by a wooden beam? Considering that their only defense was the use of deadly force—yes. For all their threats, they were unwilling to pull the trigger. As soon as the crowd began to understand this, the police, deputies, and jailors lost what little authority they still possessed.

The *Bee* later reported that a deputy sheriff had threatened to shoot the first man who entered, but forbore to shoot gray-haired Jimmy Cannon. As had happened to Sheriff Boyd, the deputy's bluff was called.

Again, Uncle Jimmy went inside, soon followed by a host of men. They stopped at the steel gate which led to the corridor. Through the bars the men could see their next opponents: Captain Cormack, fresh from his triumph at the south door, and three other officers.

"Stand back, gentlemen," Cormack said authoritatively. "You are violating the law and I must keep you out, even at the risk of your lives. I mean you be careful."

As the *World-Herald* phrased it, he "might as well have addressed himself to the wild waves." Crowbars and sledge hammers were called for, and soon the work began on the steel gate.

But where was Chief Seavey and the rest of the police?

Jailor Lynch stood behind the gate, trying to persuade the men that it was useless to try to break through the heavy steel bars. But he was talking to skilled machinists who knew better. They made short work of it; the door gave way.

Then Governor Boyd appeared in the office window, tried again to address the crowd.

"Beware of what you are about to do," he warned. No one was listening.

Inside, the men were spilling into the corridor, working their way ever deeper into the jail. By now, the police and jailors stood aside or followed along with the crowd. They watched, but did not interfere. The door which opened into the large lower-floor cell was broken next. Two black men were taken from their cells, but neither proved to be Smith.

"He is in Neal's cell!" other prisoners advised.

The crowd went upstairs, breaking yet another door and entering a large room, at one end of which stood a steel cage. In a back corner of the cage crouched a man wrapped up in a blanket. A howl of delight echoed through the jail and was quickly repeated outside.

A South Omaha man was perched on a post in the yard where he could see directly into the upstairs window near the cage. From here he relayed news and instructions to the crowd.

"He says he's a burglar," the man said of Smith. "The son of a bitch—he says he's a burglar!"

Loud hurrah from the crowd.

"They don't want no more help . . . Get cold chisels! They can't get into the cell without cold chisels!"

The cage itself was a marvel. Here is how the *Bee* described it:

> The solitary is known as the "Pauley Vault cell," and is constructed of bars two inches wide and one-half inch thick. The formation is in alternate layers of chilled [i.e., tempered] steel and wrought iron. The resistance is wonderful as the hardest cold chisel will have no effect upon the

steel, while the layers of iron makes it impossible
to break the bars by blows. The door is secured by
a heavy foot bar, held in place by a combination
Norwegian lock, while at the top and middle, bars
two inches in thickness shoot out over the door.
The lock is in a chilled steel box, doubly locked.[29]

The men tried battering the cage in with a rail, then called for cold chisels and more sledgehammers. A nearby street railway repair shop was raided, and the men inside the jail soon had all they could ask for—except the keys.

They set to work. Someone identified a weakness in the cage's design, and all effort was concentrated on that point. Inside, the clash of steel on steel was sharp and deafening; outside, the rhythmic clatter kept the crowd tense with anticipation. They were about 8,000 strong, ghostly in the bluish glare of the electric-arc streetlights, unchallenged in their authority, spilling out onto the streets, blocking the streetcars, talking, threatening, cheering, hissing, shouting . . . and waiting.

Part III: "You'll Need No Coat Where You're Going."

"The newspapers are all to blame," Police Chief Seavey said bitterly. He had finally arrived on the scene about 11 p.m. He talked with the captains and several other officers, but the police did nothing just yet. Even if every man on the force had been present, Seavey could have mustered fewer than a hundred men.[30] The mob had him outnumbered better than eighty to one, and was still growing.

A few officers near the jailor's office tried to take possession of a rope, but the crowd pulled it away from them. In moments, the rope disappeared into the crowd, ready to reappear when it was needed.

Another group of police tried to force their way inside the jail. Before they got close, however, the people realized what they were up to. The officers were picked up and carried back to the edge of the crowd.

Seavey managed to get near the building. Like the other officials before him, he tried ordering the crowd away, and like them, failed miserably. Standing on a ladder which led up to a window near the cage, Seavey tried to speak. Straining to be heard above the hissing of the crowd before him and the incessant hammering behind him, he called on the crowd to desist, telling them that "the little girl whom this man assaulted is not dead as reported, but was running about her home today."

This reminder of the crime, along with the presumption of guilt which was embedded in Seavey's words, only served to further enrage the crowd. Some went for the ladder on which he was so precariously perched. At the same time, the window above and behind him shattered, showering him with broken glass. Seavey hesitated a moment, then got down. Soon, he was seen gathering the entire day police force near the north door of the jail. Like the mob, the police would have to wait for Smith to appear.

The cage was resilient. As the crowd became impatient, rumors began circulating.

"The soldiers from the fort are coming," people cried out. "Hurry up! We want that damned nigger at once!" Certainly the fort (Fort Omaha, just north of town) was close enough for the soldiers to march in. But would the fort commander commit his troops to a civilian affair? They would have to wait and see.

Suddenly, a new sound was added to the din, the sound of rapid hoofbeats and of heavy wheels rolling over rough pavement. A new player was entering the field. Soldiers? No, it was the fire department. Chief Seavey and Mayor Cushing would later disagree as to whose idea it had been, but either way, they came, rolling in from all directions. If calm words couldn't cool off the crowd on this brisk October night, maybe jets of cold water could.

Working fast, the firemen unrolled hoses and connected to a hydrant at Eighteenth and Harney. Drivers whipped up the horses for the run toward the jail.

"Cut the hose!" someone in the crowd shouted.

The people charged, wielding axes, sharp pieces of iron, chunks of pavement—anything with an edge. When the water was turned on, twenty fountains spouted from the ruined hose that ran along Harney Street.

"Don't leave the hose here! Carry it away!" came the cry. Immediately, the crowd began gathering up fire hose and running off with it.

The firemen left, but soon returned. This time they brought with them all the rubber piping they could find. But again the crowd charged, and again the firemen were driven back. When they departed a second time—by then many were hatless, coatless, and bruised—they had no intention of returning for a third round.

The updates from the man on the pole continued:
"The door is giving way! . . . The nigger is praying! . . . The outside door is open! . . . They have cut a four inch bar in the second door!"

Then the hammering stopped and an eruption of shouting echoed from within the jail.

"We've got him! We've got him!"

"Bring him out! Bring him out!" the crowd responded.

Inside the cage, Smith was calling for help which he knew would not come. "Help! Police!" he cried out. A few police were nearby, but did nothing. A noose was placed about Smith's neck.

In one of those irrationalities which sometimes occur under great stress, Smith asked to take his coat with him.

"Never mind," he was told. "You'll need no coat where you're going."

"Then I want my gum," he said. Opening one of Ed Neal's Bibles, he took out a piece of chewing gum.[31]

George Smith was alone in the crowded cell. With him he had no family, no friends, no legal representation. When he was dragged out of the cage, he took nothing with him but the clothes on his back and a piece of chewing gum.

He was dragged down the stairs, through the corridor and into the jailor's office. Outside the window stood 10,000 people waiting to kill him. Inside, a sheriff's deputy began arguing that this man was not Smith. Judge Doane, who had managed to work his way inside, pleaded for Smith's life.

With death waiting through the open window, some of the men began to think that maybe it was best to go slow.

"Perhaps he is the wrong man," a *World-Herald* reporter said, or quoted himself as saying, "Let us send for the father and have him identify the negro."

After some argument this was agreed to. The reporter appeared in the window with a police sergeant and told the crowd what they were going to do. Some approved; others just wanted to "hang him now."

An hour's delay followed while the reporter and the police sergeant went to fetch Mr. Yeates. It was probably after midnight when, for the second time, Yeates stood face-to-face with George Smith.

He immediately recognized Smith, and admitted as much to Smith's captors. But there was no joy in it. He knew what was to follow.

"Men, I am not sure," he said. "My little girl is alive and doing well. Let the law take its course and I will be satisfied."

Smith was led to the window.

Just before he was taken outside, someone asked Smith if he had any message for his mother.

"Is she here?" he asked. He was told she wasn't. In fact, she lived less than three blocks away. If she wasn't out there, somewhere, among that vast crowd, then she was near enough to hear what was happening, and to know what it meant.

"Then I don't want to see her," Smith said.[32]

Outside, the ground was black with people. From Sixteenth to Eighteenth, Harney Street was filled with a howling mob. A row of electric streetcars sat motionless, unable to proceed through the throng. Crowd estimates ranged from 8,000 to 15,000, 10,000 being the figure most widely accepted. Many women stood at the outskirts of the mob, where the tight jam of humanity was less intense. Mayor Cushing, merely a spectator by now, waited near a stone wall at the edge of the courthouse grounds. Across the street from the mayor, a small group of prominent men waited in equal helplessness—Governor Boyd, Councilman Ed Morearty, and *World-Herald* publisher Gilbert Hitchcock among them. Morearty said he came upon the others "deploring the sad condition of things." Whether anyone questioned Hitchcock's right to deplore a situation that was at least partly of his own making, Morearty does not say.[33]

On the north side of the jail, between the jail and courthouse, the people were "packed in like sardines in a box." There, near the north door, Chief Seavey and the bulk of the Omaha Police Department waited to make their move.

It was time. At 12:25 a.m., near the office window, men began shouting "Fall back! Fall back!" as they prepared to bring Smith out. As the crowd screamed with excitement and surged backwards and forwards, a desperate struggle ensued. Smith began to fight, and the men around him struggled to shove him out the window. At the same time, a squad of police charged in to rescue Smith. Not wanting to risk a bloodbath, the police did not draw either their revolvers or their clubs, and as such, were overpowered. One group of men held them back while another choked Smith into submission and shoved him through the narrow window.

The rope was held by a hundred pairs of hands. From the jail to the street was a driveway about fifty yards long, paved with "rough granite." Along this surface Smith was dragged through the crowd toward the street.[34] "The mob rushed upon him," the *Bee* reported, "Kicking and jumping upon him as he was jerked down over the rough pavement, his clothing almost entirely torn from his body, and the skin and flesh bruised and bleeding in a shocking manner.

"It is about seventy yards from the jail window to the corner of the court house square. This run of death was made in less time than it takes to tell it."

Then some sort of delay occurred. The *World-Herald*, contradicting the *Bee,* says that a rope could not be found. The *Bee* says that men climbing a telegraph pole could find no suitable projectile over which to throw the rope. This pause in the action, according to the *World-Herald*, allowed Smith to speak,

"Am I guilty? Am I guilty?" he cried. "No, I am not! I am the man that was arrested but I am innocent! I am innocent!"

Just then a hack was driven through the crowd, stopping near the corner of the street. Suddenly, the police charged in and grabbed Smith, carrying him as they fought their way toward the hack. "The struggle," said the *Bee*, "was one of giants." No sooner did the police get Smith into the hack than the horses were unhitched and the police overpowered. Again, Smith was dragged away.

"You are killing me!" he is reported as saying.

Again, the police made a rush for Smith; again they stuffed the broken and bleeding man into a hack. In a moment, the carriage was overturned. The crowd smashed it to pieces.

In the confusion, Smith was lost; some even thought he had escaped. In fact, he was difficult to see because he was on the ground, being dragged by his neck along the street. Naked except for his shoes and part of a shirt, chunks of his shins had been torn away; his body was bruised and bleeding from the kicking and stomping he endured as he passed through the crowd.

Finally, he was dragged no further. At the northeast corner of seventeenth and Harney, Smith's captors stopped and bound his arms behind him. "Quivering with excitement," a man shinnied up a pole and threw one end of the rope over the electric streetcar wire.

"It won't hold him!" some shouted.

"Don't make a botch of it!"

The crowd's concern was unnecessary. The wire did not break as the rope grew taut, and it held as Smith's battered, naked body was raised.

> *Then, in the bluish glare of the electric arc lights, a head, a pair of shoulders, and then a body, rose out of the dense throng. It was steadily raised till it was over the heads of the people, and then it began to swing a little, and turn like a dangling scarecrow.*

But it didn't matter whether or not the wire held. The hanging was superfluous. George Smith was already dead.

A coroner's report would show that Smith's neck had been broken in three places, an injury unexplainable by the slow hanging from the electric wire. The real hanging had taken place on the ground, where Smith was dragged against the resistance of the thousands who stomped him and trampled upon him. His death, therefore, was even in its most technical sense not the act of one executioner, but of a multitude.

It was 12:35 a.m., and the crowd could hardly believe that the limp figure hanging before them was real.

"That is a dummy!" some shouted, and men moved in for a closer look. The pressure of body on body was almost unbearable for those near the center, and some grew faint. But at last the crowd became convinced that it was indeed George Smith who hung before them. "Then such a yell!" the *Bee* reported. "It sounded like the chorus that arises from the camp of a band of Indians engaged in a war dance."

Soon only about a thousand people remained, blocking the streets near the dangling corpse. Across the street, a well-dressed man was climbing into a fine carriage. Suddenly, the crowd recognized him and shouted. *Governor Boyd! Speech! Speech!* They wouldn't listen to him earlier; now they wanted him to speak, perhaps somehow to sanctify the event. Governor Boyd ignored them. His carriage drove right past the crowd. In a few moments it disappeared around the corner.

Part IV: Murder in the First Degree

In the morning, George Smith's body was put on display at Heafey and Heafey's undertaking parlor. The corpse of Ed Neal, enormously popular a day earlier, was put aside in a closed casket. Smith lay covered with a tarpaulin on a "cooling board," his head exposed, the rope still about his neck.

At 8 a.m., the doors opened to a rush of visitors. Police were on hand to keep them in line. For two hours they came, men, women, and children—6,000 in all—filing by to gaze on the swollen face of George Smith, just as many of them had gazed on Ed Neal the day before. Some cut off pieces of the rope for souvenirs.

Back at the jail, Sheriff Boyd inspected the damage which the building had suffered in his absence. The jail's appearance, said the *Bee*, "gave one the idea that the building had been besieged and captured by a war like enemy." Outside, the battering rams lay where they had been dropped. Chisels, crowbars, and sledgehammers littered the grounds, where even now curious crowds were browsing. Some people even cut pieces of wood from the telegraph pole from which Smith had been hanged.[35]

Inside, the floor in the jailor's office was covered with broken glass. The iron bars of the windows were twisted and broken. Telephone wires were cut; desks and chairs were in ruins; the gate to the corridor was wrenched off its hinges. About the only thing untouched was a small steel box on the wall. It was where the jailors locked the keys.

The trail of destruction led upstairs, where morning sunlight looked in through iron bars and broken windows upon the battered solitary cell. About the cell lay "enough tools to supply a railroad repair shop" (indeed: they had come from there). The cage's broken doors—with their smashed locks and twisted crossbeams—stood open, revealing a cell floor littered with books, papers, little ornaments, and flowers—gifts given to Ed Neal during his final days.

Mayor Cushing was calling it "the most deplorable thing that had ever occurred in the history of the county." He was also trying to make it clear that he wasn't to blame for it. And so the finger pointing began.

"I heard rumors that the negro would be lynched at 10 o'clock in the forenoon," he said. "And predicted from what I heard, that he would be. I went to Chief Seavey and apprised him of my fear; and advised him to make out the necessary papers and take Smith to the county jail. Smith was accordingly taken to the jail late in the afternoon. I also told the chief in the morning to be prepared for a mob."[36]

The local press tried to get Seavey's side of the story shortly after Smith was dead.

"I have not a word to say about it to a newspaper man tonight," he replied bitterly.

The next day, Seavey insisted that he'd had no idea that there would be a lynching until getting a phone call at 10 *p.m.* He tried calling Sheriff Boyd, but getting no response (the jail's phone lines had been cut), he went to the jail, arriving to find the mob already inside. Upon arriving at the jail, Seavey said he asked the mayor to call the fire department.

In Cushing's version, Cushing called Seavey at home after calling the fire department himself. Cushing claimed to have ordered out the entire police force, cautioning them not to fire on the crowd. Either way, Seavey did not realize the seriousness of the situation until 10 p.m., when it was too late for anything but a desperate rescue attempt.

Strangely, the story has a few personal twists for the chief of police. First, the Yeates's were his neighbors, living just half a block down the street from him.[37] For Seavey, the crime against Lizzie Yeates struck (literally) close to home. Could this have influenced his behavior?

Second, Seavey had reason to be angry with Sheriff Boyd. Being in charge of Neal's hanging, Boyd was also in the charge of the 250-odd tickets for the show. He could give them to whomever he chose, and he did not choose to give one to the chief of police. The newspapers speculated that Seavey, feeling snubbed, may not have been eager to rush to the sheriff's aid.

Mayor Cushing did not merely rely on Seavey to absorb the blame. He also maintained that whole thing was not the city's problem, but the county's.

"We turned the fellow [Smith] over to the county authorities," he said, "for the reason that the county authorities are stronger than the city authorities." In other words, Smith was "out of the city's hands at 5:00 o'clock in the afternoon, and we have nothing to do in the matter." Because of this, Cushing saw no need for the city to even investigate the matter.

He took the idea still further, adding that he didn't believe that the police had any authority over the jail/courthouse square. "I think the sheriff is a little king there," he said, explaining that while the sheriff may still call for police assistance, Sheriff Boyd did not do so.

This was complete nonsense—the city attorney said as much—but Mayor Cushing appeared to take comfort in it. According to Ed Morearty, Cushing had confessed to him months earlier that he didn't even want to be mayor any more.

What with the demands on his time and the resulting neglect of his business interests, the lousy job was costing him money.[38]

Was Mayor Cushing, Police Chief Seavey, or Sheriff Boyd more to blame? Or could any of them have done more to stop the mob? Sheriff Boyd didn't think so. "A regiment of United States troops couldn't have held that mob back," he said. "It was made up of cool, determined men, who knew just what they wanted and proposed to get it." County Attorney Mahoney, however, while not blaming the police officers and sheriff's deputies, suggested that if a squad of police had been dispatched early— when the crowd first began to gather—the trouble could have been averted. A local judge went further. The incident, he said, "demonstrates that Omaha has a chief of police who does not care whether order is preserved in the city."

Across the river, the Council Bluffs *Nonpareil* was harsher still. "There can be no question," the editors wrote, that:

> *the terrible deed of Friday night was owing to the indifference of the officials to a danger of which the prominent citizens of Omaha were warned months ago . . . If cut-throats on one side—such as Neal,—and lynchers on the other, are to rule Omaha, whenever it pleases their sweet will, better sow its site with salt, and avoid it as a modern Sodom and Gomorrah.*[39]

For the most part, the criticism was not echoed in the streets of Omaha. "I could take every man of the mob by the hand and say God bless you," the *World-Herald* quoted an Omaha woman as saying,

> *I have a little daughter. As long as twenty years' imprisonment is the only penalty for such a crime as Smith's I cannot feel that she is safe. The life of the villain is a forfeit too small for the crime. Had it been my daughter, my husband would have killed the villain on sight, else I should have despised him as a coward.*

Such was the reaction of most Omahans. A *World-Herald* editorial, probably written by the author of the anti-death penalty "A Legalized Murder," lamented "a hanging at noon, a lynching at midnight and a self-satisfied community next day." Indeed, the *World-Herald*'s pages reflected the tension between the minority who opposed the lynching and the overwhelming majority who supported it. "The overhead wire has its uses," one editor wrote wryly, while in the same column appeared a joke overheard from a poker table: "The crowd saw Smith and raised him." Mostly, outrage was saved for those who talked of prosecuting the lynchers: "The county authorities seem disposed to go through the motions of investigating the lynching. It will prove a costly and fruitless experiment."

Not all county authorities were so disposed. One county commisioner said publicly that he thought the incident "will have a good effect on the courts as well as the criminals."

Around Omaha, even many who disapproved of the lynching felt that justice had been done. "The whole affair is a disgrace to the city of Omaha," said a local doctor, "but the negro got his just deserts."

Others praised the lynching, but with qualifications, "If the boy was really guilty," said one man, "then hanging him was too mild a punishment. He had committed a most dastardly crime." Another said, "If there was no doubt of his guilt, I think he should have been hanged."

A few condemned the incident outright. Judge Estelle argued passionately against both the illegal lynching of Smith and the legal hanging of Neal:

> *Human appetite for blood is harder to appease than ravenous wolves. The lynching of Smith is the direct result of the legal execution of Neal. That execution brutalized the people and aroused the fierce passions of men. It is an argument against capital punishment which cannot be answered. Mobs encourage a disrespect of the law, hence mobs should not be encouraged.*

But another mob was already in the making.

Word on the street was that the lynching of Smith had been such a success that a repeat performance was in order. Two other black men were being held at the county jail: Jake Price, awaiting trial for the murder of Mrs. Fannie Tate, and Clinton Dixon, an army private accused of murdering a corporal. These two were to go the way of George Smith. The white prisoners could be left to the courts.

Meanwhile, County Attorney Mahoney had to decide what, if anything, to do about the Smith lynching. The mayor wanted to drop the matter, but Mahoney was not accountable to the mayor. The public stood behind the lynching, but Mahoney had little use for public sentiment. Calling the lynching "a cowardly, cold-blooded murder," he argued that both the city and county were "compelled to take hold of the matter and ferret out the perpetrators."

That is precisely what he did. Learning that fifteen of the mob's ringleaders had been identified by police, Mahoney issued warrants for their arrest. By 5 p.m. Saturday, seven of the fifteen stood before the police court for their arraignment. One can imagine their disbelief when the charge was read: *Murder in the first degree*. Mahoney was going for it all, and he would be ready to try the cases sometime Monday.

The defense attorney tried to get the men released on bail, but Mahoney refused. For one of the prisoners, an offer of $100,000 bail was made. Mahoney didn't budge. By 5:30, the seven prisoners were loaded into a patrol wagon and taken to the county jail. Within half an hour, two more lynchers were arrested and received similar treatment.

To reporters, Mahoney pointed out that under Nebraska law, *anyone* who took part in a lynching was guilty of first degree murder, a crime—incidentally—which was punishable by hanging. "It is disgraceful," Mahoney fumed. "There is no positive assurance that the mob dealt with the guilty party. There was no positive identification."

No positive identification? Mahoney was directly contradicting the newspapers, which even before the lynching had clearly stated that Smith had been identified by his victim. We will look into the evidence—such as it is still available—shortly. For the time being, we cannot pause long enough to consider evidence. The people of Omaha certainly didn't.

To many Omahans, the idea of these otherwise law-abiding men sitting behind bars like common criminals—and charged with a capital crime—was outrageous and intolerable. The planned second attack on the county jail now had two motives: death for the black prisoners and freedom for the lynchers of George Smith.

By 8:45 p.m., a crowd of nearly 4,000 had assembled outside the battered jail. Soon, Jailor Horrigan came out to talk to the crowd. He told them that Price and Dixon had been taken to Lincoln and that the nine lynchers had all been released on bond. Of course no one believed him.

Chief Seavey was still at police headquarters at 9 p.m. when the phone rang. It was Chris Hartman, a police officer. Another mob had gathered near the jail, he said, and if Seavey intended to do anything about it, he had better act quickly. Immediately, Seavey dispatched a platoon of twenty-two police officers to Seventeenth and Harney. Lining up across Harney, the officers faced west and marched toward a crowd of nearly 4,000. They were greeted with howls and jeers.

Hartman got back on the phone with Seavey. It wasn't working, he said. Soon, Seavey himself arrived with a patrol wagon and twenty more police. Standing on the wagon, the police chief tried to make a speech, but the crowd drowned him out with hoots and hisses.

They had gotten the better of him last night, but now Seavey was not ready to back down. He gave the order to clear the streets.

Over at the jail's front door, the crowd was calling for the "nigger." Jake Price, charged with murdering a woman, was the man they really wanted; Clinton Dixon was secondary. A man named Donnelly tried to reason with the crowd. To a cry of "Hang the nigger!," Donnelly replied,

"Yes, you hanged a colored man last night, but are you sure he was guilty? Now you would hang Jake Price and every one of you know that there are grave doubts about him being the man who murdered Fannie Tate."

This would have gotten nowhere had it not been for Jailor Horrigan's offer to the crowd. They didn't believe him when he said that neither Price nor Dixon nor the nine lynchers were there? They could put it to a test. Horrigan suggested that the crowd appoint a committee of five or ten men. He promised to show them every cell, and had only one condition:

"I know that many of you men are drunk," Horrigan said, "and right here I want to tell you that no drunken man can come inside this jail tonight."

This sounded like a good deal—to the sober men, anyway. But this was just the sort of offer that Sheriff Boyd had refused the night before. What was Horrigan doing?

He was telling the truth. That afternoon, Sheriff Boyd had arranged for Price and Dixon to be removed from the jail and sent to the state penitentiary in Lincoln. Reportedly, they were taken to the Union Pacific Depot disguised in women's clothing and put aboard before the crowd realized what was going on.

The lynchers were gone too. About an hour after Mahoney's refusal of bail, a judge had intervened and issued bail bonds. Even as the crowd gathered to demand their release, they were already at home and unaware of the standoff.

Out in the street, the police began marching up and down Harney, clubs drawn, encouraging the people to go home.

"Move on, ye's! What're ye here for? Move on, I say!"

The crowd offered little direct resistance. They moved, but kept coming back as soon as the police passed by.

Meanwhile, the jail committee returned from their tour of the cells, satisfied that Jailor Horrigan had been telling the truth. Even so, the crowd did not disperse immediately. Slowly, with the full police force on hand, Seavey began to get control of the situation. By 11 p.m. the streets were quiet and deserted.

The next morning's *Bee* proclaimed the "COLLAPSE OF A MOB" and credited "prompt action by the police" for the successful dispersal of the crowd. But did anyone really think that the crowd would have been so compliant had Horrigan refused the committee, as he surely would have done had any of the sought-after men been inside? Regarding the planned lynching, probably the only thing that prevented it was the absence of any black prisoners.

County Attorney Mahoney never did get any convictions from the George Smith lynching. From the beginning, he had to have known that it would be so. No jury would convict a lyncher because they believed that Smith—however ugly the lynching had been—had gotten what he deserved for his crime.[40]

But was he the right man?

To most Omahans in 1891, that would have seemed a silly question. The evidence was overwhelming. Consider this report from the *World-Herald*, which appeared the morning after the lynching:

> *George Smith was fully identified yesterday by the child, Lizzie Yeates, and her grandmother. The police found the suit of clothes which Smith had worn on the evening of the assault, hidden in a trunk in the shanty on Nicholas street where they had arrested him. They dressed him in these clothes and the victim and her grandmother identified the clothes.*[41]

How could there be any doubt?

Comparing the *World-Herald* with that morning's *Bee*, however, a careful reader would notice important contradictions. A *Bee* reporter visited the Yeates' home Friday evening, shortly after the police brought Smith there, and just hours before the lynching. The reporter was told, as we have already learned, that Lizzie did *not* identify Smith, that the grandmother was *not* "willing to swear positively" as to Smith's identity, and that Smith was *not* dressed in the blue checkered suit, but in a different suit of clothes from what the assailant had worn. Nor was the *World-Herald's* Saturday morning report of Smith's arrest at his home consistent with earlier reports by both the *World-Herald* and the *Bee*.

It isn't clear where the *World-Herald* got its information, but it seems highly unlikely that the *Bee* reporter, after visiting the family when he did, could have been mistaken about such crucial details.

But there was still more evidence against Smith. In an article titled, "IT WAS HIS FIFTH," the *World-Herald* provided more details about the "Cut-Off" case involving little Dottie Gunn. The article reported that at Smith's hearing in Council Bluffs, Dottie's mother said "that she personally knew of three other cases at that time in which Smith had committed similar assaults on young girls, but in every case the parties who should have made the complaint were afraid to make a complaint, for fear that Smith or his friends would seek revenge." The article added that "Previously, other colored people say, Smith stood charged with a like criminal assault upon his step-sister and an unknown girl at the High school grounds."

Whether or not any of the above is true is a mystery. Considering the rest of the *World-Herald*'s reporting on the case, one has to be a little skeptical.

In September, the Council Bluffs grand jury failed to indict Smith for the Dottie Gunn assault. The *World-Herald* explained that the grand jury decided that "the assault, if committed at all, was on the Nebraska side of the boundary line. The testimony in the preliminary hearing was quite conclusive as to the young brute's guilt and it was a cause of considerable feeling in the Bluffs that he escaped so easily."[42]

Several questions arise. First, why would Council Bluffs citizens decide that the valuable Cut-Off property belonged to Nebraska, even as their state government fought to keep it in Iowa? Why would a white grand jury fail to indict a black man on such a serious charge if there was "quite conclusive" evidence suggesting his guilt? Why was Smith released, rather than being handed over to the Nebraska authorities; or, if the law required his release, why was he not quickly arrested in Omaha and brought before a Nebraska grand jury? And finally, why was the Council Bluffs decision so uncontroversial? Never mind what the *World-Herald* said later about "considerable feeling in the Bluffs"; the truth is that the Council Bluffs papers said nothing about Smith's release. It is hard to believe that the

Dottie Gunn case would have been handled this way if the charge had had any merit.

This brings us back to the Lizzie Yeates case. After the assault, the police had only a vague description of a black man to go on, yet they made an arrest within twenty-four hours. How? It seems almost certain that George Smith's recent arrest and transport to Council Bluffs on a similar charge would have made him a prime suspect. Even if neither charge against Smith had merit, each reinforced the other in the public mind. And Smith's panicked behavior—hiding, then giving an alias to the police—only made him look more guilty.

The strongest evidence in favor of Smith's innocence comes to us second hand from Ed Morearty, the city councilman who inadvertently started the assault upon the jail. In his 1917 memoir, Morearty said that "had the evidence been adduced it would have disclosed the fact that he was not guilty of the crime, which could and would have been proven had he had his preliminary hearing."[43]

We don't know upon what evidence Morearty based his judgment. We only know that as a lawyer and a member of the city council, he was in a position to know what he was talking about.

The best we can say of the mob who killed George Smith is that they really thought he was guilty when they killed him. They were incited by unprofessional and misleading journalism, were encouraged by city officials who publicly presumed Smith's guilt, were defended by a national culture which held that a minority of the people were not entitled to the legal protections which the majority took for granted.

They did not know for sure that they had the right man, but they killed him anyway. They killed him blow by blow as they trampled him, pull by pull on the rope as they dragged him; it was not one person's will, but the sum of their wills that ended his life. Mahoney charged fifteen men with murder; given enough names he could have charged ten thousand.

Or—in a moral sense—even more. Mahoney's failure to convict the lynchers showed not a lack of skill or of evidence on his part, but a lack of will on the public's part. Ida B. Wells, in her famous 1892 pamphlet, *Southern Horrors*, argued that:

> *The men and women . . . who disapprove of lynching and remain silent on the perpetration of such outrages, are particeps criminis, accomplices, accessories before and after the fact, equally guilty with the actual law-breakers who would not persist if they did not know that neither the law nor militia would be employed against them.*[44]

Such was indeed the case in Omaha in 1891. No lynchers were ever punished, and the Lizzie Yeates case was closed, the public being satisfied that justice had been done. But if Ed Morearty was right, then the real rapist was never captured, but went on, perhaps, to other homes, other towns, other little girls—free—because the people of Omaha, so jealous of their daughters' safety that they would commit murder, never looked for him.

Part V: Epilogue

"The city will suffer from the disgrace for years to come," County Attorney Mahoney had warned.[45]

He was wrong.

Omaha's lynching received relatively little national press, and was quickly forgotten. As an event, the lynching of George Smith wasn't remarkable enough or rare enough to merit the prolonged attention of an indifferent public. Why, for instance, focus on George Smith, accused of rape and lynched at Omaha, Nebraska, and not Edward Peyton, accused of strike rioting and lynched at Marianna, Arkansas? Or Ben Patterson, accused of strike rioting and lynched at Hackette, Arkansas? Or Sam Wright, accused of rape and lynched at Helena, Alabama? Or John Russ, accused of murder and lynched at Columbia, Louisiana? Or Leo Green, accused of murder and lynched at Linden, Texas? Or a man named Snowden, accused of arson and lynched at Monroe, Louisiana? Or John Brown, lynched for testifying against whites at Childersburg, Alabama? Or Jack Park, accused of murder and lynched at Abitz Springs, Louisiana? Or James Scott, accused of rioting and lynched at Clifton Forge, Virginia? Or an unknown negro, lynched at Poole's Landing,

Louisiana, for reasons unknown? How do you pay attention to each of these eleven men—ten black and one white—who died at the hands of lynch mobs in October 1891? And then what do you do with November's list?

Perhaps you ignore them all.

The twelve names are taken from a book published by the NAACP in 1919, *Thirty Years of Lynching in the United States, 1889-1918*. The list of lynching victims, which includes only those cases which could be reliably documented, includes 194 entries for the year 1891, and 3,224 for the three decades covered by the study. In such a list, the only thing mildly remarkable about George Smith's lynching is that it occurred in a relatively large, Northern city.[46]

"It is not worth while to try to keep history from repeating itself," Mark Twain said, "for man's character will always make the preventing of the repetitions impossible."[47] On September 28, 1919, during the turbulent year following the end of World War I, a black man named Will Brown was lynched outside the Douglas County Courthouse. Accused—falsely, it turned out—of raping a young white woman, Brown was dragged from the courthouse, beaten, shot, hanged, cut down, dragged away, and burned on a bonfire at Seventeenth and Dodge. Surrounded by a crowd of 25,000, the new courthouse (which still stands today) suffered a million dollars' worth of damage.

As Brown was being taken outside, one man waded into the crowd to try to save him. That was Mayor Ed Smith. But the crowd turned on the mayor, threw a noose about his neck, and hanged him. Rescued by police, who cut him down and rushed him to a hospital, Mayor Smith survived—but barely.

With the courthouse a fire-charred shambles and the mayor in the hospital, little boys dragged Will Brown's charred remains through Omaha's streets till the early hours of the morning. Martial law was declared the next day, and federal troops arrived to set up machine gun nests on downtown street corners.[48]

And the usual suspects were blamed, the "Reds," the "Soviets," the International Workers of the World labor union. And people were shocked and the governor proclaimed that he "could hardly have believed that anywhere in Nebraska mob violence would have been exerted to the extent of perpetrating a public lynching . . . ."[49] And the newspapers recalled in brief articles the lynching twenty-eight years earlier of "Joe Coe" (*Bee*) or "James Smith" (*Omaha Daily News*).[50] An aging Ed Morearty again protested his innocence in the window-breaking incident and saw to it that the *Bee* published his version of the story—the excerpt from his memoirs in which he proclaims Smith's innocence.[51]

One wonders, considering the fate of Will Brown, what change had twenty-eight years wrought? What wisdom did Omaha possess in 1919 as a result of the lynching of George Smith in 1891? If his death could somehow be seen as sacrificial, what benefit had the city gained from it? In short, what had Omaha learned?

Precisely nothing.

Chapter 20 notes

1Ida B. Wells, *Southern Horrors: Lynch Law in All Its Phases* (1892; reprinted in Ida B. Wells-Barnett, *On Lynchings: Southern Horrors, A Red Record, Mob Rule in New Orleans*, New York: Arno Press, 1969), 14.

2*Omaha Morning World-Herald*, October 8, 1891.

3Ed F. Morearty, *Omaha Memories: Recollections of Events, Men and Affairs in Omaha, Nebraska, from 1879 to 1917*, Omaha: Swartz Printing Co., 1917, 42.

4Lawrence H. Larsen and Barbara J. Cottrell, *The Gate City: A History of Omaha*, Pruett Publishing Co., 1982, 82, 122; Morearty, 50.

5Rudyard Kipling, "Omaha Between Trains," in *Roundup: A Nebraska Reader*, edited by Virginia Faulkner, Lincoln: University of Nebraska Press, 1957, 168.

6Morearty, 44.

7*Morning World-Herald*, October 8, 1891.

8*Morning World-Herald*, May 4, 1892.

9*Morning World-Herald*, May 9, 1892.

10Wells, 7-12.

11*Bee* (evening), October 8, 1891.

12*Morning World-Herald*, October 9, 1891.

13James W. Savage and John T. Bell, *History of the City of Omaha Nebraska*, New York: Munsell & Co., 1894, 137-138.

14*Bee* (morning), October 9, 1891.

15*Bee* (morning), October 10, 1891; *Morning World-Herald*, October 10, 1891.

16*Bee* (morning), October 10, 1891; *Morning World-Herald*, October 10, 1891.

17*Bee* (evening), October 9, 1891.

18*Bee* (morning), October 11, 1891.

19*Bee* (morning), October 10, 1891.

20*Bee* (morning), October 10, 1891; *Morning World-Herald*, October 10, 1891.

21*Council Bluffs Globe*, October 9, 1891.

22Federal Writers' Project, *Omaha: A Guide to the City and Its Environs* (Works Progress Administration, 1939), 141-142; Richard Orr, *O & CB: Streetcars of Omaha and Council Bluffs,* Omaha: Richard Orr, 1996, 22-23.

23*Morning World-Herald*, October 11, 1891.

24*Sunday World-Herald*, March 15, 1891; *Bee* (evening),, March 16, 1891.

25*Morning World-Herald*, October 10, 1891; *Bee* (morning), October 10, 1891.

26Except where noted, Parts II and III are drawn from the *Morning World-Herald*, October 10, 1891; and the *Bee* (morning), October 10, 1891.

27James C. Olson and Ronald C. Naugle, *History of Nebraska*, 3rd Ed. (Lincoln: University of Nebraska Press, 1997), 231-232.

28Morearty, 45.

29*Bee* (morning), October 11, 1891.

30*Orff's Tri-City Business Directory, 1890-91*, (n.p.), 92.

31*Globe*, October 10, 1891.

32*Globe*, October 10, 1891.

[33]Morearty, 46.

[34] *Council Bluffs Nonpareil*, October 10, 1891.

[35]Except where noted, Part IV is drawn from the *Bee* (morning), October 11, 1891; and the *Morning World-Herald*, October 11, 1891.

[36] *Morning World-Herald*, October 10, 1891.

[37] *Omaha City Directory 1891*, (n.p.), 791.

[38]Morearty, 45.

[39] *Nonpareil*, October 11, 1891.

[40]Savage and Bell, 138-139.

[41] *Morning World-Herald*, October 10, 1891.

[42] *Morning World-Herald*, October 10, 1891.

[43]Morearty, 46.

[44]Wells, 21.

[45] *Morning World-Herald*, October 11, 1891.

[46]National Association for the Advancement of Colored People, *Thirty Years of Lynching in the United States, 1889-1918*, 1919; reprint, New York: Arno Press and New York Times, 1969.

[47] *The Quotable Mark Twain: His Essential Aphorisms, Witticisms and Concise Opinions*, ed. R. Kent Rasmussen, Chicago: Contemporary Books, 1997, 127.

[48] *Bee* (morning), September 29, 1919; *Evening World-Herald*, September 29, 1919.

[49] *Bee* (morning), October 1, 1919.

[50] *Bee* (morning), October 5, 1919; *Omaha Daily News*, September 29, 1919.

[51] *Bee* (morning), October 6, 1919.

Chapter Twenty-One

CHARLIE THE HOBO

October 1897

Three years was just too long. Standing outside the Army recruiting office at Seventeenth and Farnam, Charlie made his decision—again. He had stood here before, reading over and over the pay and conditions the Army offered, always reaching the same conclusion. One year would be all right, even two—but three? It was too much, too long a commitment. Yet he kept coming back, reconsidering. It had been the same in Denver and Kansas City.

Charlie was nineteen years old and bound by no commitments of any kind. He was lean and wiry, about 140 pounds, and traveled light. The son of Swedish immigrants, he had straight brown hair hanging over his forehead, a boyish face with high, sharp cheekbones, and hazel eyes that seemed to change color with the changing light. At present, he lived and worked at the Mercer Hotel, on the northwest corner of Twelfth and Howard. Washing dishes brought him $1.50 a week—or would, when he got paid. He'd been in town for two weeks and hadn't yet seen a cent of his wages.

But the beauty of the arrangement was that he could leave it at any time. He was nineteen. He didn't know what he wanted out of life. He had a vague sense of ambition and restlessness, but had no direction. He was a hobo, a "gaycat," riding the

Durham Western Heritage Museum
Howard Street, circa 1900, looking west from Tenth.
Today the area is known as the "Old Market."

rails from town to town, finding work when there was work to be found, moving on when there was none, moving on whenever he got restless.

Back home in Illinois he had thought of suicide, but had found the desire to live too strong. He still had his "bitter and lonely hours," but so, he now knew, did everyone else. "There was such a thing as luck in life," he said later, "but if the luck didn't come your way it was up to you to step into [the] struggle and like it."

For Charlie, the struggle—with identity and adulthood, with ambition and direction, with the reality of economic hard times—had led him to the open road. He was one of tens of thousands of men riding the rails in those days. In Omaha, which lay along one of the main hobo routes to the West, he was as he had been in the other cities he'd visited: another anonymous young stranger, lately arrived and soon to depart. With cold weather coming, he was drifting homeward, toward Illinois. The greater part of his adventure was behind him.

He had worked as a harvest hand in the Kansas wheat fields,

been floored by a brakeman's fist in an open coal car on the plains, seen the Rocky Mountains in Colorado, fallen asleep during a late-night ride standing on the "bumpers" between railroad cars—and woke up in time to realize "what a stupid reckless fool I was." He had lived and talked with bums, misfits, dreamers, criminals. An introvert by nature—intelligent and brooding—he had listened to and had told many stories in the "hobo jungles" along the tracks. He had learned that "You can be loose and easy when from day to day you meet strangers you will know only an hour or a day or two."

He rode into Nebraska atop a Pullman car, climbed down at McCook, and promptly climbed back up again when a one-eyed policeman told him, "We don't want the likes of you in this town." In Nebraska City one chilly night, he and four other hoboes tried to sleep in a boxcar, but finally gave up and marched to the jail where they asked the marshall to let them in. There they spread their newspapers on a cell floor and passed the night in warmth before being ordered out of town the next morning.

So Charlie caught a freight for Omaha and found a job at the Mercer. He worked for a man named Wink Taylor, manager, a "fancily dressed tall man who slid and slunk rather than walked around the place." Charlie "didn't notice him wink at any time but he probably had the name because he was quick as a wink."

Quick, at least, at skipping town. Back at the hotel, Charlie was told that the Mercer was "closed, gone up the spout, foreclosed, and Wink Taylor vanished." Charlie's wages would never be paid, nor would the wages of the chambermaids, kitchen hands, or anyone else to whom Wink Taylor was indebted.

Charlie spent one last night at the Mercer, then again took to the rails. Soon, he arrived in Galesburg, Illinois, walking along Berrien Street "till I came to the only house in the United States where I could open a door without knocking and walk in for a kiss from the woman of the house."

And so ends the story of Charlie the Hobo and his brief stay in Omaha. There really wasn't much to it. Charlie was simply an anonymous young stranger who passed through Omaha like the thousands of drifters who had come before him and the thousands who would come after him. And he was forgotten by the city and it was as though he'd never been there.

But Charlie never forgot his great journey, and never forgot Omaha. He even wrote a poem once about Omaha, which included the lines,

> *Omaha, the roughneck, feeds armies,*
> *Eats and swears from a dirty face.*

You see, Charlie wasn't a poet of romance and exotica, but a poet of the working man and of the hard, dirty, workingman's world. In 1920 he included his poem "Omaha" in a book called *Smoke and Steel*. By then he had dropped the Americanized "Charlie" in favor of his birthname, Carl, and so it happened that while Omaha forgot young Charlie the hobo, it came to know and respect Carl Sandburg, one of the best-loved American writers of the twentieth century.[1]

Chapter 21 notes

[1]This chapter is based on Carl Sandburg, *Always the Young Strangers*, New York: Harcourt, Brace, & Co., 1953, 375-401; and on Penelope Niven, *Carl Sandburg: A Biography*, New York: Charles Scribner's Sons, 1991, 1-38. All quotations, except the lines of poetry, are from *Always the Young Strangers*. The poetry is from "Omaha," in *The Complete Poems of Carl Sandburg*, Revised and Expanded Edition, New York: Harcourt, Brace, Jovanovich, 1969-1970, 161.

Chapter Twenty-Two

NEW WHITE CITY

1898

Erastus Beadle wrote of a special place in 1857, "The more I see of it the better I like it. It is *delightful! charming!!* and by far a pleasanter location than Omaha." He was referring to the town plot of Saratoga, Nebraska, just north of Omaha. It seemed the perfect spot upon which to build a great city.[1]

But the dream city failed. Beadle, you'll recall, went home discouraged, later to make a fortune publishing dime novels. Caught in the economic aftermath of the Panic of 1857, Saratoga withered on the vine. The town folded, and the land was later annexed by Omaha. Even the river went away. Thanks to the Missouri River's habit of cutting new channels for itself, Saratoga's former steamboat landing became a back-water on Cut-Off Lake.[2]

By the summer of 1898, Beadle was three years in his grave and Saratoga but an old-timer's memory.[3] And then the great city finally arrived, bigger and gaudier than anything the pioneers of the '50s could have imagined.

It came partly as a result of Chicago's 1893 Columbian Exposition. The great Chicago fair, named in honor of the 400th anniversary of Columbus's discovery of America (albeit a year late), attracted more than twenty million visitors and inspired

Omaha Public Library
Grand Court looking west.

numerous imitators, all of whom vowed to outdo the famous "Chicago World's Fair." One of these contenders bore the pretentious title, "Trans-Mississippi and International Exposition," and was held on the old Saratoga townsite in Omaha from June through October 1898.[4]

Covering 184 acres, the Exposition grounds featured a Grand Court of white classical-style buildings. These buildings housed displays of technology, commerce, agriculture, the arts, and—in general—the entire progress of civilization, particularly that of the Western American variety. Through the length of the Grand Court ran a man-made lagoon nearly half a mile in length, its waters adorned with a large fountain encircling a statue of Neptune, and with Venetian gondolas that carried passengers on little pleasure-cruises. The grounds also featured a Wild West show, an Indian encampment, and two midways complete with shows, rides, games, restaurants, and various concessions. The Trans-Mississippi was, and remains, the largest public event ever staged in Omaha.[5]

It started as a crazy idea, of course, a scheme as far-fetched as Ed Rosewater's "Air Line to the Black Hills" back in 1875. In the mid-1890s, during the worst economic conditions the coun-

try had seen in at least twenty years, and in the midst of prolonged drought and crop failures, someone got the notion to put
on a big, expensive fair and to invite the world. As the idea
caught on, Omaha businessmen risked large sums of money on
the chance that crowds of tourists could be lured to their
depression-stricken city, a city in which some 5,000 houses
stood empty.[6] In fact, the Exposition itself was located on an
area of empty city lots that had recently been converted back to
cornfields.[7]

Not that a tourist would have guessed any of this by the
summer of 1898. By then the economy had recovered, the
drought had ended, and the cornfields of North Omaha had disappeared beneath the "New White City,"[8] with its gleaming
buildings, its towering arches, its half-dozen steam generators,
its 14,000 electric light bulbs, and its scores of Indians, Negroes,
Chinese, Turks, Egyptians, and other exotic peoples brought in
for the entertainment of the crowds.

"Impress upon the visitors that Omaha is an up-to-date
town," the *World-Herald* instructed its readers before the
Exposition opened. This, of course, was the main point of the
thing. As the *World-Herald* explained the following day, the
Exposition was "an object lesson that is to open the eyes of the
world as to the realities of western life."[9]

For us, the most fascinating thing is not the "object lesson"
itself, but what it tells us about the people who were "teaching"
that lesson to the American public. What did they think of
themselves and their city? Who did they think they had become
as a people? And what—as they approached the end of the nineteenth century, and as we approach the end of this book—did it
all mean?

The stories of two of the Exposition's biggest days will help
answer those questions.

July 4, 1898

The rush began as soon as the gates opened at 7 a.m.
Throughout the day, streetcar after electric streetcar arrived,
"loaded from floorboard to roof" with eager passengers.[10] By 10
a.m., the Exposition grounds were swarming with people, but
still they came, on into the afternoon and evening, nearly

45,000 in all by day's end.[11] This is how the *Bee* described the scene:

Flags and streamers innumerable waved over the avenues that were gorgeous with the pretty summer raiment of thousands of women. A dozen bands made the air tremulous with inspiring strains, and in the patriotic ensemble of sound and color the great white buildings glistened like celestial palaces . . . Thousands of yards of bunting waved in red, white and blue profusion from every possible vantage. A thousand flags floated from the staffs of the main building and streamers of bunting were festooned over the avenues and along the fronts of the smaller buildings.[12]

Then came the parade. "The whole plaza was black with people" as it passed.[13] Embellished with elaborate daylight fireworks from Japan, the scene was a cosmopolitan spectacle unlike anything Omaha had ever witnessed. The procession included caged wild animals, an Egyptian wedding party on camels and donkeys, cowboys and Indians from the wild west show, a Chinese band, floats advertising the Schlitz and Pabst breweries, "Montana girls who sat on their horses man-wise, without any concern for conventionalities," and assorted Greeks, French, Italians, Mexicans, Germans, and Cubans, followed by—more ominously—a float commemorating the battleship *Maine*, which earlier that year had mysteriously exploded in a Cuban harbor. [14]

During the parade, a Turkish band struck up *The Star Spangled Banner*, and created a sensation among the audience. As the exotic musicians played, their music swelled:

in sublime contrast to the blare of the zerzhonis and the rattle of the drums. At the first note a huge Turk in the line of march jumped high in the air and bringing his scimeter (sic) and shield together with a resounding clash above his head

Omaha Public Library
Nearly 100,000 people showed up when President
McKinley toured the Trans-Mississippi Exposition.

he let out a yell that might have been heard in
Constantinople. Then the crowd broke loose.
Hundreds of little flags appeared as though by
preconcerted arrangement, and were waved in
unison, with a tumult of cheers that fairly flut-
tered the bunting overhead.[15]

It appeared that the world had indeed come to Omaha, and
even the Turks were playing America's national anthem. There
was a message here. And in case that message was lost on anyone, what happened next would drive it home to even the most
obtuse fairgoer.

After the parade, the crowd gathered in the Grand Plaza to
enjoy the music of the Fourth Regimental Band. A military
band was appropriate, for the nation was at war.

We remember it as the Spanish-American War, when we remember it at all. It was a short, lopsided fight, an easy victory for the increasingly powerful United States against a decrepit Spanish empire. It began just before the Exposition opened, and ended before the fair was half-over.

But that is hindsight. On July 4, the war was still on, and the people were filled with hopeful anxiety. What had started as a Cuban war for independence from Spain had grown to involve the U.S., Spain, Cuba, and the Philippines (then a Spanish possession). The U.S. Navy had already destroyed the Spanish fleet in the Philippines, but the fight in Cuba was not yet over. Even as the revelers enjoyed their international parade, American ships and ground troops were converging on Santiago, Cuba, where the Spanish Caribbean fleet was waiting in the harbor.

SWEPT UP
THE HILL LIKE
A HURRICANE

read the *World-Herald* headline of July 3. "Cowboy Regiments Carry San Juan in Face of a Withering and Destructive Fire." Prominent among the heroes of the day were the "rough riders commanded by Lieutenant Colonel Roosevelt."

On the Fourth, the headlines were even more hopeful. And as the military band finished playing, a man took the stage to interrupt the program with a war bulletin fresh from the telegraph office. It confirmed what the morning papers had already been proclaiming. General Shafter, commander of the U.S. troops in Cuba, had sent an ultimatum to the Spanish troops in Santiago. He had them surrounded, Shafter said, and he was demanding their unconditional surrender.

"At this the people cheered loud and long," the *World-Herald* reported, and it appears to have been an understatement.[16] A little while later, a second war bulletin—this one from Admiral Sampson—boasted, "The fleet under my command offers the nation as a Fourth of July present the destruction of the whole of [Spanish Admiral] Cervera's fleet. No one escaped."[17]

Though the Spanish surrender would not come until the seventeenth, the crowd knew that the war was won. "The enthusiasm was so intense," wrote the official historian of the

Exposition, "that bedlam might be said to have broken loose among the multitude."[18]

Though the Fourth of July pioneers of '54 could hardly have imagined the scene, one thing had not changed: the people still wanted a "spread-eagle" speech. And that day's featured speaker, a Philadelphian named James Beck, gave them one.

"We can reverently thank the Ruler of Nations," Beck intoned, ". . . that upon no preceding anniversary has our country exercised so wide an influence among the nations of the earth, nor used it for any loftier or nobler purpose. . . Never did a nation make war with a less selfish purpose. . . No lust of military glory or territorial aggrandizement inspired our nation."

To anyone acquainted with the history of the Spanish-American War, those last claims seem laughably false. But Beck appeared to believe them, and the crowd took them seriously. And the first statement—that America's international influence had never been greater—was undeniable.

Just what was America to do with its growing power?, Beck wondered. "Is the western hemisphere large enough for the influence and progress of the American people, or must we surrender, commercially and politically, our policy of isolation and claim an influence which shall be as limitless as the world is round?"

Speaking with an eloquence laden with religious imagery, Beck argued at length against America's traditional isolationism. For America to "skulk and shirk behind the selfish policy of isolation," he thundered, "and to abdicate a destined world supremacy, would be the colossal crime of history."[19]

America was coming of age. No longer a weak, isolated nation of farmers and shopkeepers, the U.S. stood ready to dominate the coming century, and Beck was perceptive enough to see it coming. In the same way, within America, the West was coming of age. The frontier was settled; now the trans-Mississippi states were beginning to flex their economic and political muscle—that, of course, was the stated "object lesson" of the Exposition. And within the West, Omaha too was coming of age. No longer a frontier town, Omaha had grown into a metropolis. The Exposition proved it, and the "New White City" represented Omaha's vision of itself. Forty-four years earlier, a handful of young pioneers had crossed the Missouri River to launch an audacious scheme. They had come with big dreams of building themselves a great city. In the summer of 1898, their children announced to the world that those dreams had come true.

October 12, 1898

From the Grand Plaza's Music Pavilion, it was nearly impossible to see a spot of ground unoccupied by a human being. "The human sea was unbroken," reported the *Bee*, "from the Horticultural Building to the East Midway, and even the young trees and the roofs of the buildings were populated by ambitious spectators." And still the people poured in, about 70,000 of them, until the mass of humanity was so tightly packed that hundreds could not even get within sight of the Grand Plaza.[20]

A band was playing patriotic songs and the Second Nebraska Regiment—lately returned from the war—stood proudly in their blue uniforms, lining either side of the entrance to the Exposition grounds.

At 11 a.m., a column of carriages entered the plaza, proceeding slowly through the path held open by the Nebraska troops. In the lead carriage rode William McKinley, President of the United States.

McKinley is hardly remembered today—seems to be merely the last of the bland, paunchy, anonymous presidents who filled in time between Abraham Lincoln and Theodore Roosevelt—but in the fall of 1898 he was at the height of his power and popularity. Two-and-a-half years into his presidency, the Ohio Republican had presided over both an economic recovery and a successful war. It didn't matter that his rival in the '96 election had been a Nebraskan—the fiery William Jennings Bryan. McKinley was coming into Bryan's home state, and to the Exposition that had been partly Bryan's idea, and could nonetheless expect a hero's welcome.

Which is precisely what he got. "The passage of the presidential carriage through the crowd was accompanied by the most extravagant demonstrations," reported the *Bee*, "The crowd was wedged so closely that it was almost impossible to move, but the people managed to get their hands above their heads long enough to wave a greeting with hats and handker-chiefs and flags, while their voices united in a succession of tremendous cheers that made the Plaza ring." Before the day ended, the crowd would swell nearly to 100,000.

For McKinley, the day was filled with an exhausting round of giving and listening to speeches, shaking thousands of hands, and attending banquets and socials with Omaha's wealthy and respectable class. He even managed to see a little of the fair.

But there was one thing that McKinley didn't want to miss, and he cut other engagements short in order to fit it in. He wanted to see the Indians.

An important part of the Trans-Mississippi and International Exposition was the "Indian Congress," an encampment of Indians from various tribes that served as a liv-ing history exhibit for curious whites. The camp was open to the public during certain hours, and the Indians staged popular "sham battles" and demonstrated their ceremonies and tradi-tions.

For whites, the old fear of Indians was gone. The tribes were all confined to reservations now, and the Indian wars were fad-ing into a mythic past. Even the ghost dance had lost its power to terrify. In 1890, fear and misunderstanding of the ghost dance religious movement had led to the murder of Sitting Bull and to a massacre of Indians at Wounded Knee, South Dakota. Less than eight years later, the ghost dance was performed without incident at the Exposition grounds in Omaha. Spectators watched, and the Stars and Stripes flew proudly above the scene.[21]

McKinley wanted to see the Indians, and so they were brought before him. Under the headline, "GREAT FATHER AND INDIAN," the *Bee* devoted a lengthy article to the historic meeting, opening with this revealing paragraph:

> *Yesterday morning President McKinley received the homage of a hundred thousand rep-resentatives of a race that stands at the pinnacle of the greatest civilization of the world's history and of a nation that in the opinion of many states-men is just commencing to play its great part*

*upon the stage of the universe. In the afternoon the
president was rendered honor by a thousand representatives of a passing civilization that was in
its way great and of a dying nation that acted
within its limitations as magnificent a part in the
past as its successor in the present. The one set of
the subjects of the stars and stripes was but a
comparatively small part of the millions that
inhabit the twenty-four transmississippi states;
the other was an alarmingly large proportion of
the remnant of the Indian race.*[22]

It was believed that the Indians were on their way to extinction, that in another generation they would be all but gone. It
was assumed, therefore, that the Indian Encampment was not
only the first time that the representatives of so many native
tribes would come together, but also that it would be the last.

As McKinley and his entourage sat in a grandstand, the
tribes were presented one by one. Each tribe's name was
announced, and its chief introduced. Wichita, Sioux, Omaha,
Blackfoot, Crow, Tonkawa, Flathead, Sac and Fox, Assiniboine,
Kiowa, Apache.

*First came the women in blankets of brilliant
combinations of red, blue, yellow and green, some
with toddling children as gaudily clothed as
themselves by their sides and some with pappoos-
es upon their backs, some silent and shy, and others singing and chanting and with smiling faces.
Then came the warriors on foot, some with a
superfluity of gaudy costumes and others with
none at all, every man with all of his exposed
body, arms, legs, trunk and face fantastically
painted in brilliant hues. Finally came the horse-
men as brilliantly decorated, dashing up and
halting with perfect horsemanship at the foot of
the stand.*

For some, the display was amusing, and there was much talk

about the awkward manners of the Indians and their "gaudy" costumes. But the President was quiet and thoughtful. He "appeared to study rather than to take amusement out of the spectacle."

The Apaches came forward and stood before the grandstand. Just then an old Apache chief "dashed up behind his tribe, halted in front of them and lifted up his eyes" to the crowd. He was a small man, tough and wiry, his hair streaked with gray, his brown face creased like old leather. Unlike the others, he was dressed not in native costume, but in the uniform of an army scout. His name, when announced, brought a murmur of recognition from the crowd.

It was Geronimo.

Through the years, countless Indians fought against the steady encroachment of the whites into tribal territories. Of the native leaders, many names are legendary: Pontiac, Tecumseh, Osceola, Black Hawk, Crazy Horse, Sitting Bull, Chief Joseph— just to name a few. Of these leaders, Geronimo was the end of the line. After all other tribes had been restricted to reservations, he and his band of Chiracahua Apaches were the last to challenge the might of the U.S. Army. Geronimo's 1886 surrender at Skeleton Canyon, Arizona, closed the final chapter of the Indian wars—though, as mentioned earlier, a bloody epilogue had yet to be played out at the so-called "Battle" of Wounded Knee in 1890.

The reader will recall that one of Geronimo's adversaries was the formidable George Crook, who requested a transfer after being ordered to break faith with the Apaches. Crook was replaced with General Nelson Miles, and it was Miles, not Crook, who received Geronimo's final surrender. In their negotiations, Miles told Geronimo that if he surrendered, he would be exiled to Florida for a time, but eventually would be allowed to return to Arizona.

That promise, like so many others, was not kept. Geronimo and his followers were sentenced to hard labor, were kept away from their families for months, and were never allowed to return to their homeland. Even in 1898, Geronimo arrived at the Exposition as a military prisoner and was housed in an army tent.

George Crook had died years earlier, but Miles was alive and well. In fact, he was a guest at the Exposition and sitting in the grandstand that day with the President's entourage. During a similar presentation earlier that week, Geronimo had spotted his old adversary among the crowd, had stared at him long and hard, then dismounted his horse and climbed into the grandstand, working through the crowd until he reached the General. There is sometimes a strange bond between warriors who have fought against each other. For Geronimo, this bond was apparently a strong one, stronger even than imprisonment and the government's broken promises. That day, Geronimo had greeted Miles with a hug.

On this day, President's Day, Geronimo took off his broad-brimmed hat and smiled up at the crowd—though whether he was looking at McKinley or Miles is unclear. Either way, the great warrior paid his public respects to the government that had conquered him.

After the presentation of the tribes, an officer led them all in three rousing cheers for the president. The formal program then ended with an enthusiastic mock battle between two groups of Indians.

But there was still one more thing. The Indians asked to meet the president, and he agreed. Escorted by an army officer, McKinley came out onto the grounds where the Indians waited in a long line—chiefs, warriors, women, and children all together. Hat in hand, bowing politely as he worked his way down the line, the President greeted them all.

At one point he stood face-to-face with Geronimo. For a moment, the two men regarded each other, white man and native, conqueror and conquered, president and prisoner. It was, apparently, a friendly moment, both men standing bareheaded out of respect for each other, perhaps even smiling. The president bowed and moved on. If he and Geronimo said anything to each other, it is not recorded.

But the dignity and the seriousness with which McKinley behaved toward the Indians spoke clearly enough. Like the *Bee* reporter who wrote about the meeting, McKinley seems to have sensed the sorrow inherent in the situation. If there was joy in the pageantry and battle of that afternoon, it was the joy of a wake. The old America—the America of the endless frontier, the America of pioneers and Indians, the America where a town like Omaha City could spring up overnight out on the prairie somewhere, where a fistfight could break out on the floor of the territorial legislature, where packs of stray dogs roamed the muddy streets and three-card monte men prowled the wooden sidewalks, the America where the rest of the world was so far away that you didn't have to send your best boys off to try to save it—that was gone now, never to return. A new century was coming, and all around was a new world, a new America, a new white city.

Incidentally, the Exposition's "New White City"—the beautiful Grand Court—was all torn down within a few years. Despite appearances, the elaborate buildings were little more than plaster of Paris over cheap wooden frames. The frontier may have been closed, but in 1898 a little of Omaha's old boomtown spirit lived on.

Chapter 22 notes

[1]Beadle, 23.

[2]Known today as Carter Lake.

[3]Albert Johannsen, *The House of Beadle and Adams and Its Dime and Nickel Novels: The Story of a Vanished Literature*, Vol. I, Norman: University of Oklahoma Press, 1950, 68.

[4]The Exposition grounds included what is now Kountze Park (between 19th and 21st, Pinkney and Pratt Streets).

[5]Description of Exposition grounds: James B. Haynes, *History of the Trans-Mississippi and International Exposition of 1898*, (Published Under Direction of the Committee on History as Authorized by the Board of Directors, June 30, 1902), 1910, 29-53.

[6]Larsen and Cottrell, *The Gate City*, 82.

[7]Haynes, 31.

[8]*Morning World-Herald*, June 2, 1898.

[9]*Morning World-Herald*, May 31, June 1, 1898.

[10]*Bee* (morning), July 5, 1898.

[11]Haynes, 246.

[12]*Bee* (morning), July 5, 1898.

[13]*Bee* (morning), July 5, 1898.

[14]*Morning World-Herald*, July 5, 1898. See also Haynes, 80-83.

[15]*Bee* (morning), July 5, 1898.

[16]*Morning World-Herald,* July 5, 1898.

[17]Haynes, 83.

[18]Haynes, 84.

[19]Haynes, 388-389, 393.

[20]*Bee* (morning) October 13, 1898. See also Haynes, 89, 247.

[21]Haynes, 227.

[22]McKinley and the Indians: *Bee* (morning), October 13, 1898. See also Haynes, 219.

Extra! Extra!

ASSAULTED HIS BRIDE
A Young Husband Grows Hilarious
on His Wedding Night.

Edward Stansberry is a loo-loo, although his wife does not make that allegation in the complaint filed against him this morning . . .
> —*Omaha Evening Bee*, March 14, 1891

* * *

JOHN CHINAMAN: "Omiha Blee belly good plaper. Use hlim wrap up washee in."
> —*Omaha World-Herald*, March 15, 1891

* * *

HANGED THEM BOTH.

Mississippi Lynchers String Up a Man and a Woman.
> —*Omaha Daily Bee, September 29, 1891*

* * *

Bald Heads and Greatness
The London Lancet denounces as false the doctrine that abundant hair is a sign of bodily or mental strength in a man. It says that despite the Samson precedent, the Chinese are mostly bald, yet they form the most enduring of races. The average madhouse furnished proof that long and thick hair is not a sign of intellectuality. The easily wheedled Esau was hairy while the mighty Caesar was bald. "Long haired men are generally weak and fanatical, and men with scant hair are the philosophers and statesmen and soldiers of the world."
> —*Omaha Daily Bee*, October 9, 1891

* * *

Scott's EMULSION
of Pure Cod Liver Oil and
HYPOPHOSPHITES of Lime and Soda
is endorsed and prescribed by leading physicians because
both the Cod liver Oil and Hypophosphites are the recognized
agents in the cure of Consumption. It is as palatable as milk.

Scott's Emulsion is a perfect emulsion. It is a wonderful
Flesh Producer. It is the Best Remedy for CONSUMPTION,
Scrofula, Bronchitis, Wasting Diseases, Chronic Coughs and
Colds. Ask for Scott's Emulsion and take no other.
—Omaha World-Herald, October 9, 1891

* * *

Don't be
Careless About
Your Complexion
It is woman's chiefest physical charm. It is often her only
capital. It is always worth a great deal to her, in business, love
or social affairs. No matter how browned, or rough, or sallow
your skin may be, or how much it is disfigured with freckles,
moth-patches, blackheads or pimples
MRS. GRAHAM'S
Face Bleach
will remove every blemish and leave your skin as pure as
clear and white as it was in baby days. Your complexion will
then be as nature made it. Instructions go with each bottle how
to keep it so. Price $1.50. All druggists sell it.
Mrs. J. M. Crissey, druggist, corner Lake and 4th streets,
and all the leading Omaha druggists sell it.
—Omaha World-Herald, October 11, 1891

* * *

The signal service man is throwing out dark hints about
snow. In the present temper of the community, he would better
be careful.
—Omaha World-Herald, October 14, 1891
(Three days after the George Smith lynching.)

* * *

LYNCHED, AS USUAL.
LITTLE ROCK, ARK., May 24.
—Omaha World-Herald, May 25, 1892

* * *

A BRUTAL NEGRO TROOPER.
———

A Bestial Colored Soldier in Jail for a Terrible Crime.
—Omaha World-Herald, May 25, 1892

* * *

ARE HIT HARD BY CUPID.
———

Omaha Teachers Finding Places in the Matrimonial Market.

Under the languorous influence of warm sunshine and April rains Cupid has made a successful assault on the ranks of the Omaha teachers, and during the last week or two scarcely a day has passed without bringing news of another prospective marriage that will deprive the schools of valuable teachers. The worst of it is that the young men most intimately concerned have had the good taste to make their selections from among the best teachers whose places it will be difficult to fill. . . . It is understood that as a sort of antidote to the contagion that seems to have developed into an epidemic, Superintendent Marble will address the next meeting of the Teachers' association on "The Undesirability of Husbands, and How to Avoid Them."   *—Omaha Bee*, April 12, 1895

* * *

Petty thieves continue to do a thriving business. Jail sentences are no longer a terror to this class of criminals. A rock pile and chain gang would be.   *—Omaha Bee*, April 24, 1895

* * *

*With apology for the repetition we pause long enough to
remark that Mr. Rosewater is very mad.*
—*Omaha Sunday World-Herald*, October 3, 1897

* * *

*Go where you will, to attend a fair, circus, exposition—or
any other big event—and you will surely see him. His is the
worst nuisance that ever happened. We refer to the young man
who sees a beer cork in his pathway and immediately becomes
hilariously drunk and sets about letting the entire world know
that his a confirmed "rounder."*

*With his hat set rakishly on the side of his addlepate, and
with a "Whoop! Ain't I a dead game sport?" expression on his
weak face, he staggers about through the crowds, making loud
remarks and courting attention.*

*. . . It is really too bad that the exposition guards are not
allowed to use their discretion about killing some people.*
—*Omaha World-Herald*, June 3, 1898
(During the Trans-Mississippi and International Exposition)

* * *

*The pretty young man with a tri-colored ribbon on his natty
straw hat and the bottom of his trousers turned up just so high
approached the soda water stand and called for lemon phos-
phate. As he was sipping it he glanced at the trim young lady
who served him and smilingly asked:*

*"I presume you have to answer an awful lot of fool questions,
do you not?"*

"Yes," replied the young lady with a weary air.

*"So I thought. Charming day. What particular question is
fired at you oftenest from the hayseeds?"*

"That one."

"Which one?"

"The one you just asked."

*And as the young lady carefully rinsed the glass the pretty
young man wandered away in a trance.*
—*Omaha World-Herald*, June 8, 1898
(During the Trans-Mississippi and International Exposition)

* * *

The question whether tonight ends the nineteenth century is still being fiercely debated. The people who sit up, however, to witness the transition from the old year to the new will not know the difference.

—*Omaha Bee*, December 31, 1899

* * *

USHERED IN VERY QUIETLY.

———

Year 1900 Arrives at Omaha With But Little of the Vociferousness Usual at This Time.

———

Although the direct cause of columns of vexing arguments, unaccountable cases of madness, disruptions of friendships untold, provocative of much dispute and pulling of hair, the year 1900 was ushered in by Omaha very quietly last night. There was little of the chiming of bells, volleying of firearms and shrieking of whistles that often marks the turning of the year.

—*Omaha World-Herald*, January 1, 1900

* * *

TWENTIETH CENTURY IS BORN

———

Dawning of a New Cycle Marked by Saturnalia of Gunpowder and Glad Hurrahs.

———

The twentieth century is here. It was ushered in at midnight amid a saturnalia of gunpowder, clanging of bells, shrieking of whistles and the tumultuous hurrahs of young America and some old ones, too. The streets were thronged with pedestrians until after 12 o'clock and there was a general recognition of the fact that not only a new year, but a new century was dawning.

—*Omaha Bee*, January 1, 1901

Omaha Daily Bee, October 9, 1891

Adelina Patti was a famous
opera singer of the period.

Epilogue

THE YOUNG STRANGERS

They seemed to be no more than casual acquaintances. A young man and a young woman boarded an electric streetcar in Council Bluffs and paid their fare to Omaha. The conductor took no other notice of them.[1]

It was Saturday, March 13, 1897, a day in which a fat, late-winter snow was falling and turning the brown world white again.

They sat quietly as the streetcar glided high over the Missouri River through the steel truss of the Douglas Street Bridge. To their left stood the Union Pacific Railroad Bridge, completely rebuilt since the days of John Pierson and the tornado. To their right, on the riverbank, lay the site of the Lone Tree Landing, where a generation earlier a rickety ferryboat had deposited some Fourth of July revelers eager to build themselves a city. By now, the tree was long gone and the site covered by sprawling railroad tracks and Union Pacific maintenance shops.

They entered Omaha on Douglas Street, passing by Anna Wilson's palatial brothel at Ninth, and heading west toward Twelfth. Looking out the windows, craning their necks, they began scanning the sidewalks, as though searching the crowds of pedestrians for someone in particular.

At Twelfth and Douglas—where, nearly thirty years earlier, a whitewashed barrel had stood in a mudhole bearing the warning, "No Bottom!"—the car stopped to let passengers on and off. The young man stood, looking over the heads of the crowd, searching, but not finding the person he was expecting. Leaving his seat, he went up to the conductor with a strange request. *Could the car be held here for just a few minutes longer?* And when he explained why, the conductor agreed.

It's hard to have a private conversation on a public streetcar. Several passengers overheard the young man's request and its reason. But the delay did not upset them. Quite the contrary. Immediately, the word spread excitedly into the street that there was going to be a wedding, "a society wedding, a swell affair," right there aboard the streetcar.

Within minutes the car was jammed with passengers, most of whom had no other reason for riding than to share the happiness of the young strangers from over the river. Among the new passengers was the minister, "a short, pleasant-faced" man. The bridegroom asked the conductor to go ahead. The conductor rang a bell twice, and the motorman—standing outside on a platform at the car's front end—eased the car ahead up Douglas Street.

Plowing on through the snow, the wedding party passed one of the blocks where Canada Bill and his cappers used to play their tricks on travelers. They passed the corner where the *Herald* staff used to write their stories in an office above a billiard saloon. Turning south on Fourteenth, they passed the scene of the great editorial "mill" between Rosewater and Balcome. They passed near the old site of Drexel & Maul's undertaking parlors, where the Coffin Club had once worked its mischief. They passed the corner of Fourteenth and Farnam, where the Grand Central Hotel had once stood, and where the cesspool had overflowed, and where heavyweight champion Tom Allen had boasted to reporters of his coming victory. They passed the undertaking parlors of Heafey & Heafey, where crowds had lined up to leer at the battered corpse of George Smith.

The wedding took place on Fourteenth Street, in the three blocks between Douglas and Howard. At a stop, the certificate of marriage was filled out, the conductor and motorman signing as witnesses.

And then the minister and the well-wishers departed, and the car headed east on Howard into a relatively new area that would one day be known as the Old Market. At Twelfth, the car turned north, heading back toward Douglas, and passing the Mercer Hotel, where in a few months a young stranger named Carl Sandburg would be washing dishes for a promised $1.50 a week.

And new passengers came and went, by now unaware of what had just taken place aboard Car #55. But the newlyweds remained aboard until the streetcar had crossed back over the bridge into Council Bluffs. Their story was strange and interesting, and would appear in the next day's *Bee*. But like all the other stories—the sites of which the young couple had passed by unaware—their story would soon fade from memory.

They finally departed where they had come aboard, at the corner of Pearl and Broadway in Council Bluffs. After they had gone, the conductor and motorman realized that they couldn't remember their names. The young man and woman had simply stepped off the streetcar and walked away, disappearing into the falling snow.

Epilogue notes

[1]This story is taken from the *Bee* (morning), March 14, 1897. Streetcar route: Richard Orr, *O & CB*, 87.

INDEX

THE AUTHOR

David Bristow

David L. Bristow has lived in Omaha since 1992. He writes for various magazines and is currently working on a novel. *A Dirty, Wicked Town* is his first book. More of his work is available at the website he maintains, **www.david-bristow.com.**

Other Books About Plains History
From CAXTON PRESS

Massacre Along the Medicine Road
A Social History of the Indian War
of 1864 in Nebraska Territory

ISBN 0-87004-389-7 Cloth $32.95
ISBN 0-87004-387-0 Paper $22.95
6x9, 40 photographs, 8 maps, 500 pages

Wild Towns of Nebraska
ISBN 0-87004-325-0
8 1/2 x 11, 147 pages, 121 illustrations, paper $14.95

Bad Men and Bad Towns
ISBN 0-87004-349-8
8 1/2 x 11, 180 pages, illustrated, paper $14.95

Blood at Sand Creek
ISBN 0-87004-361-7
6x9, 214 pages, illustrations, paper $8.95

Plain Enemies
ISBN 0-87004-364-1
6x9, 312 pages, illustrated, paper $14.95

Deadly Days in Kansas
ISBN 0-87004-379-x
8 1/2 x 11, 140 pages, illustrated, paper $14.95

For a free Caxton catalog write to:

CAXTON PRESS
312 Main Street
Caldwell, ID 83605-3299

or

Visit our Internet Website:

www.caxtonpress.com

Caxton Press is a division of The CAXTON PRINTERS, Ltd.

WC